Intelligent Fashion Forecasting Systems: Models and Applications

Tsan-Ming Choi • Chi-Leung Hui • Yong Yu
Editors

Intelligent Fashion Forecasting Systems: Models and Applications

Springer

Editors
Tsan-Ming Choi
Business Division
Institute of Textiles and Clothing
The Hong Kong Polytechnic University
Hong Kong
People's Republic of China

Chi-Leung Hui
Business Division
Institute of Textiles and Clothing
The Hong Kong Polytechnic University
Hong Kong
People's Republic of China

Yong Yu
Business Division
Institute of Textiles and Clothing
The Hong Kong Polytechnic University
Hong Kong
People's Republic of China

ISBN 978-3-642-39868-1 ISBN 978-3-642-39869-8 (eBook)
DOI 10.1007/978-3-642-39869-8
Springer Heidelberg New York Dordrecht London

Library of Congress Control Number: 2013954375

Printed on acid-free paper

Springer is part of Springer Science+Business Media (www.springer.com)

Preface

Forecasting is a crucial function for companies in the fashion apparel industry. Despite the fact that there is no "perfect" forecast, forecasting for highly structured data (e.g., the time series with high seasonality or trend) is known to be "easy" because there are many well-established models which provide the needed analytical formulations. However, for many real-life forecasting applications in the fashion industry, the data patterns are notorious for being highly volatile, and it is very difficult, if not impossible, to analytically learn about the underlying pattern. As a result, many traditional methods (such as statistical models) will fail to make a sound prediction. Over the past decade, advances in artificial intelligence technologies have provided an alternative way of generating precise and accurate forecasting results for fashion (e.g., sales forecasting, color trend forecasting).

Although being an important and timely topic, there is currently an absence of a comprehensive reference source that provides the state-of-the-art findings on both theoretical and applied research on the intelligent fashion forecasting systems. In view of the above, we have edited this Springer handbook which features several peer-refereed papers. To be specific, this handbook contains three parts that cover (i) introductory, review, and exploratory materials related to fashion forecasting; (ii) theoretical modeling research on fashion forecasting; and (iii) intelligent fashion forecasting applications and analysis. The specific topics covered include the following:

- Introduction to Intelligent Fashion Forecasting
- Sales Forecasting in Apparel and Fashion Industry: A Review
- Collaborative Planning Forecasting Replenishment Schemes in Apparel Supply Chain Systems: Cases and Research Opportunities
- Measuring Forecasting Accuracy: Problems and Recommendations
- Forecasting Demand for Fashion Goods: A Hierarchical Bayesian Approach
- Forecasting Fashion Store Reservations: Booking Horizon Forecasting with Dynamic Updating
- Fuzzy Forecast Combining for Apparel Demand Forecasting

- Intelligent Fashion Colour Trend Forecasting Schemes: A Comparative Study
- Neural Networks Based Forecasting for Romanian Clothing Sector

We are pleased to offer through this handbook new analytical and empirical results with valuable insights, which will contribute to the literature. To the best of our knowledge, this research handbook is the first one which specifically examines intelligent fashion forecasting.

Before ending, we would like to take this opportunity to thank Niels Peter Thomas, Emmie Yang, and Michelle Feng of Springer for their kindest support and advice along the course of carrying out this book project. We are grateful to all the authors who have contributed their research to this handbook and the anonymous reviewers who have helped review the papers. We also acknowledge the editorial assistance of Na Liu and Hau-Ling Chan.

Hong Kong, China Tsan-Ming Choi
Hong Kong, China Chi-Leung Hui
Hong Kong, China Yong Yu

Contents

Part I
Introduction, Review and Exploratory Studies

Chapter 1
Introduction: Intelligent Fashion Forecasting

Tsan-Ming Choi, Chi-Leung Hui, and Yong Yu

Forecasting is a classic topic of information systems [1] and it is a crucial part for companies in the fashion apparel industry. Despite the fact that there is no "perfect" forecast, forecasting for highly structured data (e.g., the time series with high seasonality or trend) is known to be "easy" because there are many well-established models which provide the needed analytical formulations [13, 18]. For example, Hott [1] develop analytical models with closed-form expressions for forecasting time series with prominent features of seasonality and trend by using the exponentially weighted moving average method. In addition, more sophisticated statistical methods such as SARIMA [2] and ARIMA have also been widely applied for these structured forecasting problems with good performance. However, for many real life applications in the fashion industry, the data patterns are notorious for being highly volatile and it is very difficult, if not impossible, to analytically learn about the underlining pattern and hence the well-established and traditional statistical methods will fail to make a sound prediction. As a result, recent advances of artificial intelligence (AI) technologies have provided the alternative way of providing precise and more accurate forecasting result for fashion sales time series. For example, Au et al. [4] explore the fashion sales forecasting problem for fashion retailers by using evolutionary neural networks (ENN). They find that ENN can substantially enhance the forecasting accuracy compared to various other traditional methods. Although AI methods such as ENN can produce highly accurate forecasting results for volatile data sets, they suffer a major drawback in which they are slow (e.g., ENN can take hours in order to generate the forecasting results). This shortcoming becomes a major barricade which hinders the application of AI methods for forecasting in real world. Recently,

T.-M. Choi (✉) • C.-L. Hui • Y. Yu
Business Division, Institute of Textiles and Clothing, The Hong Kong Polytechnic University, Hung Hom, Kowloon, Hong Kong
e-mail: jason.choi@polyu.edu.hk

T.-M. Choi et al. (eds.), *Intelligent Fashion Forecasting Systems: Models and Applications*, DOI 10.1007/978-3-642-39869-8_1,

in the literature, there are some innovative proposals and studies from different perspectives for establishing intelligent efficient forecasting systems with a focus on speed. Many of these proposed systems and models are inspiring and can lead to many promising applications. For example, El-Bakry and Mastorakis [5] propose an innovative approach which speeds up the prediction stage. To be specific, their method improves the forecasting speed by applying cross correlation between the whole input data and the weights of neural networks in the frequency domain. El-Bakry and Mastorakis prove analytically that this proposal can speed up the whole forecasting process and they call the resulting neural network a high speed neural network (HSNN) and discuss its use in time series forecasting. In Choi et al. [2], in order to enhance the accuracy and versatility of SARIMA in conducting fashion sales forecasting, a novel hybrid approach by wavelet transform is developed. To be specific, Choi et al. propose a scheme in which the original fashion sales time series is decomposed into components by wavelet transform. By conducting forecasting at the component level, the respective prediction results are obtained. Finally, in order to get the time series forecast for the original sales data, the component-level forecasts are transformed back to the original time series forecast. This hybrid wavelet transform SARIMA method has been tested with real and artificial data sets. Its performance is compared to both the pure statistical methods as well as some traditional AI methods, and is found to be satisfactory. Most recently, inspired by the strengths and weaknesses of pure statistical method (PSM) and the extended extreme learning machines (EELM), Yu et al. [6] develop a novel algorithm which combines the EELM and the pure statistical model (PSM) to conduct intelligent fast forecasting for fashion sales time series. Their method has employed a sophisticated scheme to determine the optimal parameters of the algorithm which can achieve the best possible (expected) accuracy with EELM and PSM within the given time limit constraint. In addition to the pure statistical method, there are other newly emerged models which are fast and can yield comparable forecasting accuracies. For instance, the Grey Model (GM) [25] is one of such models. The GM has been employed in the study of fashion trend forecasting, and very favorable results have been reported in [22]. Such models like GM are also suitable candidates for modeling the fashion forecasting problems. Similarly, research work as in [24] would also require an algorithm which intelligently chooses between the models to accomplish efficient forecasting tasks.

Motivated by the importance of intelligent fashion forecasting, this book project is organized and it features a collection of peer-refereed papers which are organized into three parts, namely Part I – introductory, review and exploratory materials related to fashion forecasting, Part II – theoretical modeling research on fashion forecasting, and Part III – intelligent fashion forecasting applications and analysis. In the following, we introduce each featured paper.

First of all, in Chap. 2 (Part I), Sebastien reviews studies of sales forecasting methods and their implementation in the supply systems of fashion companies over the past decade. The main purposes of this paper are to provide the reader a synthetic understanding of the fashion industry especially from the forecast point of view. With this objective, the author discusses the emerging issues, such as sustainable development, and proposed various new research trends, such as the fast fashion or the mass customization. In addition, he reviews and explores the current state-of-the-arts scientific forecasting methods which can be applied to cope with the existing and coming industrial challenges of the fashion industry.

In Chap. 3 (Part I), Ho and Choi examine the timely industrial practice known as collaborative planning, forecasting and replenishment (CPFR) scheme. They first focus on studying an individual case on an Asian garment manufacturer. After that, they review and explore with good details the American denim supply chain and identify various important inventory management practices and the role played by CPFR. Finally, they discuss and propose various future research directions which include (i) the importance of having the right type of fashion forecasting applications in place, (ii) the robust mechanism for enhancing fashion supply chain performance under CPFR, (iii) the cluster strategy and off-shore production in fashion supply chain, and (iv) the analytical models which can quantify the benefit brought by CPFR for fashion companies.

Forecast adjustment commonly occurs when organizational forecasters adjust a statistical forecast of demand to take into account factors which are excluded from the statistical calculation. In Chap. 4 (Part II), Davydenko and Fildes investigate how to measure the accuracy of such adjustments. Owing to specific features of the demand data, they reveal that many existing error measures are generally not suitable to the task. In order to ensure an interpretable and unambiguous evaluation, they recommend the use of a metric based on aggregating performance ratios across time series using the weighted geometric mean. They demonstrate that this measure has the advantage of treating over- and under-forecasting even-handedly, has a more symmetric distribution, and is robust. Furthermore, their empirical analysis using the recommended metric shows that, on average, adjustments yielded improvements under symmetric linear loss, while harming accuracy in terms of some traditional measures. This provides further support to the critical importance of selecting appropriate error measures when evaluating the forecasting accuracy.

In Chap. 5 (Part II), Yelland and Dong present a forecasting model that tackles the difficulties presented by the pronounced and variable life cycles of many fashion apparel goods, particularly those in the so-called fast fashion segment. Demands of this nature are notoriously difficult to forecast, since standard extrapolative methods (such as exponential smoothing in its various forms) fail to capture the dynamics of the life cycle, while more specialized techniques that are attuned to life cycle can be wildly inaccurate when calibrated early in a product's life, since initial observations of actual demand (if indeed any are available) often provide little indication of long term life cycle trends. They address these problems using a hierarchical Bayesian forecasting model with an explicit representation of the product life cycle. The latter correctly accommodates the effects of life cycle dynamics on demand, while the hierarchical Bayesian structure allows accurate forecasts to be made early in a product's life based on prior histories of comparable products. They take a novel approach to establish the applicability of their model; they use an agent-based simulation model of a fashion market, in which individuals and their purchasing decisions are concretely represented.

Using their simulation model, they demonstrate that forecasts produced with their model substantially out-perform those of a sophisticated off-the-shelf forecasting system.

In Chap. 6 (Part II), Haensel explains and develops a new method for updating booking/reservation horizons when parts of the horizon become known. In most sales situations there is a high correlation between early and late reservations, which means taking this information into account can help to significantly improve the forecast accuracy. The forecasting methodology comprises two steps: first a dimension reduction of the general forecasting problem by singular value decomposition and second a dynamic forecast and updating procedure which uses penalized least squares. The procedure considers the correlation within the booking horizon as well as correlation between successive horizon instances. The proposed method is tested on three simulated datasets with different characteristics and he finds that forecasting with updating clearly outperforms forecasting without updating.

In Chap. 7 (Part III), Kaya et al. present a novel and practical approach to generate demand forecasts at SKU and store detail in the apparel industry. The generated forecasts help constitute the core input of a larger decision support system that aids apparel managers in matching supply and demand across stores. Their paper makes important contribution in two ways. First, they develop a method that generates forecasts based on the inherent seasonal demand pattern at product category level. This pattern is identified by estimating lost sales and the effects of special events and pricing on demand. The method also allows easy integration of product managers' qualitative information on factors that may affect demand. Second, they develop a fuzzy forecast combiner. The combiner calculates the final forecast using a weighted average of forecasts generated by independent methods. Combination weights are adaptive in the sense that the weights of the better-performing methods are increased over time. Forecast combination operations employ fuzzy logic. They illustrate their approach with a simulation study that uses data from a Turkish apparel firm and shows very promising performance.

The forecasting of fashion colour trends has long been a very challenging problem and the practitioners simply rely on advice of the industrial experts. Unfortunately, it is not scientifically sound and its performance is far from ideal. In Chap. 8 (Part III), Yu et al. propose a novel scientific method to examine the forecasting of colour trends, where the historical observations of fashion colour sales are used for learning the patterns of colour changes. Moreover, this allows learning and forecasting colour trends objectively from the time series data. They report a comparison study among different forecasting methods and models. They find that while the statistical models like Auto Regression Integrated Moving Average (ARIMA) can produce sound forecasting results, the artificial intelligence models like Artificial Neural Network (ANN) can perform slightly better. In addition, with the Fuzzy Neural Network (FNN)-based models, the forecasters do not need to pay attention to the settings of "terms" which correspond to the changing of colour trends, while they get the forecasting result in the forms of descriptive terms directly from the model. This improves the usability of the proposed models.

In Chap. 9 (Part III), Banica et al. explore two forecasting approaches for the clothing industry based on the case in Romania, namely the macroeconomic level (by taking into account the interest of potential investors in this field) and the microeconomic level (representing the analysis of the results of an operational company and the identification of trends that could improve its performances). The authors examine various important questions which include whether: (i) financial forecasting in the fashion sector a method to improve the foreign direct investments in Romania, (ii) sales forecasting of a fashion company is a method to increase the profit and improve the company management. Substantial discussions on the topic are reported and industrial insights are generated.

As we can see from the above introduction, the papers featured in this book have explored different aspects of fashion forecasting with a lot of important insights. A lot of critical issues in fashion forecasting are examined. We believe that this book has generated many new research results which can advance the practice of fashion forecasting and probably also inspire new research on the topic. Moreover, to the best of our knowledge, this book is the first one which scientifically studies to fashion forecasting with the focal point on intelligent systems. Thus, it is in fact the pioneering text on this important topic.

References

1. Holt CC (2004) Forecasting seasonals and trends by exponentially weighted moving averages. Int J Forecasting 20:5–10
2. Choi TM, Yu Y, Au KF (2011) A hybrid SARIMA wavelet transform method for sales forecasting. Decis Support Syst 51:130–140
3. Yu Y, Hui CL, Choi TM, Au R (2010) Intelligent fabric hand prediction system with fuzzy neural network. IEEE Trans Syst Man Cybern C 40:619–629
4. Au KF, Choi TM, Yu Y (2008) Fashion retail forecasting by evolutionary neural networks. Int J Prod Econ 114:615–630
5. El-Bakry HM, Mastorakis N (2008) A new fast forecasting technique using high speed neural networks. In: Proceedings of the 8th WSEAS international conference on signal, speech and image processing (SSIP'08). Spain, pp 116–138
6. Yu Y, Choi TM, Hui CL (2011) An intelligent fast sales forecasting model for fashion products. Expert Syst Appl 38:7373–7379
7. Sun ZL, Choi TM, Au KF, Yu Y (2008) Sales forecasting using extreme learning machine with applications in fashion retailing. Decis Support Syst 46:411–419
8. Yu Y, Choi TM, Hui CL, Ho TK (2011) A new and efficient intelligent collaboration scheme for fashion design. IEEE Trans Syst Man Cybern A 41:463–475
9. Kandil MS, El-Debeiky SM, Hasanien NE (2001) Overview and comparison of long-term forecasting techniques for a fast developing utility: part I. Electr Pow Syst Res 58:11–17
10. Goldstein DG, Gigerenzer G (2009) Fast and frugal forecasting. Int J Forecasting 25:760–772
11. Huang GB, Zhu QY, Siew CK (2006) Extreme learning machine: theory and applications. Neurocomputing 70:489–501
12. Sun ZL, Au KF, Choi TM (2007) A neuro-fuzzy inference system through integration of fuzzy logic and extreme learning machines. IEEE Trans Syst Man Cybern B Cybern 37:1321–1331
13. Hanke JE, Wichern DW (2009) Business forecasting. Prentice Hall, Upper Saddle River

14. Box GEP, Jenkins GM, Reinsel GC (2008) Time series analysis: forecasting and control. Wiley, Hoboken
15. Choi TM, Li D, Yan H (2008) Mean-variance analysis for the newsvendor problem. IEEE Trans Syst Man Cybern A Syst Man 38:1169–1180
16. Singh R, Balasundaram S (2007) Application of extreme learning machine method for time series analysis. Proc World Acad Sci Eng Technol 26:361–367
17. Jana PK, Sinha BP (1997) Fast parallel algorithms for forecasting. Comput Math Appl 34:39–49
18. Willis HL, Parks TW (1983) Fast algorithms for small area electric load forecasting. IEEE Trans Pow Ap Syst PAS-102(10):3425–3432
19. Yu Y, Choi TM, Au KF, Kwan CY (2008) A web-based system for fashion sales forecasting. Res J Text Apparel 12:56–64
20. Yu Y, Hui CL, Choi TM, Ng SFF (2011) A new approach for predicting Fabric Hand. Text Res J 81:574–584
21. Yu Y, Choi TM, Hui CL (2012) An intelligent quick prediction algorithm for industrial control and loading problems. IEEE Trans Autom Sci Eng 9(2):276–287
22. Yu Y, Hui CL, Choi TM (2012) An empirical study of intelligent expert systems on forecasting of fashion color trend. Expert Syst Appl 39:4383–4389
23. Choi TM, Hui CL, Ng SFF, Yu Y (2012) Color trend forecasting of fashionable products with very few historical data. IEEE Trans Syst Man Cybern C 42(6):1003–1010. Doi: 10.1109/TSMCC.2011.2176725)
24. Choi TM, Hui CL, Yu Y (2012) Fashion time series forecasting with limited time and limited data. Working paper
25. Deng JL (1989) Introduction to grey system theory. J Grey Syst 1(1):1–24

Chapter 2
Sales Forecasting in Apparel and Fashion Industry: A Review

Sébastien Thomassey

Abstract The fashion industry is a very fascinating sector for the sales forecasting. Indeed, the long time-to-market which contrasts with the short life cycle of products, makes the forecasting process very challenging. A suitable forecasting system should also deal with the specificities of the demand: fashion trends, seasonality, influence of many exogenous factors, ... We propose here a review of the different constraints related to the sales forecasting in the fashion industry, the methodologies and techniques existing in the literature to cope with these constraints and finally, the new topics which could be explored in the field of the sales forecasting for fashion products.

2.1 Introduction

The clothing industry includes many companies from the spinning to the distribution which are involved from the transformation of the fibre until the final garment (Fig. 2.1). Consequently, the creation of a garment requires a quite long and complex process with many manufacturing steps. The fashion and ephemeral aspect of the finished products contrasts with this long manufacturing process. However, the main actor of this network is the distributor downstream of the process. It makes orders for the upstream companies and supplies the consumer with their products: it is the driver of the all flows in the process.

These different stages with quite long and fluctuated manufacturing times involve a management based on a push flow strategy which makes the supply chain very sensitive to the bullwhip effect. In this context, sales forecasting emerges as a key

S. Thomassey (✉)
ENSAIT-GEMTEX, University Lille Nord of France, 2 allée Louise et Victor Champier, 59100 Roubaix, France
e-mail: sebastien.thomassey@ensait.fr

T.-M. Choi et al. (eds.), *Intelligent Fashion Forecasting Systems: Models and Applications*, DOI 10.1007/978-3-642-39869-8_2,

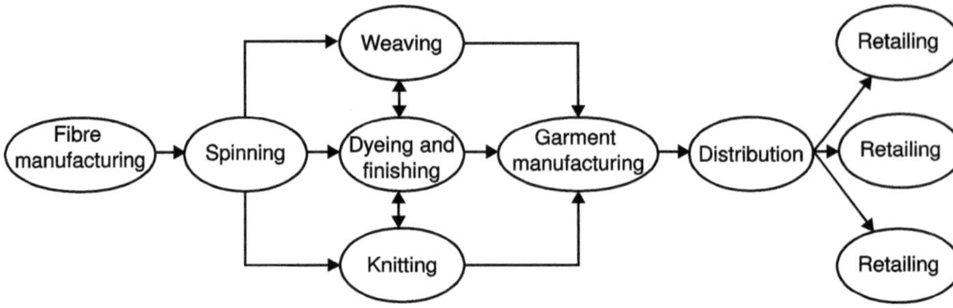

Fig. 2.1 The apparel supply chain

success factor of the supply chain management [59, 68]. However, the specificities of sales in the clothing sector make the forecasting process very complex. Indeed, the long and incompressible manufacturing and shipping lead times required to be provided with long term forecasts. Forecasting systems have also to take into account the particularities of the clothing itself:

- Strong relationships between most garments and the weather make the sales very seasonal. Seasonal data give general trends but unpredictable variations of weather involve significant peaks or hollows.
- Sales are disturbed by many exogenous variables such as end-of-season sale, sales promotion, purchasing power of consumers, etc. ...
- Fashion trends provide very volatile consumer demands [55]. The design and style should be always up to date and most of the items are not renewed for the next collection. Consequently, historical sales are often not available since most of items are ephemeral.
- Product variety is huge. Indeed items are declined in many colour alternatives to meet the fashion trend, and in various sizes which should match with morphologies of the target consumers.

All these constraints make the sales forecasting for apparel companies very specific and complex. Therefore the implementation of such forecasting systems requires not only a strong background in the field of forecasting, but also a full and precise knowledge of the operations and challenges of the fashion industry and its supply chain.

For these reasons, this exciting topic has led to many works in the literature for decades [33, 68].

The next section deals with the main features of the fashion industry and more particularly the requirements in term of sales forecasting. It describes the specificities of the fashion sales which should absolutely be taken into account in the forecasting systems.

The Sect. 2.3 deals with the impacts of forecast errors on the supply chain. A review of the literature of simulations of supply combined with a forecasting system enables to show the real benefits of the reduction of forecast errors.

The Sect. 2.4 investigates the methods used by companies to respond to the constraints of the fashion industry and then suggests existing advanced methods to perform more accurate and reliable sales forecasts. These methods include fuzzy logic, neural networks and data mining.

The last section concludes and suggests some topics which currently arise for the sales forecasting in fashion industry. Sales discount, unsold management, new products, ... are specific cases in the sales forecasting point of view which should be deeply investigated in the near future.

2.2 The Fashion Industry and Its Requirements for Sales Forecasting

Usually, the decision process in the fashion company starts with the definition of budget for the collection and/or the sourcing. When designers have selected the items which should be included in the collection, the mix of budget and sales forecasting enables managers to launch the purchases or the production [67].

In fashion industry, it is commonly known that consumer demands are very volatile [21,55]. Indeed, consumers are very unfaithful and generally their selection is first based on the price of the product. Facing these constraints, companies try to reduce their production costs by keeping a high service level. Thus, most of manufacturing processes, detailed in Fig. 2.1, are performed in far away and low cost countries. This strategy leads to the increase in the lead time and the lot size of supplies. Consequently, the supply chain management has to be optimized to avoid delay, out of stock, unsold and to keep the right inventory level. Therefore, many supply chain management tools have enabled companies to improve scheduling and synchronizing of material and information flows. Most of these tools can be customized to the specific constraints of the clothing retailing, however their efficiency is mostly dependent of the accuracy of sales forecasts.

In order to perform suitable sales forecasting for the supply chain management, it is crucial to perfectly know the product, the sales features and how the distributor will use the forecasts [8], especially in the very specific environment of the fashion industry.

The following subsections describes the main characteristics which should be taken in account to design a sales forecasting system for the fashion industry.

2.2.1 Horizon

The forecast horizon is one of most important feature of the forecasting system. Indeed, higher is the horizon, better is the anticipation, but higher are the errors of forecasts. Consequently, it is important to rigorously define the required horizon.

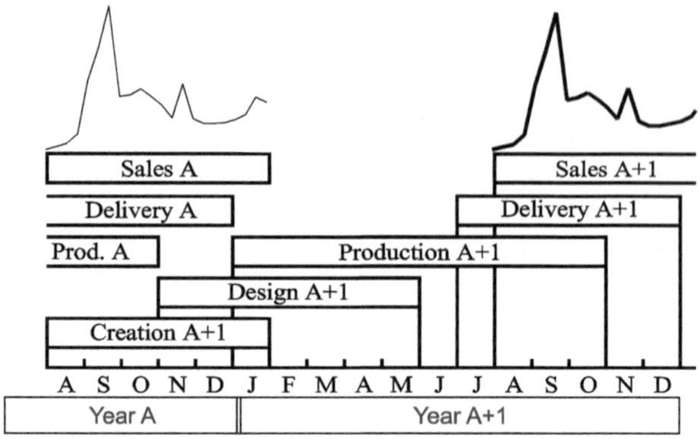

Fig. 2.2 Example of planning for autumn-winter items

With the supply strategy defined previously, many decisions are based on sales forecasting: purchases, orders, replenishments, inventory allocations, ... All these decisions should be considered in a sufficient time according to the incompressible lead times for production, shipment,transportation, quality control, ...

Furthermore, the supply strategy of clothing companies is generally composed on two steps:

1. A first order at the beginning of the season to enable the supply of the stores and to achieve to a right inventory level in warehouse.
2. One or more replenishments for some items during the season.

Considering the schedule of design/production/distribution of clothing items given for instance in Fig. 2.2, this strategy involves two horizons of forecast:

- A long term horizon, i.e. 1 year, to plan the sourcing and the production,
- A short term horizon, i.e. a few weeks, to replenish if necessary and to adjust the orders and deliveries of local stores.

Consequently, the sales forecasting system should provide two forecasts with two different horizons. The methods and models used to compute the forecast are obviously different according to the considered horizon.

2.2.2 *Life Cycle*

For most of the products, the life cycle is generally composed of four phases: the launch (or the implantation), the rise, the maturation and the decline. However in fashion industry, it is commonly known that life cycle of products is quite short especially compared with their long supply process [21, 55, 64].

Furthermore for clothing products, different categories should be differentiated according to the nature of items:

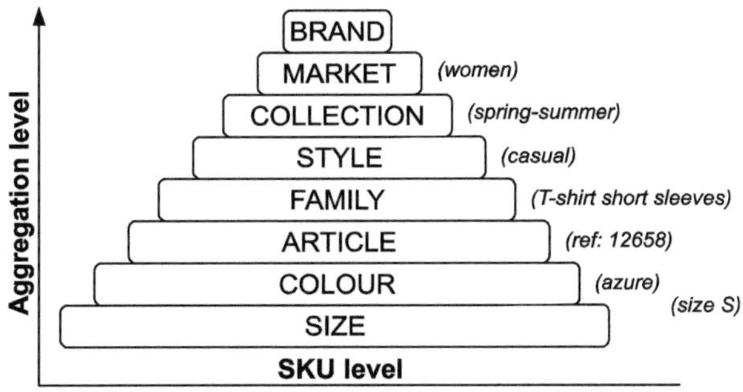

Fig. 2.3 Example of data aggregation by topology of products

- Basic items which are sold throughout the year (for instance denims) or each year (for instance basic white T-Shirt).
- Fashion items, including "one shot" items, which are sold punctually in a short period. They are generally not replenished.
- Best selling items are sold each year with slight modifications according to the fashion trends and could be replenished during the season.

The high variety of products generates strong differences in term of life cycles and it would be simplistic to assume that they all have the same behaviour.

In terms of forecasting, basic items and "best-selling" items are usually taken into account in sales forecasting system, while fashion items with "one shot" supply are often not considered in the "traditional" forecasting process. In fact, this category of products, widely used by the "fast fashion" brands, has specific forecasts, especially for the allocation of stocks in the stores and management of shelves [16].

2.2.3 *Aggregation*

In fashion industry, the product variety is one of the heaviest constraint. Indeed, the fashion trends involve many styles and colours. Combined with the variations in sizes, the product variety becomes huge [55, 64] and makes the management of Stock Keeping Unit (SKU) very complex.

In the point of view of sales forecasting, this variety, the short lifespan and the reference changing for each collection, require the company to aggregate the data. The main issue is then to select the right level and criteria for the aggregation. Classification methods based on quantitative or qualitative attributes could be implemented (see Sect. 2.4.2.2), but companies usually prefer to conveniently aggregate their data from a hierarchical classification of the topology of products [24] (Fig. 2.3). The suitable level for sales forecasts based for instance on time series techniques, is the lower level which enables the company to get historical data of several years ("family" level in Fig. 2.3). In the lower levels, for instance the SKU level, data are ephemeral and no historical data are available. Thus, other techniques based on data mining and classification should be implemented.

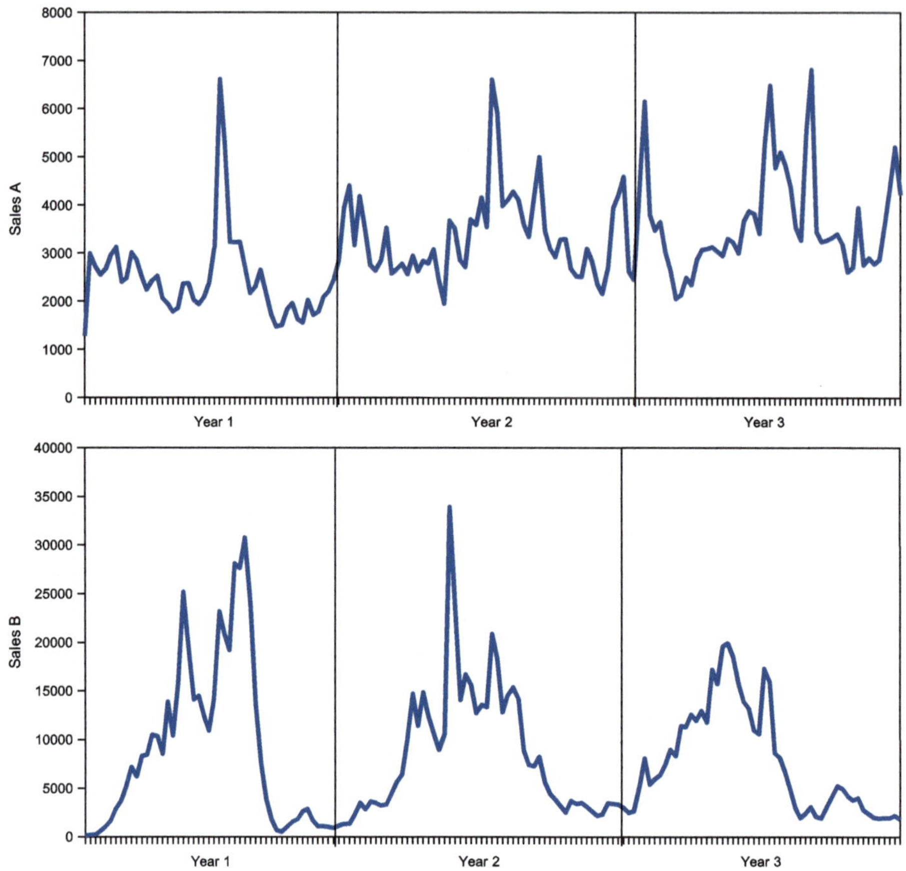

Fig. 2.4 Example of sensitivity to the seasonal variation: underpants (A) and short sleeve T-shirts (B) sales

2.2.4 *Seasonality*

Seasonality is also an important feature which has to be taken into account for every time series analysis, such as sales forecasting and which has been widely investigated in literature [18, 28, 36].

However in fashion industry, some items are logically very sensitive to the seasonal variation, such as swim wears or pull overs, others are not impacted, such as underpants. The Fig. 2.4 illustrates the sales of two basic items with a different behaviour in term of seasonality:

- (A) Underpants are not sensitive to seasonal variations. Their sales do not clearly show any periodic fluctuations

- (B) Short sleeve T-shirts are seasonal products. The amount of their sales is obviously larger during the hot period of each year.

Thus, according to the sensitivity of the considered item, the seasonality should be more or less integrated into the forecasting system for clothing sales.

2.2.5 *Exogenous Variables*

The clothing market is strongly impacted by numerous factors which make the sales very fluctuated. These factors, also called explanatory variables, are sometimes not controlled and even unknown. Some of them involve an increase of the purchase decision, others modify the store traffic [43]. Hence, the difficulty to exactly identify them and to quantify their impact [25].

Figure 2.5 illustrates the variables which are commonly taken into account by marketing experts (non-exhaustive list) for their influence on store traffic and/or purchase decision [43].

The impact of these factors could be very dissimilar on sales. Indeed, some factors generate punctual fluctuations without significantly affecting the overall volume of sales, for instance a temporal price discount produces peaks of sales as illustrated in Fig. 2.6. Others impact more globally the sales such as macro-economic data or strategy of retail. For instance, sales of the year 3 in Fig. 2.6 show an unexpected decline which could be explained from these kind of factors.

Regarding the previous remarks, practitioners have to keep in mind when building the forecasting system that [59]:

- Explanatory variables are essential to model the clothing sales and if possible the most relevant ones have to be integrated in the computation of the forecast.
- These variables are many and varied and it is not possible to establish an exhaustive list.
- The impact of each of these variables is particularly difficult to estimate and it is not constant over time.
- These variables can be correlated on them. This strongly complicates the understanding and the modelling of their impact on sales.
- Some variables are not available (i.e. competitor data) or predictable (i.e. weather data) and thus can not be integrated in the forecasting system.

2.3 Impacts of Forecast Errors

The direct effects of forecasting on efficiency, costs, inventory levels, or customer service levels is difficult to understand [4, 58]. In literature, many works rely on more or less complex simulations of a supply chain or more frequently a sample of a supply chain with different scenarios in many industrial fields.

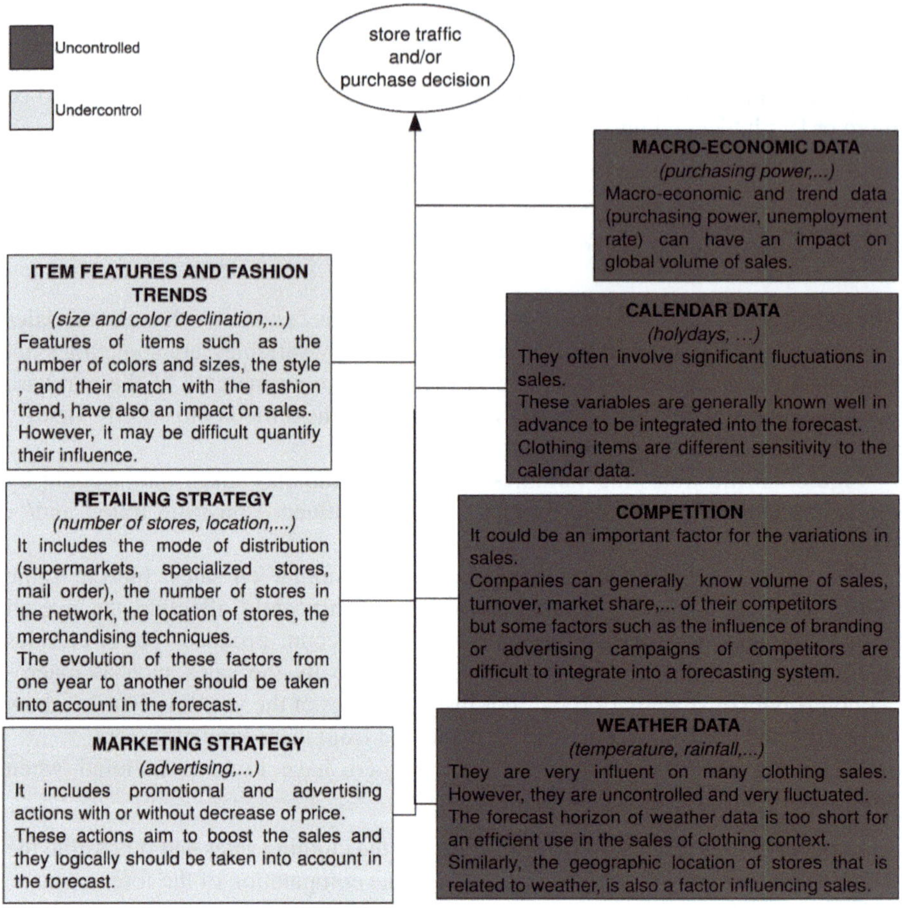

Fig. 2.5 Exogenous factors (non exhaustive list) related to the sales of clothing items

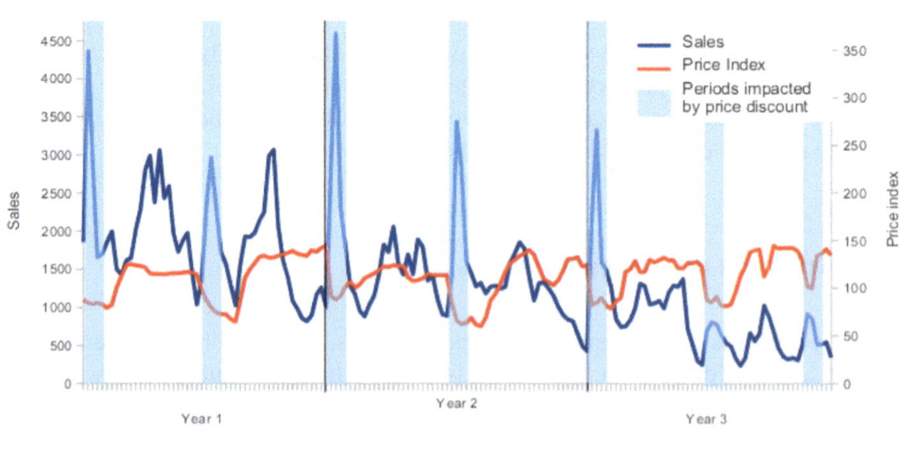

Fig. 2.6 Sales sensitivity to the price discount

It generally emerges that for most companies, based on push flow supply chain, sales forecasting arises as an important factor for the supply chain management. Indeed, many researches has demonstrated that a reduction of forecast errors leads to better supply chain performances [10, 29, 54, 75].

In [34], the authors investigate seven supply chains in different industrial sectors and they conclude that a suitable forecasting model enables to stabilize the supply chain especially for price-sensitive products.

In [9], an empirical analysis of the sales of more 300 SKUs of a superstore, clearly exhibits the relationship between forecast errors, inventory holdings and inventory costs.

In [29], the authors simulate a MRP method to understand and quantify the effect of forecasting on different indicators such as cost, inventory level, service level, ... they find that reducing the errors of forecast provides better benefits than choosing inventory decision rules. They also show that a misspecification of the forecasting method definitely increases costs.

In the same way, [2] investigates the relationship between forecasting and operational performances in the supply chain in chemical industry. They showed that the choice of the forecasting method strongly impacts the customer service and the costs.

Information sharing, and more especially the sharing of forecast data, also strongly impacts the supply chain management [3, 15, 42, 73]. In [78], a simulation is achieved on a sample of supply chain composed of a manufacturer and a retailer. Different scenarios are investigated including sharing information and forecast accuracy. They conclude that even if the manufacturer can get the same level of forecast accuracy as the retailer, the manufacturer would still prefer to share the forecasting demand of the retailer, instead of forecasting it himself. Thus, forecast effort should be done downstream of the supply chain, i.e. as close as possible of the demand of final users.

Some studies deal with the case of fashion industries with the constraints defined in Sect. 2.2 (long lead times, ephemeral and fashion items, etc. ...). It generally emerges that the forecast accuracy arises as one of the successful factors in supply chain management especially for fashion products [45]. The benefits of the implementation of advanced forecasting techniques can be evaluated at different levels:

- Reduction of the bullwhip effect [56, 71] without major supply chain reorganization [17].
- Possibility for the supplier to smooth out production, to optimize its resources, to decrease costs, and to improve the effectiveness of retailer's sourcing strategy [74].
- Reduction of lost sales, markdowns and consequently increase profit margin [45].

In [59] a simulation of the sourcing process of a retailer and a manufacturer is performed to quantify the impact of the forecast accuracy specifically on clothing supply chain. This simulation takes all the constraints into account described in

Sect. 2.2 and is implemented on real data of 20 items .... The sourcing strategy, including minimum reorder size, replenishment decision, ... is based on a Quick Response method [6].

Concerning the forecasts, this simulation implements sales forecasting at SKU level for a long-term horizon (a whole season). This forecasting system enables the retailer to estimate the sales in the stores at the beginning of the season. The forecasts of the whole season are shared with the manufacturer.

Different forecast scenarios are then simulated:

1. A scenario called "data mining based forecast" which uses the data mining based forecasting system developed in [60]. This system performs accurate forecasts.
2. A scenario called "average profile" forecast where forecasts are the average of the sales profiles of historical items of the same family. This method could be considered as the method commonly used technique in many companies.
3. A scenario called "flat profile forecast" where forecasts are the weekly average of the sales quantity of the whole season. This is a very basic forecast used as a benchmark.

The quantitative results of this study show that the scenario 1, using the more advanced forecasting system, enables significant reduction of the inventory level of the retailer (between 11.5 and 18 % according to the scenario), the inventory level of the manufacturer (around 11 %), the lost sales in stores (between 4.5 and 11 %) whereas the gross margin rises (between 8 and 14 %) (see [59] for more details).

Finally, these results obviously demonstrate the beginning of a bullwhip effect on a two stage supply chain and they suggest a significant amplification on the whole supply chain.

As per these studies, it seems obvious that fashion companies have to implement a suitable forecasting system and share their forecasts, and then have to try to restructure and/or rethink their supply chain to reduce the lead times and minimum order quantities.

2.4 Sales Forecasting Methods for Fashion Industry

Time series forecasting methods are probably the most used techniques for prediction of sales data. These statistical techniques include various well-known models that have formal statistical foundations [23]: exponential smoothing [13], Holt Winters model [66], Box & Jenkins model [12], regression models [51] or ARIMA. These methods have been implemented in different areas and they provide satisfactory results [40]. However, their efficiency strongly depends of the field of application, the forecast goal (especially the horizon) or the user experience [8]. Consequently, for the reasons described in Sect. 2.2, these methods are not easily and not efficiently implemented in the textile-apparel environment and more generally in any fashion sectors, especially because most of time series methods require large historical data sets, a complex optimization of their parameters, a certain experience of the operator, and they are limited to linear structure.

Many commercial softwares are based on these statistical techniques and enable the operator to automatically select the more suitable methods according to the considered data set [37]. Thus, ARIMA, Holt winters, Box & Jenkins or regression methods are implemented in various software such as *Autobox* of AFS, *Forecast Pro* of BFS, *SmartForecasts* of SmartSoftware, ... Few softwares, *SPSS Neural Networks* of IBM or *Forecaster* of Alyuda, use advanced computing techniques such as neural networks. In the last decade, the main trend is the implementation of forecasting tools into integrated softwares such as ERP: *Aperia Forecaster* of Aperia, *SAP Demand planning* of SAP, *TXT-Integrated Retail planning* of TXT Group, ... Some companies propose also specific systems for apparel and fashion industry: *Forecast Management* of Demand Solutions, *Optimate* of SEI. These softwares provide to the users useful tools which enable the management of the splitting by size and colour and the Point Of Store (POS) data.

2.4.1 Usual Methods

Despite of the various and advanced methods implemented in commercial softwares, they are seldom used in the textile-apparel industry. Their cost could be one reason but not only. Indeed, to obtain an optimized automatic treatment, the implementation of such systems on huge and customized databases could be very fastidious. Moreover, and maybe the main cause, practitioners want and need to keep control on their forecasts. No company agrees to let forecasting decision to a software, although it is very accurate. In fact, automatic forecasts from softwares, if they exist, are generally used as baseline for the final forecasts of the practitioners.

Due to the constraints described in Sect. 2.2, for ease of interpretation and understanding, and for cost reduction, companies have attempted to implement their own forecasting system. These customized systems, based on practitioner experiment, generally achieve relatively acceptable accuracy. Each companies use its own tips to perform what should be the best forecast.

The main frame is generally composed of a baseline forecast, extracted of a specific software or more basically sales of last year. The practitioner then reworks this baseline according to explanatory variables which are taken into account. For instance, the practitioner modifies the curves according to the price reduction periods and of course his knowledge of the market. The result could be very accurate since seasonality and impact of main explanatory variables are taken into account. However, this method has various drawbacks:

- The number of variables treated is limited, if not the analysis becomes too complex and imprecise,
- This work can be very tedious if the number of items is large,
- The results are fluctuating according to the experience of the operator.

For these reasons, the practitioner needs to use more advanced techniques to increase the accuracy of sales forecasts. These techniques are introduced in the following section.

2.4.2 Advanced Sales Forecasting Methods

The first parameter to take into account when designing a forecasting model is the availability of historical data. As shown in Sect. 2.2.3, fashion industry mainly needs forecasts at two levels of data aggregation:

- The "family level" composed of items of same category (T-Shirts, trousers, ...) which enables companies to plan and to schedule purchase, production and supply at mid term. For this aggregation level, historical data usually exist.
- The "SKU level" which is required to replenish and to allocate inventory in stores at a shorter horizon. At this level, references (SKU) are ephemeral since they are created for only one season. Thus, historical data are not available, even if many items more or less similar have usually been sold in previous seasons.

2.4.2.1 Forecasting Methods with Historical Data

When historical data are available, the forecasting system has to extract the maximum information as possible from the past years. For fashion items such as garments, these information are the traditional trend and seasonality but also the impact of exogenous factors. If the two firsts should require many attentions and skills, the last one is very difficult to model and to control (see Sect. 2.2.5) and requires advanced techniques.

Among these techniques, neural networks (NN) are probably the more used techniques in sales forecasting especially for short-term forecast where the main issue is to be reactive to the last known sales [69]. NN perform generally well for sales forecasting if the demand is not seasonal and quite non fluctuating [67]. Consequently, if NN are directly implemented without advanced pretreatment of data or learning techniques, they are not suitable for fashion items. Therefore, many hybrid techniques based on NN have emerged to fit the features of the considered demand.

Recently, extreme learning machine (ELM) algorithms has been widely described and implemented in the literature for sales forecasting issues, and more especially for the learning process of NN [19, 35, 57, 67, 68, 77]. Comparing with NN based models with gradient learning algorithms, ELM should be better in generalization and faster in learning [67].

In [57], a NN model with extreme learning machine for fashion sales forecasting with a short term horizon is proposed. Their model enables to quantify the relationship between sales amount and some significant fashion product attributes such as colour, size and price.

In [67], the authors propose a sales forecasting method for fashion retailing, which performs mid-term forecasts (from annual to monthly forecasts) by item categories or cities. The proposed method relies on a hybrid intelligent model comprising a data pre-processing component and a forecaster (based on ELM). This method is claimed to overcome the limitations of NN and to tackle the sales forecasting problems in the fashion retail supply chain.

If ELM have demonstrated their effectiveness in sales forecasting problem, even in fashion industry, they still may suffer, like gradient or back propagation methods, of over-fitting or under-fitting especially for fashion sales data.

In [68], the authors have performed a hybrid model based on ELM with adaptive metrics of inputs to avoid over-fitting problem. Their model provides more accurate forecasts than other sales forecasting models (AR and ANN) implemented on fashion retailing data.

However, results obtained in this works only concern one-step-ahead point forecasting with monthly data.

In [19], another neural network methodology is proposed: a forecasting model based on a Gray relation analysis integrated with extreme learning machine (GELM) for the retail industry. According to experimental results, this hybrid system enables to select more significant influential factors, to increase the learning speed and to improve the forecasting performance comparing with other advanced models based on GARCH model and back-propagation network

Other soft computing techniques for sales forecasting have also been successfully implemented in fashion industry.

Fuzzy logic and Fuzzy Inference Systems (FIS) are commonly used to model uncertain knowledge and non-linear, fluctuating, disturbed and incomplete data [70]. These characteristics lead to implement fuzzy inference systems to model complex relationships between data, such as the influence of exogenous factors on sales [39].

For instance, a such system has been implemented on real data in [62]. The FIS is first used to quantify and to remove the influence of exogenous factors on historical sales. Statistical models based on seasonality can be then applied to forecast the sales of the future season without exogenous factors. The influence of exogenous factors existing in the future season are obtained by the FIS and are added on the seasonality based forecast to provide the final forecast. The inference rules and parameters of the FIS are extracted and optimized from the historical database with genetic algorithm. In this study, considered exogenous factors are the price, the holidays and season period.

Comparing with traditional forecasting models on real sales of 322 item families, this fuzzy based system improves significantly the accuracy of the mid-term forecast (one season ahead).

This result demonstrates that the right estimation of influences of exogenous factors is a key point for the sales forecasting of fashion items.

To conclude, advanced techniques such as ELM or FIS enable to improve the forecast accuracy compared with traditional time-series methods or traditional NN models. But different works never achieve a benchmark with real forecasts of retailers, which could be the only criteria for retailers to implement the model or not.

2.4.2.2 Forecasting Methods Without Historical Data

Most of fashion items are sold during only one season. Companies have to estimate the sales without any historical data: the forecasting system should be then designed for new product sales forecasting. New product forecasting is one of the most difficult forecasting problem [20]. Indeed, forecasting methods described in Sect. 2.4.2.1 are not suitable. In this context, a two-step methodology seems emerged:

1. To cluster and to classify new products to forecast their sales profile (mid-term forecast).
2. To adapt and to readjust this profile according to the first weeks of sales (short-term forecast).

If no historical data exists for the considered item, but similar products have already been sold in previous seasons. Indeed, new products usually replace old ones with almost the same style and/or functionality (i.e. T-shirt, pull over, ...), it is thus possible to use historical data of similar products to estimate the sales profile of the new products [53].

Thus, to forecast the sales profiles of new products such as garments with clustering and classification techniques, descriptive attributes (price, life span, sales period, style, ...) of historical and new products should be taken into account. The aim is to model the relationship between historical data, i.e. between sales and descriptive criteria of related items, and then to use these relationships to forecast future sales from descriptive criteria of new items.

These relationships are often complex and non-linear [5]. For this kind of problem, machine learning methods have demonstrated their efficiency for building simple and interpretable pattern classification models [41, 48].

This methodology has been successfully implemented in [60] and [61] for fashion sales forecasting. The process consists to:

1. Cluster the historical products which have similar sales profiles.
2. Establish links between sales profiles and descriptive criteria of historical products.
3. Assign each new product to one sales profile from its descriptive criteria.

The choice of the clustering and the classification methods varies according to the type and the number of data.

The clustering procedure could be based on the classic and straightforward k-means method if the number of data is reasonable, whereas more advanced techniques based on neural techniques such as Self Organizing Map (SOM) [38] should be preferred if dataset is larger, noisier or contains outliers [65].

For the classification procedure, neural networks and decision trees are considered as the most competitive techniques for this kind of applications [41, 63]. Neural networks are generally preferred for their generalization ability [76] and provide best results with numerical data. Decision trees obviously outperform neural networks in term of interpretability [72], seem less sensitivity to reductions in sample size and perform best with non-numerical data [14, 44].

As for any machine learning system, the main drawback of this method is that the data have to be reliable and relevant, especially for the descriptive criteria.

If the forecast of the sales profiles is very useful for a mid-term horizon at SKU level, it should be improved for short term forecasting. Indeed, allocation of inventory, replenishment of stores, ... require accurate weekly and sometimes daily sales forecasting.

For this purpose, the strategy of "pre-sales" is often implemented for fashion products and more generally for new product forecasting.

Whenever it is possible, i.e. when replenishments are possible at low cost and with reasonable lead time, companies can supply some new products in a small sample of selected stores for a short period before the selling season. The analysis of these sales gives precious information for the whole supply.

In other cases, different models have been performed to extrapolate the future sales from few weeks of sales. In [30], pre-sales data enable to cluster stores of fashion merchandise. The pre-sales data at the representative stores is then used to estimate the sales at all the other stores in the same cluster.

In [31], 3 weeks of sales are used to determine the success or the failure of a new product. These 3 weeks enable them to define sales forecast ratio and to perform weekly forecasts.

Another method is based on a truncated Taylor Series [46]. The sales forecast is assumed as a Taylor Series where the first derivatives are the most important component. The final forecast is computed from a weighted sum of historical data with more weight to more recent data.

In [47], a diffusion model is implemented to forecast new product sales. Under some assumptions, the sales are extrapolated from a non-linear symmetric logistic curve considering saturation level, inflection point and delay factor of life cycle of products.

In [20], the authors propose an original decision support system for new product sales forecasting. This system automatically selects the best model according to the characteristics of the data and the requirements of the user. The models implemented are classical time-series models but also the specific models previously described. They obtained good results on real data but this system as not been tested on fashion items.

In any case, these methods require that products have already been classified according to their sales profiles.

2.5 Conclusion and Scopes

Sales forecasting in fashion industry is a challenging issue for many years. A lot of efforts has been done to improve the accuracy of forecasting systems with the specific constraints in this interesting field.

Advanced techniques such as extreme learning machine have enabled searchers to increase the capacity of systems to extract information from historical data, even if these data are strongly disturbed.

Data mining techniques and extrapolation techniques based on "pre-sales" can be very powerful when no historical data are available.

All these techniques will be improved again and again in the near future. However, other topics could be also very interesting to investigate. Indeed, the fashion industry is a very dynamic sector. New markets emerge and consequently new constraints and new requirements for the forecasting systems. These evolutions are attractive opportunities for researchers in the next decades.

Among these new trends, mass customisation strategy currently represents a small sample of products but could rise and change the needs in term of forecast and supply.

A further interesting trend is the fast fashion strategy [16]. Some famous brands successfully use this strategy and their requirements in sales forecasting are very specific.

Finally, another way of improvement for the fashion sales forecasting could be a deeper investigation of the management of the price discount, promotion, unsold, ... Indeed, fashion items are very price sensitive. Managers usually drive their sales with price discounts during the selling period to avoid end season inventory.

A decision support system based on sales forecasting to help companies to manage their sales and also their profits according to the price of the product could be very useful system. In a such system, the forecast engine should be able to accurately model the relationship between sales and price of a product.

Many studies have focused on the effect of promotions on sales in different industrial fields [1, 11, 22, 26, 27, 49, 50].

In [52], the authors implement a structural equation modelling [32] to understand how different demand factors, such as promotional factors, influence sales. Their proposed method was developed using weekly sales data of individual products of a leading Soft Drink Company.

In [7], a simulation of a two echelon supply chain with price sensitive demand is carried out. This simulation aims to investigate the impact of price discount on the profits of the manufacturer, the retailer and the consumer according to different strategies. This work demonstrates that relationships between price and the real profits of the actors of the supply chain is very complex.

Therefore, many profitable improvements specific to the fashion industry and using advanced forecasting techniques, could be done in this purpose.

References

1. Abraham M, Lodish L (1987) PROMOTER: an automated promotion evaluation system. Mark Sci 6(2):101–123
2. Acar Y, Gardner ES (2012) Forecasting method selection in a global supply chain. Int J Forecast 28(4):842–848
3. Agrawal S, Sengupta RN, Shanker K (2009) Impact of information sharing and lead time on bullwhip effect and on-hand inventory. Eur J Oper Res 192(2):576–593

4. Ali MM, Boylan JE, Syntetos AA (2012) Forecast errors and inventory performance under forecast information sharing. Int J Forecast 28(4):830–841
5. Altam EI, Macro G, Varetto F (1994) Corporate distress diagnosis: comparison using linear discriminant analysis and neural networks. J Bank Finance 18:505–529
6. Al-Zubaidi H, Tyler D (2004) A simulation model of quick response replenishment of seasonal clothing. Int J Retail Distrib Manag 32(6):320–327
7. Arcelusa FJ, Satyendra Kumar, Srinivasand G (2008) Pricing and rebate policies in the two-echelon supply chain with asymmetric information under price-dependent, stochastic demand. Int J Prod Econ 113:598–618
8. Armstrong JS (2001) Principles of forecasting – a handbook for researchers and practitioners. Kluwer, Norwell
9. Babai MZ, Ali MM, Boylan JE, Syntetos AA (2013) Forecasting and inventory performance in a two-stage supply chain with ARIMA(0,1,1) demand: theory and empirical analysis. Int J Prod Econ 143(2):463–471
10. Bayraktar E, Koh S, Gunasekaran A, Sari K, Tatoglu E (2008) The role of forecasting on bullwhip effect for E-SCM applications. Int J Prod Econ 113(1):193–204
11. Blattberg RC, Levin A (1987) Modelling the effectiveness and profitability of trade promotions. Mark Sci 6(2):124–146
12. Box GEP, Jenkins GM (1969) Time series analysis forecasting and control. Prentice Hall, Englewood Cliffs
13. Brown RG (1959) Smoothing forecasting and prediction of discrete time series. Prentice Hall, Englewood Cliffs
14. Bryson KMO (2004) Evaluation of decision trees: a multi-criteria approach. Comput Oper Res 31:1933–1945
15. Byrne PJ, Heavey C (2006) The impact of information sharing and forecasting in capacitated industrial supply chains: a case study. Int J Prod Econ 103(1):420–437
16. Caro F, Gallien J (2010) Inventory management of a fast-fashion retail network. Oper Res 58(2):257–273
17. Chandra C (2005) Application of multi-steps forecasting for restraining the bullwhip effect and improving inventory performance under autoregressive demand. Eur J Oper Res 166(2): 337–350
18. Chatfield C (2003) The analysis of time series: an introduction. Chapman & Hall/CRC, New York
19. Chen FL, Ou TY (2011) Sales forecasting system based on Gray extreme learning machine with Taguchi method in retail industry. Expert Syst Appl 38:1336–1345
20. Ching-Chin C, Ieng AIK, Ling-Ling W, Ling-Chieh K (2010) Designing a decision-support system for new product sales forecasting. Expert Syst Appl 37:1654–1665
21. Choi TM (2007) Pre-season stocking and pricing decisions for fashion retailers with multiple information updating. Int J Prod Econ 106(1):146–170
22. Christen M, Gupta S, Porter JC, Staelin R, Wittink DR (1997) Using market level data to understand promotion effects in a nonlinear model. Mark Res 34(3):322–334
23. Chu CW, Peter Zhang GQ (2003) A comparative study of linear and nonlinear models for aggregate retail sales forecasting. Int J Prod Econ 86:217–231
24. Correa J (2007) Optimization of a fast-response distribution network. M.S. thesis, LFM, Massachusetts Institute of Technology
25. De Toni A, Meneghetti A (2000) The production planning process for a network of firms in the textile-apparel industry. Int J Prod Econ 65:17–32
26. Divakar S, Ratchford BT, Shankar V (2005) CHAN4CAST: a multichannel, multi-region sales forecasting model and decision support system for consumer packaged goods. Mark Sci 24(3):334–350
27. Dube J-P (2004) Multiple discreteness and product differentiation: demand for carbonated soft drinks. Mark Sci 23(1):66–81
28. Franses PH (1996) Recent advances in modelling seasonality. J Econ Surv 10(3):299–345

29. Fildes R, Kingsman BG (2010) Incorporating demand uncertainty and forecast error in supply chain planning models. J Oper Res Soc 62:483–500
30. Fisher M, Rajaram K (2000) Accurate retail testing of fashion merchandise: methodology and application. Mark Sci 19(3):266–278
31. Goldfisther K, Chan C (1995) New product reactive forecasting. J Bus Forecast Methods Syst 13(4):7–9
32. Hair JF, Black WC, Babin BJ, Anderson RE, Tatham RL (2006) Multivariate data analysis, 6th edn. Prentice-Hall, New Jersey
33. Hammond JH (1990) Quick response in apparel industries. Havard Business school, Cambridge
34. Hill A, Doran D, Stratton R (2012) How should you stabilise your supply chains? Int J Prod Econ 135(2):870–881
35. Huang GB, Zhu QY, Siew CK (2004) Extreme learning machine: a new learning scheme of feedforward neural networks. In: Proceedings of the international joint conference on neural networks (IJCNN2004), Budapest, pp 25–29
36. Hylleberg S (1992) Modelling seasonality. Oxford University Press, Oxford
37. Jain, CL (2007) Benchmarking forecasting software and systems. J Bus Forecast Methods Syst 26(4):30–33
38. Kohonen T (2001) Self-organizing maps. In: Springer series in information sciences, 3rd edn. Springer, Berlin
39. Kuo RJ (2001) A sales forecasting system based on fuzzy neural network with initial weights generated by genetic algorithm. Eur J Oper Res 129:496–517
40. Kuo RJ, Xue KC (1999) Fuzzy neural networks with application to sales forecasting. Fuzzy Sets Syst 108:123–143
41. Lee KC, Oh SB (1996) An intelligent approach to time series identification by a neural network-driven decision tree classifier. Decis Support Syst 17:183–197
42. Lee H, So K, Tang C (2000) The value of information sharing in a two-level supply chain. Manag Sci 46(5):626–643
43. Little JDC (1998) Integrated measures of sales, merchandising and distribution. Int J Res Mark 15:473–485
44. Mak B, Munakata T (2002) Rule extraction from expert heuristics: a comparative study of rough sets with neural networks and ID3. Eur J Oper Res 136:212–229
45. Mattila H, King R, Ojala N (2002) Retail performance measures for seasonal fashion. J Fash Mark Manag 6(4):340–351
46. McLean, BL, Wortham AW (1988) Methodology aids forecasting with limited amounts of data. Ind Eng 20(2):18–22
47. Morrison J (1996) How to use diffusion models in new product forecasting. J Bus Forecast Methods Syst 15(2):6–9
48. Muller W, Wiederhold E (2002) Applying decision tree methodology for rules extraction under cognitive constraints. Eur J Oper Res 136(2):282–289
49. Naik PA, Raman K, Winer RS (2005) Planning marketing-mix strategies in the presence of interaction effects. Mark Sci 24(1):25–34
50. Nair H, Dube J-P, Chintagunta P (2005) Accounting for primary and secondary demand effects with aggregate data. Mark Sci 24(3):444–460
51. Papalexopoulos AD, Hesterberg TC (1990) A regression-based approach to short-term system load forecasting. IEEE Trans Power Syst 5:1535–1547
52. Ramanathan U, Muyldermans L (2010) Identifying demand factors for promotional planning and forecasting: a case of a soft drink company in the UK. Int J Prod Econ 128:538–545
53. Saaksvuori A, Immonen A (2005) Product lifecycle management, 2nd edn. Springer-Verlag, Berlin and Heidelberg GmbH & C
54. Saeed K (2008) Trend forecasting for stability in supply chains. J Bus Res 61:1113–1124
55. Sen A (2008) The US fashion industry – a supply chain review. Int J Prod Econ 114:571–593
56. So KC, Zheng X (2003) Impact of supplier's lead time and forecast demand updating on retailer's order quantity variablility in a two-level supply chain. Int J Prod Econ 86:169–179

57. Sun ZL, Choi TM, Au KF, Yu Y (2008) Sales forecasting using extreme learning machine with applications in fashion retailing. Decis Support Syst 46:411–419
58. Syntetos AA, Nikolopoulos K, Boylan JE, Fildes R, Goodwin P (2009) The effects of integrating management judgement into intermittent demand forecasts. Int J Prod Econ 118:72–81
59. Thomassey S (2012) Sales forecasts in clothing industry – the key success factor of the supply chain management. Int J Prod Econ 128:470–483
60. Thomassey S, Fiordaliso A (2006) A hybrid sales forecasting system based on clustering and decision trees. Decis Support Syst 42(1):408–421
61. Thomassey S, Happiette M (2007) A neural clustering and classification system for sales forecasting of new apparel items. Appl Soft Comput 7(4):1177–1187
62. Thomassey S, Happiette M, Castelain JM (2005) A short and mean-term automatic forecasting system – application to textile logistics. Eur J Oper Res 161(1):275–284
63. Tsujino K, Nishida S (1995) Implementation and refinement of decision trees using neural networksTsujinoK for hybrid knowledge acquisition. Artif Intell Eng 9:265–275
64. Vaagen H, Wallace SW (2008) Product variety arising from hedging in the fashion supply chains. Int J Prod Econ 114(2):431–455
65. Vesanto J, Alhoniemi E (2000) Clustering of the self-organizing map. IEEE Trans Neural Netw 11(3):586–600
66. Winters PR (1960) Forecasting sales by exponential weighed moving averages. Manag Sci 6:324–342
67. Wong WK, Guo ZX (2010) A hybrid intelligent model for medium-term sales forecasting in fashion retail supply chains using extreme learning machine and harmony search algorithm. Int J Prod Econ 128(2):614–624
68. Xia M, Zhang Y, Weng L, Ye X (2012) Fashion retailing forecasting based on extreme learning machine with adaptive metrics of inputs. Knowl Based Syst 36:253–259
69. Yoo H, Pimmel RL (1999) Short-term load forecasting using a self-supervised adaptive neural network. IEEE Trans Power Syst 14(2):779–784
70. Zadeh LA (1994) Soft computing and fuzzy logic. IEEE Soft 11(6):48–56
71. Zhang X (2004) The impact of forecasting methods on the bullwhip effect. Int J Prod Econ 88:15–27
72. Zhou ZH, Jiang Y (2004) NeC4.5: neural ensemble based C4.5. IEEE Trans Knowl Data Eng 16(6):770–773
73. Zhao X, Xie J (2002) Forecasting errors and the value of information sharing in a supply chain. Int J Prod Res 40(2):311–335
74. Zhao X, Xie J, Lau RSM (2001) Improving the supply chain performance: use of forecasting models versus early order commitments. Int J Prod Res 39(17):3923–3939
75. Zhao X, Xie J, Leung J (2002) The impact of forecasting model selection on the value of information sharing in a supply chain. Eur J Oper Res 142(2):321–344
76. Zhou ZH, Wu J, Tang W (2002) Ensembling neural networks: many could be better than all. Artif Intell 137(1–2):239–263
77. Zhu Q, Qin A, Suganthan P, Huang G (2005) Evolutionary extreme learning machine. Pattern Recognit 38(10):1759–1763
78. Zhu X, Mukhopadhyay SK, Yue X (2011) Role of forecast effort on supply chain profitability under various information sharing scenarios. Int J Prod Econ 129(2):284–291

Chapter 3
Collaborative Planning Forecasting Replenishment Schemes in Apparel Supply Chain Systems: Cases and Research Opportunities

Daisy Ka-Yee Ho and Tsan-Ming Choi

Abstract Fashion apparel industry is dynamic, and is highly affected by the ever-changing market trend and consumer needs. With the constant change of consumers' preferences, concepts such as fast fashion arise and become more and more dominant. Many of these concepts are made feasible only with a highly efficient and responsive supply chain. In this paper, collaborative planning, forecasting and replenishment (CPFR) schemes and various inventory management practices in apparel supply chains are explored. We first focus on studying an individual case on a garment manufacturer. We then investigate the American denim supply chain and reveal various inventory management practices and the role played by CPFR. Some future research directions are discussed.

Keywords Collaborative planning • Forecasting and replenishment • CPFR • Supply chain management • Fashion apparel

3.1 Introduction

Nowadays, fashion apparel industry is selling more and more fast-moving fashion products. This is especially the case for the fast fashion brands in which their products are categorized by having a very short life cycle. Since these products

---

This paper is based on the graduation project of the first author, in which the second author is the advisor

D.K.-Y. Ho • T.-M. Choi (✉)
Institute of Textiles and Clothing, Faculty of Applied Science and Textiles, The Hong Kong Polytechnic University, Hung Hom, Kowloon, Hong Kong
e-mail: jason.choi@polyu.edu.hk

T.-M. Choi et al. (eds.), *Intelligent Fashion Forecasting Systems: Models and Applications*, DOI 10.1007/978-3-642-39869-8_3,

are highly seasonal-based, the respective market trend is basically unpredictable and consumer demand is very volatile [31, 35]. This makes product forecasting, inventory planning and replenishment challenging.

There is no doubt that inventory management [30] is an important aspect in the apparel industry. An optimal inventory level enables profit maximization and reduces unnecessary costs. With the recent uprising trend of fast-fashion, fashion retailers and garment manufacturers are looking for methods to enhance their stock turnover. In order to maximize profit, fashion retailers and garment manufacturers all strive to shorten production lead-time, adopt efficient inventory replenishment policy and enhance product quality such that they can stay competitive in the market [26, 27, 29]. Regarding modern inventory management practices in fashion apparel, supply chain strategic alliance schemes such as quick response (QR) have been widely applied in various segments along the supply chain. With the advance of information technology and the popularity of information systems such as the enterprise resource planning (ERP) systems, a supply chain practice known as collaborative planning, forecasting and replenishment (CPFR) emerges as a highly significant and useful scheme. In fact, in fashion apparel, CPFR is a strategic concept specifying how fashion retailers and their suppliers (i.e. garment manufacturers) cooperate to achieve an efficient and effective supply chain through a close collaboration on their inventory planning, forecasting, and replenishment practices. In fact, CPFR commonly includes production and purchase planning, demand forecasting and order management among the supply chain partners [1]. The ultimate goal of CPFR is to minimize the risks from poor inventory decisions among the supply chain agents and lower expenses by sharing information and synchronizing the individual agents' decisions. It is well-reported that CPFR helps improve the efficiency of the supply chain, lower inventory levels and reduce operational costs through the deep collaboration of chain partners.

In light of the importance of inventory management and CPFR in the global apparel supply chains, this paper first conducts a case study on a garment manufacturer with respect to its CPFR relate practices. After that, the American denim industry [25, 28] is also selected as an area of investigation for the respective inventory management and CPFR operations. Notice that the existing literature on inventory management and CPFR forms the basis of the analysis. Findings are revealed and some managerial insights are generated.

3.2 Literature Review

Lean manufacturing is a well-developed managerial concept in fashion apparel. It requires a few basic elements such as bar coding system implemented on merchandise, computerized information technology on transferring data, well-organized distribution centers for logistical supports, and a set of regulations to enable the flow in the apparel supply chain. It is known that Wal-Mart, JC Penney and the Gap Inc. are all examples which adopt lean manufacturing concept in their supply chains, and their sales increased steadily throughout the 1980s till the end of 1990s [2]. From the suppliers' point of view, lean manufacturing creates a revolutionary change on their production and operations. Since retailers are trying to avoid excess inventory in their retail channels, they treat the excess inventory as a variation of demand fluctuation. To be specific, in case of any abrupt changes, the excessive inventory will be re-packaged or re-employed for further applicable situation. This relates to the further and recent development of mass customization business model in the apparel supply chain where manufacturers try to minimize the finished merchandise inventory and best serve consumers' customized needs [3].

The concept of safety stock management also arises in apparel inventory management. The safety stock is the quantity of inventory kept to prevent stock-out. Obviously, it relates to customers' demand and the level of inventory services [33]. More importantly, it helps to protect stockout during delivery periods. Safety stock helps to prevent sales loss in case of the sudden increase of demand [4]. There are always trade-offs between keeping sufficient safety stocks and minimizing inventory holding costs. Even though a shorter lead time reduces the safety stock level and the loss caused by stock-outs, improves customer services level, and increases the competitive advantages of business [5], the expenses incurred by increased delivery frequency cannot be ignored. Therefore, a fashion company should maintain a good balance between safety stock and the cost minimization to optimize its business performance [38].

In addition to safety stock concept, a lot of inventory management related supply chain management [27] measures, with the focal point on the use of information [6, 7], have been widely applied in the apparel industry. For example, vendor-managed inventory (VMI) is a way that suppliers are responsible to take care of the retailers' stock replenishment needs [8]. Under VMI, the challenge is to ensure timely delivery among companies through a consistent data transfer and proper information sharing. It is known that the ultimate goal of VMI for the supply chain is to lower the operations costs and maintain a low safety stock in a multi-echelon setting [9]. Another supply chain concept which also benefits the flow of the inventory is known as Quick Response (QR) which is an initiative developed in the American fashion apparel industry back to the 1980s (see [10]). Essentially, compressing production time, ensuring product quality and providing excellent (inventory) customer services (which reduce stockout and markdown) are the strengths of QR [11]. Both QR and VMI require a high level of collaboration and partnership between the supply and demand sides of the two supply chain partners. The use of modern information technology for enhancing information flow is highly regarded as a critical element for implementing QR and VMI. Again, the goal of an efficient apparel supply chain is to maximize its profitability with cost reduction.

In fact, in between QR and VMI (in terms of the degree of alliance and commitment), there exists a scheme known as CPFR. To be specific, CPFR is an emerging methodology in supply chain management and was first introduced in the mid 1990s in the United States, it includes three critical parts of the standard operations process, namely planning, forecasting and replenishment [1, 36]. Under CPFR, at the beginning, a mutual agreement among all agents along the supply chain is required, and then they define the key metrics and develop a joint plan, such as replenishment rate, minimum order quantity, and promotion strategies.

From the aggregate sales data of the shared information, the planning side of the fashion supply chain should forecast the potential deviation and expected growth of the company. Inventory strategies can then be formulated to meet the sales target by summarizing the forecast of the different parties. Afterwards, the manufacturing part of the supply chain can produce the required quantity of products under the allowable production capacity, and they can minimize the safety stock. Notice that the collaborating firms will make adjustment based on the up-to-date market demand, because they can identify any on-going issues and understand the constraints through forecasting together. Last by not least, the replenishment plan will be established after the order forecast is confirmed and put into production [12]. In fact, it is proposed that CPFR extends the focus of supply chain among partners' collaboration. It can synchronize business processes and activities so that the supply chain agents can share their expertise in a timely basis [13]. Notice that CPFR puts a strong emphasis on collaborative forecasting and there are prior reports indicating failure cases in which the supply chain partners running CPFR have mistaken "sharing demand related information" is equal to having common forecast.[1] Compared to QR, CPFR requires a greater commitment in co-ordination and frequent meetings between partners are necessary, whereas the commitment is less than VMI. Since the eventual objective is to increase sales and improve customer services, communication is an important aspect in CPFR across the supply chain. It begins and focuses on a few relationships among partners, and concentrates on the processes which are required to improve. Once the relationships are strongly bonded and certain procedures are improved, the goal can be set for a long-term partnership. However, from a managerial perspective, CPFR should have measurable results coming from the supply chain by solving current problems. Since CPFR requires a huge investment on developing the procedures stated earlier, there might be a conflict between the temporary objective and the long term goal of the company [14]. Trust in partnership becomes a crucial aspect in CPFR. Observe that naturally firms have diverse interests in short-term benefits, and these unforeseen conflicts will alleviate their commitment to the supply chain [15].

There are several benefits for choosing CPFR as the inventory management strategy in the apparel supply chain. First of all, it improves the fulfilment rate of merchandise because suppliers, manufacturers and retailers decide and plan the produced quantity together. The amount of safety stock can then be reduced and kept at a low level (especially at the supplier's warehouse in the upstream supply chain); ultimately, the downstream supply chain does not have to carry a large amount of unsold merchandise. Besides, CPFR enhances the speed of production processes because production and distribution are linked, and thus production scheduling is improved. Besides information-sharing under CPFR, another benefit of applying this concept into the supply chain is that resources and expertise can be shared among partners [15]. Inventory carrying costs will also be decreased.

[1] The two are not the same as different companies can have different forecasting results even if they are given the same set of demand data because they may employ different forecasting methods.

By using CPFR, customer demand, order shipment and delivery status can be tracked by computerized information systems easily because information is more transparent throughout the supply chain (i.e. the inventory visibility is enhanced). Once inventory is reduced, the company enjoys a better cash flow because the overall capital decreases. The company can then use the extra money for further investment or expansion.

3.3 A Case Study on an Apparel Manufacturer X

In this section, we focus on a single company case on an apparel manufacturer X (AMX[2]). AMX is a well-established apparel manufacturer in Asia. It focuses a lot on advanced research and development on apparel products, and provides supply chain services to its retail customers with consistent quality and reliability. AMX has branch offices in Asia and the United States and its customers include many big name American retailers such as JC Penney and Nordstrom. AMX is known as the pioneer of many apparel innovations. In terms of product creativity, AMX is well-recognized as the pioneer of various advances in using new materials and fabrics for producing high quality functional apparel. From a supply chain management standpoint, AMX has been proven in records that it is very successful in reducing total logistics expenses, lowering inventory costs, increasing the turnover of stock and improving customer satisfaction among its competitors. For inventory management practices, CPFR is rather popularly adopted between AMX and its retail customers. In fact, AMX first began CFPR by working with a mass market American retailer (MMAR) almost two decades ago. The reason for adopting CPFR at that time was mainly driven by the fact that forecasting was very inaccurate in the respective supply chain under the old practice (in the absence of CPFR). In fact, AMX and its American retail customer MMAR used different methods and models to estimate sales for upcoming seasons. Moreover, a lot of promotional events were misunderstood by both parties which led to big communication error. Under their CPFR strategy, AMX and MMAR implemented a new forecasting system to make forecasting consistent. Top managements of both companies also maintained constant communication through weekly video and tele-conferencing to update each other on sales and strategic planning. As a result of this CPFR scheme, AMX and MMAR report significant sales improvement and operation costs reduction, and they improve their customer services [37] all at the same time. CPFR is hence a proven success at AMX and it is a value-adding service that AMX can offer to its retail customers.

---

[2] All the company names in this section are fictitious names while they represent real companies in practice.

3.4 Inventory Practices and CPFR: Denim Industry in the United States

3.4.1 *Industrial Background and Evolution*

In this section, the supply chain of denim apparel in the United States is portrayed. To be specific, we explore from a macro perspective of a typical US apparel supply chain along with the benefits of free trade agreements. To a certain extent, the American importing and exporting partnerships with various countries explain their ideas of inventory management and CPFR. Denim serves as an everyday wear for people. As the society gradually transforms and becomes more and more modernized, consumers' preferences on denim jeans have changed overtime for the past decades. Nowadays, denim is a kind of "must-have" fashion item in most people's wardrobes. In the American textile apparel market, the demand of denim has revolutionized for the past 20 years. In order to meet the market demand, the flow of importing and exporting of denim fabric has been changed, as well as the supply chain strategy in the US denim apparel companies. In addition, with the effects of free trade agreements between the United States and different countries, the supply chain of denim has changed drastically. Consumer consumption on denim jeans has increased for the past years in the United States market. According to the data in "Lifestyle Monitor 2007 Denim Issue", from 1997 to 2007, American men increased denim ownership from 7.2 to 7.4 pairs, while that of American women increased from 6.6 to 8.1 pairs [16]. Since the demand of denim consumption has gone up over time, import of denim fabric has increased over the past 20 years. Drawing from the data from the Office of Textiles and Apparel (OTEXA), the total denim imports of the United States were 58.847 million dollars in 1990 and 219.665 million dollars in 2000. The import countries have changed by the effect of North American Free Trade Agreement (NAFTA) [32] in that particular period also. In 1990, the top 5 denim importing regions were mainly from Asia, including Hong Kong, Taiwan, Argentina, China and Brazil. In 2000, Mexico ranked the first of importing denim, followed by Hong Kong, Canada, Taiwan and India. In 1990, Levi's played a major role of in men's jeans with 48.2 % of market share. However in 2000, Levi's dropped its market share to 25 % because other competitors, such as Gap and Tommy Hilfiger, increased their share in denim apparel market [17]. Therefore, managing an effective supply chain is very important in the American denim market.

Before the commencement of NAFTA, the United States had a cluster of jeans manufacturers in Texas, which dominated the denim production for the US consumers. El Paso, a city in Texas, was a famous denim manufacturing town which concentrated on stonewashing from the 1980s to mid 1990s. At that time, stonewashed blue jeans, lighter in color and softer in feel than unwashed denim was very popular in the American fashion market [18]. The reasons of having jeans stonewashing plants in El Paso were because of its proximity to Mexico, its water resources and labor's low wages. For example in 1990, El Paso's wage was only 73 % of that in Texas, and in 1997, per capita income in El Paso was 64 % of that in Texas [18]. However, with the effect of NAFTA beginning in 1994, El Paso's leading role of stonewashing denim has altered, and manufacturing plants have migrated to Mexico. Torreon, an industrial city in Mexico, was a 4 h driving distance from the United States border. Since many US denim manufacturing plants have already relocated to that region, Torreon has gradually transformed into a manufacturing cluster, focusing on denim production. From 1993 to 2000, 360 apparel factories in Torreon increased employment from 12,000 jobs to 75,000. Moreover in the early 1990s, Mexico was one of the leading apparel exporters to the US. From 1993 to 2000, denim fabric used in Torreon for exporting jeans increased from 2 % to 15 % [19]. The reason of US denim buyers choosing Torreon to import jeans was that Torreon acquired a strong networking system of connecting local factories to the US exporters. In the past, the US and Mexico shared denim production in different procedures. In the early 1990s, the US manufacturers produced the fabric locally, trimmed and cut the fabric, and delivered them to Mexico. Torreon firms then assembled different parts of jeans and sent them back to the US for further finishing and distribution. After the NAFTA has implemented, Mexico is able to develop higher production capabilities. In the past, the US manufacturers sourced raw material from Asian regions, such as Taiwan and Hong Kong. Towards the late 1990s, Mexico manufacturers gradually built up a full-package of production services to their customers. They received orders from the US buyers, and they sourced raw materials, developed fabrication and produced the final goods. They then exported to the US for distribution. Compared with importing goods from Asian countries, Mexico provided faster production and delivery to the US retailers. Moreover, the depreciation of Peso in the mid 1990s increased denim textile trade between Mexico and the United States. Between December 1994 and mid-1995, the peso depreciated more than 50 % [20]. This attracted even more US denim manufacturers to develop their production plants in Torreon region, enjoying low labor costs and anticipating a quicker response from market and serving their consumers better. As a consequence, big fashion brands (i.e. Calvin Klein and Tommy Hilfiger), and budget retailers (i.e. including Kmart and JC Penney) imported denim jeans from Torreon manufacturers towards the late 1990s and 2000s [17]. On the other hand, the United States textile apparel manufacturing firms vanished under the influence of NAFTA implementation. Many leading North Carolina-based textile companies reduced the number of employees in their domestic market, because they shifted their production processes to Mexico. These production shifts deprived job opportunities away from the American textile workers, and the nature of the American textile industry has altered its role from apparel production to brand and distribution management. By the end of 1990s, the flow of supply chain in the US became more efficient with NAFTA, and both countries encountered benefits and losses for such production shift. In the twenty-first century, the American denim manufacturers continued seeking ways of outsourcing their production to lower cost production countries. China was the rising nation of denim importers to the US because of their WTO membership in 2001. On the other hand, the US denim market has a greater diversification on branding and consumers' preferences now, which also affects the supply chain development of different denim manufacturers. With all these changes in the millennium era, the denim supply chain performs differently than the past decade.

Mexico enjoyed success of providing full package services to denim manufacturers in the United States in the late 1990s with the effect of NAFTA. However, price and production capacity became a concern for the US buyers due to the rise of manufacturing nations in Asia. Moreover, there were more external reasons causing the downturn in Mexican denim production. The 9/11 event in 2001 created uncertainty in the US economy and security concerns. A lot of small and mid-size denim firms in La Laguna region shut down because larger manufacturers were unwilling to spare facilities and productions. At that time, around 20–30 % of the garment business decreased, which caused a lay-off of 30,000 Mexican workers in that region in 2001. In the following year, manufacturers began either upgrade their production facilities to decrease the use of labor, or relocated their production plants to inner Mexico with lower labor costs. As a result, the La Laguna region lost its competitive advantages of clustering denim production plants relative to other countries, and the US denim manufacturers continued in searching for a better and cheaper location for production [21]. Since Mexico lost its competitiveness as a denim importer to the US, with the identity of being a WTO member, China was able to export goods to the members (i.e. the United States) with quota and tariff free advantages. Although certain textile products were put into safeguards by the US government until 2008, denim products were not categorized to be one of them. As such, China increased their denim import from 1.7 million in 1990 to 27.17 million US dollars by the year of 2007 (Drawing data from OTEXA). Similar to the La Laguna region, China adopted the cluster strategy for textile production. Cluster strategy is geographic concentrations of interconnected companies, firms in related industries, specialized suppliers, associated institutions and service providers in a particular field that compete but also cooperate. China has three main textiles cluster regions: Pearl River Delta (PRD), Yangtze River Delta (YRD) and Bohai-Rim Region (BRR). For denim products, the production plants mainly cluster at the Guangdong Province, which belongs to the Pearl River Delta region. These regions are located near the coastal area and big developed cities, i.e. Hong Kong and Shanghai. The clusters can then easily gain access to potential buyers from there. Also, the cluster manufacturers provide full-package services from production to distribution to their customers, and these services enable them to monitor the whole supply chain effectively. Moreover, they can share technology development, market trend and resources because of their proximity. As a result, denim production in China gained these competitive advantages among other countries and became the major importer to the US market [22].

As discussed above, the American denim supply chain has undergone a revolution for the past decades. Nowadays, besides China, India and Japan are the emerging countries for exporting denim to the US. Similar to China, India serves the low and mid-tier denim market, usually producing in mass quantity and exporting the finished products to the US. Japan, however, is keen on developing valuable and delicate denim fabric, which serves the premium denim market. It helps to reduce the sewage, and the development of eco-friendly denim products is going to be a trend in the textile market.

3.4.2 Cluster Strategy, Inventory Management, and CPFR

Observed from the trend of denim supply chain in the United States, export countries, such as Mexico and China, have widely adopted the cluster strategy in various cities in order to standardize their manufacturing sectors. Cluster strategy enhances the flow of information and resources sharing among similar manufacturers, and reduces transshipment costs. For demand side, fashion retail buyers do not have to jump from one place to another to source their right suppliers, since their locations are concentrated and segmented into different parts of that particular country. For the supply side, apparel manufacturers can have access to more resources and information. Ultimately, costs of production can be minimized throughout the supply chain. Since the inventory control in the cluster is under coordination among manufacturers among the particular region, the bullwhip effect of the entire supply chain tends to reduce [23]. This example of denim supply chain delineates another characteristic of inventory management, along with the concept of lean manufacturing through cluster strategy. Thus, adopting cluster strategies for exporting countries is a good inventory management method.

On the other hand, denim firms are striving to improve their supply chain operations in order to cope with the market need in the United States. Since apparel product is always a consumer-driven based market, consumer preferences play an important role in the denim supply chain as well. In the past, denim was considered to be uniforms for heavy duty workers. Nowadays, denim jeans become a daily wear for all genders and age groups, for both casual and important occasions. As driven by the market needs and the industrial trend, more denim manufacturers and retailers are also collaborating in different degrees nowadays. For example, Levi's and Wal-Mart utilized the CPFR strategy to maximize their profitability and increase efficiency of the supply chain and we discuss their case in the following.

Levi's, the denim jeans originator, dominated the denim market share during the 1970s–1980s. It has been an iconic American brand for several decades. As other fashion labels aggressively developed their denim line, i.e. GAP, Tommy Hilfiger and Abercrombie & Fitch, Levi's market share in the younger consumers' market dropped. Levi's sales reached 7.1 billion US dollars in 1996 but dropped to 4.1 billion US dollars in 2003. Since Levi's faced a very competitive situation at that time, especially with the youngster market, it's essential for it to acquire a bigger volume of sales in order to secure the company's profit. Thus, Levi's cooperated with Wal-Mart to launch a less expensive product line called Signature. In order to work with this giant retailer, Levi's first set up extra distribution ports (in Los Angeles, Texas and Florida) for serving Wal-Mart's demand. Since Wal-Mart has an enormous number of retail stores, Levi's had to figure out their daily sales activities and display quantity. Levi's then implemented a software system to work with Wal-Mart EDI, and they collaborated on demand forecast, product modifications and order planning together (i.e. running CPFR). With all these data, Levi's could provide supports from ordering to delivery to Wal-Mart [24]. The CPFR scheme enhances inventory visibility and it enables a greater efficiency throughout the supply chain of Wal-Mart and Levi's. Moreover, it provides a faster stock replenishment and reacts to the spontaneous market change. Although the investment cost was huge, Levi's and Wal-Mart performed CPFR effectively, increased profits of both corporation and decreased redundancy of their supply chain.

3.5 Findings and Concluding Remarks

Inventory management in fashion supply chain management is always crucial, and different sectors of the supply chain strive to seek for ways to minimize all possible costs in order to maximize profit. This paper has explored various inventory management practices related to collaborative planning forecast and replenishment (CPFR) in the fashion industry. A successful industrial company on AMX has been examined by a single case study. Another industrial case on the American denim supply chain has been extensively reviewed and discussed. From the case studies, a few future quantitative research opportunities are proposed,

1. Since forecasting is a crucial part on CPFR. In addition to having a consistent forecasting method in place, the performance of the respective forecasting method is critically important. Thus, for future research, it is promising to examine what specific kind of forecasting method will be applicable and especially useful for CPFR in fashion. Some existing methods based one statistical models and artificial intelligence models are good candidates to study further.
2. Besides sharing sales data and collaborating in forecasting and replenishment with a goal of improving supply chain inventory management, the supply chain partners should also consider critical issues such as risk sharing, financial arrangement, and cash flow management [34]. Ideally, CPFR should help to achieve a win-win situation in the supply chain for the participating agents. Despite being a rather obvious goal, this is challenging to achieve because bargaining power tends to rule the division of benefit and risk. As a result, new research should be conducted to investigate the robust mechanism under which win-win situation, in the presence of bargaining powers of the participating partners, can be achieved.
3. Cluster strategy and off-shore production are two important elements we have observed from the American denim supply chains. How these strategies relate to CPFR deserves deeper explorations. In addition, from the global supply chain perspective, how the change of local economics situation of each country affects

the respective denim supply chain and the implementation of CPFR is another interesting topic for further studies.

4. Despite realizing that CPFR is useful, it is important to quantify the benefits of it for both the upstream manufacturer and the downstream retailer. This calls for more quantitative research on the topic.

References

1. Fliender G (2003) CPFR, an emerging supply chain tool. Ind Manage Data Syst 103(1):14–21
2. Abernathy FH, Dunlop JT, Hammond JH, Weil D (1999) A stitch in time: lean retailing and the transformation of manufacturing–lessons from the apparel and textile industries, 1st edn. Oxford University Press, New York
3. Stratton R, Warburton RDH (2003) The strategic integration of agile and lean supply. Int J Prod Econ 85(2):183–198
4. Takahashi M (2007) Consideration for chance losses with inventory optimizations. Int J Comput Sci Netw Secur 7:52–58
5. Ouyang LY, Wu KS (1997) Mixture inventory model with backorders and lost sales for variable lead-time. J Oper Res Soc 24:875–882
6. Choi TM, Li J, Wei Y (2013) Will a supplier benefit from sharing good information with a retailer? Decis Support Syst. Doi: 10.1016/j.dss.2013.05.011
7. Cui R, Allon G, Bassamboo A, Van Mieghem JA (2013) Information sharing in supply chains. An empirical and theoretical valuation. Working paper, Northwestern University
8. Choi TM (2011) Coordination and risk analysis of VMI supply chains with RFID technology. IEEE Trans Ind Inform 7:497–504
9. Kaipia R, Holmstrom J, Tanskanen K (2002) VMI: what are you losing if you let your customer place orders? Prod Plann Control 13(1):17–25
10. Choi TM (2013) Optimal apparel supplier selection with forecast updates under carbon emission taxation scheme. Comput Oper Res 40(11):2646–2655
11. Christopher M, Lowson R, Peck H (2004) Creating agile supply chains in the fashion industry. Int J Retail Distrib Manage 32(8):367–376
12. Danese P (2007) Designing CPFR collaborations: insights from seven case studies. Int J Oper Prod Manage 27(2):181–204
13. Jagdev HS, Thoben KD (2001) Anatomy of enterprise collaboration. Prod Plann Control 12(5):437–451
14. Larsen TS, Thernoe C, Andresen C (2003) Supply chain collaboration theoretical perspectives and empirical evidence. Int J Phys Distrib Logist Manage 33(6):531–549
15. Holweg M, Disney S, Holmström J, Småros J (2005) Supply chain collaboration: making sense of the strategy continuum. Eur Manage J 23(2):170–181
16. Cotton Inc (2007) Lifestyle monitor 2007 denim. Cotton incorporated. Lifestyle monitor 2007 denim issue (8). Nov 2006. Retrieved on 2 Oct 2008. Website: http://www.cottoninc.com/SupplyChainInsights/DenimApparelTrends/DenimApparelTrends.pdf?CFID=9703131&CFTOKEN=95467789
17. Gereffi G, Spener D, Bair J (2002) Free trade and uneven development: the North American apparel industry after NAFTA. Temple University Press, Philadelphia
18. Abel A, Phillips T (2000) The relocation of El Paso's stonewashing industry and its implications for trade and the environment. Working paper, University of Texas at Austin
19. Gereffi G, Bair J (2001) Local clusters in global chains: the causes and consequences of export dynamism in Torreon's blue jeans industry. World Dev 29(11):1885–1903

20. Shoesmith G (2000) Jobs and goods make a run for the border. The Go-to-place for management. Retrieved on 6 Oct 2008. Website: http://findarticles.com/p/articles/mi_qa5314/is_200001/ai_n21450403
21. Van Dooren R (2006) La Laguna: of exporting jeans and changing labor relations. Tijdschr Econ Soc Ge 95(5):480–490, Website: http://www3.interscience.wiley.com/cgi-bin/fulltext/118627581/PDFSTART
22. Zhang Z, To C, Cao N (2004) How do industry clusters success: a case study in China's textiles and apparel industries. J Textile Apparel Technol Manage 4(2):1–10
23. Li J, Liu C (2008) Inventory control model of cluster supply chain with time-delay based on online switched system. In: The 3rd international conference on grid and pervasive computer workshops, IEEE 2008. Kunming, China, pp 115–121
24. Girard K (2003) Supply chain partnerships: how Levi's got its jeans into Wal-Mart. *CIO*.com-business technology leadership. Retrieved on 19 Nov 2008. Website: http://www.cio.com/article/31948/Supply_Chain_Partnerships_How_Levi_s_Got_Its_Jeans_into_Wal_Mart
25. Agarwal S (2008) Japanese denim- environment friendly jeans manufacturing attempts. Denim and jeans. Retrieved on 19 Nov 2008. Website: http://www.denimsandjeans.com/japanese-denim-environment-friendly-jeans-manufacturing-attempts/2008/09
26. Boute RN, Disney SM, Lambrecht MR, Van Houdt B (2007) An integrated production and inventory model to dampen upstream demand variability in the SC. Eur J Oper Res 178:121–142
27. Christopher M (1998) Logistics and supply chain management: strategies for reducing costs and improving services. Prentice-Hall, London
28. Cotton Inc (2006) Supply chain insight: denim apparel trends. Cotton incorporated, vol 1(8). Retrieved on 23 Sept 2008. Website: http://www.cottoninc.com/supplychaininsights/denimappareltrends/denimappareltrends.pdf?CFID=9430724&CFTOKEN=35776603
29. Dutta P, Chakraborty D, Roy AR (2007) An inventory model for single-period products with recording opportunities under fuzzy demand. Comput Math Appl 53:1502–1517
30. Enrick NL (1968) Inventory management. Chandler, San Francisco, p 13
31. Fisher M, Rajaram K, Raman A (2001) Optimizing inventory replenishment of retail fashion products. Manuf Serv Oper Manage 3:230–241
32. Gereffi G (2000) The transformation of the North American apparel industry: is NAFTA a curse or a blessing? vol 84. Naciones Unidas, Santiago
33. Jeffrey MM, Butler RJ, Malone LC (2008) Determining a cost-effective customer service level. Supply Chain Manage Int J 11:225–332
34. Choi TM (2013) Multi-period risk minimization purchasing models for fashion products with interest rate, budget, and profit target considerations. Ann Oper Res, doi: 10.1007/s10479-013-1453-x, in print
35. Choi TM (2013) Local sourcing and fashion quick response system: the impacts of carbon footprint tax. Transp Res – Part E 55:43–54
36. Pramatari K, Miliotis P (2008) The impact of collaborative store ordering on shelf availability. Supply Chain Manage Int J 13:49–61
37. Storey J, Emberson C, Reade D (2005) The barriers to customer responsive supply chain management. Int J Oper Manage 25(3):242–260
38. Talluri S, Cetin K, Gardner AJ (2004) Integrating demand and supply variability into safety stock evaluations. Int J Phys Distrib Logist Manage 34:62–69

Part II
Theoretical Modeling Research

Chapter 4
Measuring Forecasting Accuracy: Problems and Recommendations (by the Example of SKU-Level Judgmental Adjustments)

Andrey Davydenko and Robert Fildes

Abstract Forecast adjustment commonly occurs when organizational forecasters adjust a statistical forecast of demand to take into account factors which are excluded from the statistical calculation. This paper addresses the question of how to measure the accuracy of such adjustments. We show that many existing error measures are generally not suited to the task, due to specific features of the demand data. Alongside the well-known weaknesses of existing measures, a number of additional effects are demonstrated that complicate the interpretation of measurement results and can even lead to false conclusions being drawn. In order to ensure an interpretable and unambiguous evaluation, we recommend the use of a metric based on aggregating performance ratios across time series using the weighted geometric mean. We illustrate that this measure has the advantage of treating over- and under-forecasting even-handedly, has a more symmetric distribution, and is robust.

Empirical analysis using the recommended metric showed that, on average, adjustments yielded improvements under symmetric linear loss, while harming accuracy in terms of some traditional measures. This provides further support to the critical importance of selecting appropriate error measures when evaluating the forecasting accuracy. The general accuracy evaluation scheme recommended in the paper is applicable in a wide range of settings including forecasting for fashion industry.

Keywords Judgmental adjustments • Forecasting support systems • Forecast accuracy • Forecast evaluation • Forecast error measures

---

This paper is an extended version of Davydenko and Fildes [8] which appeared in the International Journal of Forecasting

A. Davydenko (✉) • R. Fildes
Department of Management Science, Lancaster University, Lancaster LA1 4YX, UK
e-mail: a.davydenko@lancaster.ac.uk

T.-M. Choi et al. (eds.), *Intelligent Fashion Forecasting Systems: Models and Applications*, DOI 10.1007/978-3-642-39869-8_4,

4.1 Introduction

The most well-established approach to forecasting within supply chain companies starts with a statistical time series forecast, which is then adjusted by managers in the company based on their expert knowledge. This process is usually carried out at a highly disaggregated level of SKUs (stock-keeping units), where there are often hundreds if not thousands of series to consider [11, 27]. At the same time, the empirical evidence suggests that judgments under uncertainty are affected by various types of cognitive biases and are inherently non-optimal [32]. Such biases and inefficiencies have been shown to apply specifically to judgmental adjustments [12]. Therefore, it is important to monitor the accuracy of judgmental adjustments in order to ensure the rational use of the organisation's resources which are invested in the forecasting process.

The task of measuring the accuracy of judgmental adjustments is inseparably linked with the need to choose an appropriate error measure. In fact, the choice of an error measure for assessing the accuracy of forecasts across time series is itself an important topic for forecasting research. It has theoretical implications for the comparison of forecasting methods and is of wide practical importance, since the forecasting function is often evaluated using inappropriate measures (see, for example, [4, 5]), and therefore the link to economic performance may well be distorted. Despite the continuing interest in the topic, the choice of the most suitable error measure for evaluating companies' forecasts still remains controversial. Due to their statistical properties, popular error measures do not always ensure easily interpretable results when applied to real-world data [20, 21]. In practice, the proportion of firms which track the aggregated accuracy is surprisingly small, and one apparent reason for this is the inability to agree on appropriate accuracy metrics [17]. As McCarthy et al. [25] reported, only 55 % of the companies surveyed believed that their forecasting performance was being formally evaluated.

The key issue when evaluating a forecasting process is the improvements achieved in supply chain performance. While this has only an indirect link to the forecasting accuracy, organisations rely on accuracy improvements as a suitable proxy measure, not least because of their ease of calculation. This paper examines the behaviours of various well-known error measures in the particular context of demand forecasting in the supply chain. We show that, due to the features of SKU demand data, well-known error measures are generally not advisable for the evaluation of judgmental adjustments, and can even give misleading results. To be useful in supply chain applications, an error measure usually needs to have the following properties: (i) scale independence – though it is sometimes desirable to weight measures according some characteristic such as their profitability; (ii) robustness to outliers; and (iii) interpretability (though the focus might occasionally shift to extremes, e.g., where ensuring a minimum level of supply is important).

The most popular measure used in practice is the mean absolute percentage error, MAPE [11], which has long been being criticised (see, for example, [10, 20, 21]). In particular, the use of percentage errors is often inadvisable, due to the large number of extremely high percentages which arise from relatively low actual demand values.

To overcome the disadvantages of percentage measures, the MASE (mean absolute scaled error) measure was proposed by Hyndman and Koehler [20]. The MASE is a relative error measure which uses the MAE (mean absolute error) of a benchmark forecast (specifically, of the random walk) as its denominator. In this paper we analyse the MASE and show that, like the MAPE, it also has a number of disadvantages. Most importantly: (i) it introduces a bias towards overrating the performance of a benchmark forecast as a result of arithmetic averaging; and (ii) it is vulnerable to outliers, as a result of dividing by small benchmark MAE values.

To ensure a more reliable evaluation of the effectiveness of adjustments, this paper proposes the use of an enhanced measure that shows the average relative improvement in MAE. In contrast to MASE, it is proposed that the weighted geometric average be used to find the average relative MAE. By taking the statistical forecast as a benchmark, it becomes possible to evaluate the relative change in forecasting accuracy yielded by the use of judgmental adjustments, without experiencing the limitations of other standard measures. Therefore, the proposed statistic can be used to provide a more robust and easily interpretable indicator of changes in accuracy, meeting the criteria laid down earlier.

The importance of the choice of an appropriate error measure is justified by the fact that previous studies of the gains in accuracy from the judgmental adjustment process have produced conflicting results (e.g., [12, 14]). In these studies, different measures were applied to different datasets and arrived at different conclusions. Some studies where a set of measures was employed reported an interesting picture, where adjustments improved the accuracy in certain settings according to MdAPE (median absolute percentage error), while harming the accuracy in the same settings according to MAPE [12, 31]. In practice, such results may be damaging for forecasters and forecast users, since they do not give a clear indication of the changes in accuracy that correspond to some well-known loss function. Using real-world data, this paper considers the appropriateness of various previously used measures, and demonstrates the use of the proposed enhanced accuracy measurement scheme.

The next section describes the data employed for the analysis in this paper. Section 4.3 illustrates the disadvantages and limitations of various well-known error measures when they are applied to SKU-level data. In the fourth section, the proposed accuracy measure is introduced. The fifth section contains the results from measuring the accuracy of judgmental adjustments with real-world data using the alternative measures and explains the differences in the results, demonstrating the benefits of the proposed enhanced accuracy measure. The concluding section summarises the results of the empirical evaluation and offers practical recommendations as to which of the different error measures can be employed safely.

4.2 Descriptive Analysis of the Source Data

The current research employed data collected from a company specialising in the manufacture of fast-moving consumer goods (FMCG) which are fashionable in nature. This is an extended data set from one of the companies considered by Fildes et al. [12]. The company concerned is a leading European provider of household and personal care products to a wide range of major retailers. Table 4.1 summarises the data set and contains the number of cases used for the analysis. Each case includes (i) the one-step-ahead monthly forecast prepared using some statistical method (this will be called the system forecast); (ii) the corresponding judgmentally adjusted forecast (this will be called the final forecast); and (iii) the corresponding actual demand value. The system forecast was obtained using an enterprise software package, and the final forecast was obtained as a result of a revision of the statistical forecast by experts [12]. The two forecasts coincide when the experts had no extra information to add. The data set is representative of most FMCG manufacturing or distribution companies which deal with large numbers of time series of different lengths relating to different products, and is similar to the other manufacturing data sets considered by Fildes et al. [12], in terms of the total number of time series, the proportion of judgmentally adjusted forecasts and the frequencies of occurrence of zero errors and zero actuals.

Since the data relate to FMCG, the numbers of cases of zero demand periods and zero errors are not large (see Table 4.1). However, the further investigation of the properties of error measures presented in Sect. 4.3 will also consider possible situations when the data involve small counts, and zero observations occur more frequently (as is common with intermittent demand data).

Table 4.1 Source data summary

Total number of cases	6,882
Total number of time series (SKUs)	412
Period of observations	Mar 2004 to Jul 2007
Total number of adjusted statistical forecasts (% of total number of cases)	4,779 (69 %)
Number of zero actual demand periods (% of total number of cases)	271 (4 %)
Number of zero-error statistical forecasts (% of total number of cases)	47 (<1 %)
Number of zero-error judgmentally adjusted forecasts (% of total number of adjusted forecasts)	61 (1 %)
Number of positive adjustments (% of total number of adjusted forecasts)	3,394 (71 %)
Number of negative adjustments (% of total number of adjusted forecasts)	1,385 (29 %)

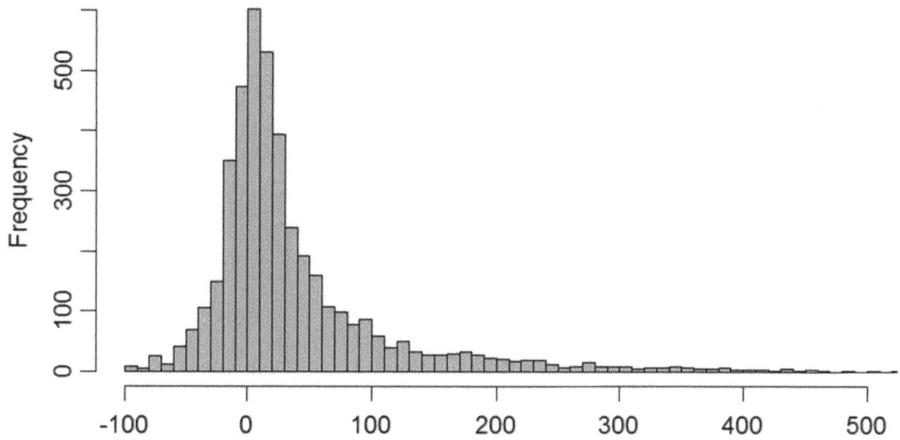

Fig. 4.1 Histogram of the relative adjustment, measured in percentages

As Table 4.1 shows, for this particular data set, adjustments of positive sign occur more frequently than adjustments of negative sign. However, in order to characterise the average magnitude of the adjustments, an additional analysis is required. In their study of judgmental adjustments, Fildes et al. [12] analysed the size of judgmental adjustments using the measure of relative adjustments that is defined as $100 \times$ (Final forecast − System forecast)/System forecast.

As the values of the relative adjustments are scale-independent, they can be compared across time series. However, the above measure is asymmetrical. For example, if an expert doubles a statistical forecast (say from 10 units to 20 units), he/she increases it by 100 %, but if he/she halves a statistical forecast (say from 20 units to 10 units), he/she decreases it by 50 % (not 100 %). The sampling distribution of the relative adjustment is bounded by −100 % on the left side and unbounded on the right side (see Fig. 4.1). Generally, these effects mean that the distribution of the relative adjustment may become non-informative about the size of the adjustment as measured on the original scale. When defining a 'symmetric measure', Mathews and Diamantopoulos [24] argued for a measure where the adjustment size is measured relative to an average of the system and final forecasts. The same principle is used in the symmetric MAPE (sMAPE) measure proposed by Makridakis [22]. However, Goodwin and Lawton [15] later showed that such approaches still do not lead to the desirable property of symmetry.

In this paper, in order to avoid the problem of the non-symmetrical scale of the relative adjustment, we carry out the analysis of the magnitude of adjustments using the natural logarithm of the (Final forecast/System forecast) ratio. Log-transformation is a common approach to restore symmetry with ratio data since $\ln(A/B) = -\ln(B/A)$ for any positive numbers A and B.

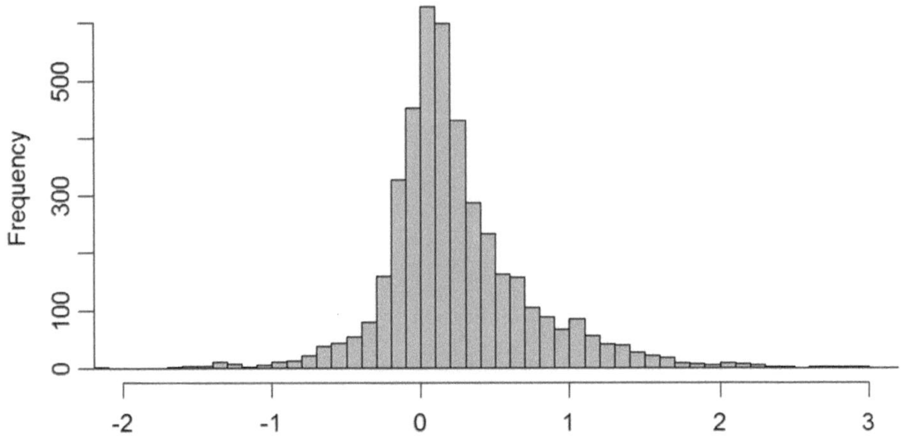

Fig. 4.2 Histogram of ln(Final forecast/System forecast)

Table 4.2 Summary statistics for the magnitude of adjustment

	ln(Final forecast/System forecast)				
Sign of adjustment	1st quartile	Median	3rd quartile	$\text{Mean}_{(2\%\ \text{trim})}$	$\exp[\text{Mean}_{(2\%\ \text{trim})}]$
Positive	0.123	0.273	0.592	0.412	1.510
Negative	−0.339	−0.153	−0.071	−0.290	0.749
Both	−0.043	0.144	0.425	0.218	1.243

From Fig. 4.2, it can be seen that the log-transformed relative adjustment follows a leptokurtic distribution and this distribution is still non-symmetrical (although not as severely as for the original data shown on Fig. 4.1). As is well known, the sample mean is not an efficient measure of location under departures from normality [34]. We therefore used the trimmed mean as a more robust summary measure of location. The optimal trim level that corresponds to the lowest variance of the trimmed mean depends on the distribution, which is unknown in the current case. Some studies have shown that, for symmetrical distributions, a 5 % trim generally ensures a high efficiency with a useful degree of robustness (e.g., [16]). However, it is also known that the trimmed mean gives a biased estimate if the distribution is skewed [23]. We used a 2 % trim in order to eliminate the influence of outliers while at the same time avoiding introducing a substantial bias.

The results presented in Table 4.2 suggest that, on average, for the dataset under consideration, the magnitude of positive adjustments is higher than the magnitude of negative adjustments, measured relative to the system forecast. Even after using a log scale to treat percentages to baseline symmetrically, the magnitude of positive adjustments is pronouncedly higher than the magnitude of negative ones. The average magnitude of a positive relative adjustment is about twice as large as the average magnitude of a negative adjustment. Also, adjustments with positive signs have much higher ranges than negative ones.

4.3 Appropriateness of Existing Measures for SKU-Level Demand Data

4.3.1 *Percentage Errors*

Let the forecasting error for a given time period t and SKU i be

$$e_{i,t} = Y_{i,t} - F_{i,t},$$

where $Y_{i,t}$ is a demand value for SKU i observed at time t, and $F_{i,t}$ is the forecast of $Y_{i,t}$.

A traditional way to compare the accuracy of forecasts across multiple time series is based on using absolute percentage errors [20]. Let us define the percentage error (PE) as $p_{i,t} = 100 \times e_{i,t}/Y_{i,t}$. Hence, the absolute percentage error (APE) is $|p_{i,t}|$. The most popular PE-based measures are MAPE and MdAPE, which are defined as follows:

$$\text{MAPE} = \text{mean}\left(|p_{i,t}|\right),$$

$$\text{MdAPE} = \text{median}\left(|p_{i,t}|\right),$$

where mean$(|p_{i,t}|)$ denotes the sample mean of $|p_{i,t}|$ over all available values of i and t, and median$(|p_{i,t}|)$ is the sample median.

In the study by Fildes et al. [12], these measures served as the main tool for the analysis of the accuracy of judgmental adjustments. In order to determine the change in forecasting accuracy, MAPE and MdAPE values of the statistical baseline forecasts and final judgmentally adjusted forecasts were calculated and compared. The significance of the change in accuracy was assessed based on the distribution of the differences between the absolute percentage errors (APEs) of forecasts. The difference between APEs is defined as

$$d_{i,t}^{\text{APE}} = \left|p_{i,t}^{\text{f}}\right| - \left|p_{i,t}^{\text{s}}\right|,$$

where $|p_{i,t}{}^{\text{f}}|$ and $|p_{i,t}{}^{\text{s}}|$ denote APEs for the final and system forecasts, respectively, for a given SKU i and period t. Fildes et al. [12] used the Wilcoxon's two-sample paired signed rank test to compare the APEs of the final and system forecasts. This is equivalent to performing a one-sample signed rank test to test the median of $d_{i,t}^{\text{APE}}$ against zero.

The sample mean of $d_{i,t}^{\text{APE}}$ is the difference between the MAPE values corresponding to the final and system forecasts:

$$\text{mean}\left(d_{i,t}^{\text{APE}}\right) = \text{mean}\left(\left|p_{i,t}^{\text{f}}\right|\right) - \text{mean}\left(\left|p_{i,t}^{\text{s}}\right|\right) = \text{MAPE}^{\text{f}} - \text{MAPE}^{\text{s}}. \tag{4.1}$$

Therefore, testing the median of $d_{i,t}^{\text{APE}}$ against zero using the above tests leads to establishing whether MAPE^{f} differs significantly from MAPE^{s} (in case if the distribution of $d_{i,t}^{\text{APE}}$ is symmetric, which is one of the assumptions of the above tests). In fact, the distribution of $d_{i,t}^{\text{APE}}$ is inherently skewed, which complicates matters and may result in drawing erroneous conclusions, but we will now not focus on this particular problem.

The results reported suggest that, overall, the value of MAPE was improved by the use of adjustments, but the accuracy of positive and negative adjustments differed substantially. Based on the MAPE measure, it was found that positive adjustments did not change the forecasting accuracy significantly, while negative adjustments led to significant improvements. However, percentage error measures have a number of disadvantages when applied to the adjustments data, as we explain below.

One well-known disadvantage of percentage errors is that when the actual value $Y_{i,t}$ in the denominator is relatively small compared to the forecast error $e_{i,t}$, the resulting percentage error $p_{i,t}$ becomes extremely large, which distorts the results of further analyses [20]. Such high values can be treated as outliers, since they often do not allow for a meaningful interpretation (large percentage errors are not necessarily harmful or damaging, as they can arise merely from relatively low actual values). However, identifying outliers in a skewed distribution is a non-trivial problem, where it is necessary to determine an appropriate trimming level in order to find robust estimates, while at the same time avoiding losing too much information. Usually authors choose the trimming level for MAPE based on their experience after experimentation (for example, [12], used a 2 % trim), but this decision still remains subjective. Moreover, the trimmed mean gives a biased estimate of location for highly skewed distributions [23], which complicates the interpretation of the trimmed MAPE. In particular, for a random variable that follows a highly skewed distribution, the expected value of the trimmed mean differs from the expected value of the random variable itself. This bias depends on both the trim level and the number of observations used to calculate the trimmed mean. Therefore, it is difficult to compare the measurement results based on the trimmed means for samples that contain different numbers of observations, even when the trim level remains the same.

SKU-level demand time series typically exhibit a high degree of variation in actual values, due to seasonal effects and the changing stages of a product's life cycle. Therefore, data on adjustments can contain a high proportion of low demand values, which makes PE-based measures particularly inadvisable in this context. Considering extremes, a common occurrence in the situation of intermittent demand is for many observations (and forecasts) to be zero (see the discussion by [29]). All cases with zero actual values must be excluded from the analysis, since the percentage error cannot be computed when $Y_{i,t} = 0$, due to its definition.

The extreme percentage errors that can be obtained can be shown using scaled values of errors and actual demand values (Fig. 4.3). The variables shown were scaled by the standard deviation of actual values in each series in order to eliminate the differences between time series. It can be seen that the final forecast errors have a skewed distribution and are correlated with both the actual values and the

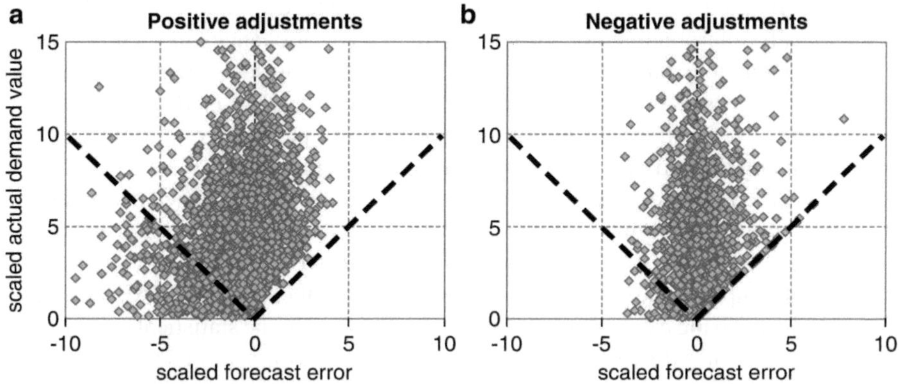

Fig. 4.3 Dependencies between forecast error, actual value, and the sign of adjustment (based on scaled data)

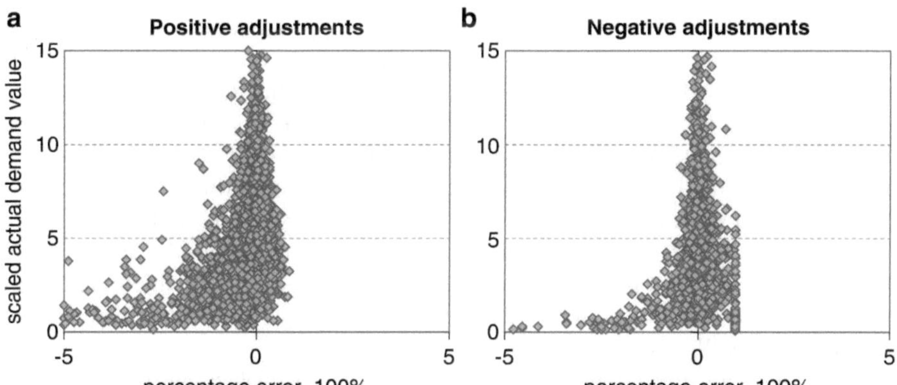

Fig. 4.4 Percentage errors, depending on the actual demand value and adjustment sign

signs of adjustments; it is also clear that a substantial number of the errors are comparable to the actual demand values. Excluding observations with relatively low values on the original scale (here, all observations less than 10 were excluded from the analysis, as was done by [12]) still cannot improve the properties of percentage errors sufficiently, since a large number of observations still remain in the area where the actual demand value is less than the absolute error. This results in extremely high APEs (>100 %), which are all too easy to misinterpret (since very large APEs do not necessarily correspond to very damaging errors, and arise primarily because of low actual demand values). In Fig. 4.3, the area below the dashed line shows cases in which the errors were higher than the actual demand values. These cases result in extreme percentage errors, as shown in Fig. 4.4. Due to the presence of extreme percentages, the distribution of APEs becomes highly skewed and heavy-tailed, which makes MAPE-based estimates highly unstable.

A widely used robust alternative to MAPE is MdAPE. However, MdAPE is neither easily interpretable nor sufficiently indicative of changes in accuracy when forecasting methods have different shaped error distributions. The sample median of the APEs is resistant to the influence of extreme cases, but is also insensitive to large errors, even if they are not outliers or extreme percentages. Comparing the accuracy using the MdAPE shows the changes in accuracy that relate to the lowest 50 % of APEs. However, MdAPE's improvement can be accompanied by remaining more damaging errors lying above the median if the shapes of the error distributions differ. In Sect. 4.5, it will be shown that, while the MdAPE indicates that judgmental adjustments improve the accuracy for a given dataset, the trimmed MAPE suggests the opposite to be the case. Moreover, the task of assessing the statistical significance of changes for MdAPE can be problematic due to the non-symmetric distributions of APEs. Therefore, additional indicators are required in order to be able to draw better-substantiated conclusions with regard to the forecasting accuracy.

Apart from the presence of extreme APEs, another problem with using PE-based measures is that they can bias the comparison in favour of methods that issue low forecasts [3, 4, 21]. This happens because, under certain conditions, percentage errors put a heavier penalty on positive errors than on negative errors. In particular, we can observe it when the forecast is taken as fixed. To illustrate this phenomenon, Kolassa and Schutz [21] provide the following example. Assume that we have a time series that contains values distributed uniformly between 10 and 50. If we are using a symmetrical loss function, the best forecast for this time series would be 30. However, a forecast of 22 produces a better accuracy in terms of MAPE. As a result, if the aim is to choose a method that is better in terms of a linear loss, then the values of PE-based measures can be misleading. The way in which the use of MAPE can bias the comparison of the performances of judgmental adjustments of different signs will be illustrated below.

One important effect which arises from the presence of cognitive biases and the non-negative nature of demand values is the fact that the most damaging positive adjustments (producing the largest absolute errors) typically correspond to relatively low actuals (left corner of Fig. 4.3a), while the worst negative adjustments (producing the largest absolute errors) correspond to higher actuals (centre section, Fig. 4.3b). More specifically, the following general dependency can be found within most time series. The difference between the absolute final forecast error $|e_{i,t}{}^{\mathrm{f}}|$ and the absolute statistical forecast error $|e_{i,t}{}^{\mathrm{s}}|$ is positively correlated with the actual value $Y_{i,t}$ for positive adjustments, while there is a negative correlation for negative adjustments. To reveal this effect, distribution-free measures of the association between variables were used. For each SKU i, Spearman's ρ coefficients were calculated, representing the correlation between the improvement in terms of absolute errors ($|e_{i,t}{}^{\mathrm{f}}| - |e_{i,t}{}^{\mathrm{s}}|$) and the actual value $Y_{i,t}$. Figure 4.5 shows the distributions of the coefficients $\rho_i{}^{+}$, calculated for positive adjustments, and $\rho_i{}^{-}$, corresponding to negative adjustments (the coefficients can take values 1 and -1 when only a few observations are present in a series). For the given dataset, mean$(\rho_i{}^{+}) \approx 0.47$ and mean$(\rho_i{}^{-}) \approx -0.44$, indicating that the improvement in forecasting is markedly correlated with the actual demand values. This illustrates

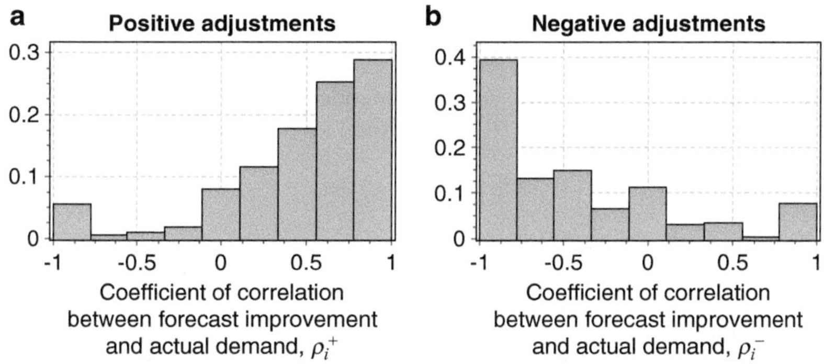

Fig. 4.5 Spearman's ρ coefficients showing the correlation between the improvement in accuracy and the actual demand value for each time series (relative frequency histograms)

the fact that positive adjustments are most effective for larger values of demand, and least effective (or even damaging) for smaller values of demand. Actually, efficient averaging of correlation coefficients requires applying Fisher's z transformation to them and then transforming back the result (see, e.g., [26]). But here we used raw coefficients because we only wanted to show that the ρ value clearly correlates with the adjustment sign.

Because of the division by the scale factor that is correlated with the numerator, the difference of APEs (which is calculated as $d_{i,t}^{\text{APE}} = 100 \times (|e_{i,t}{}^{\text{f}}| - |e_{i,t}{}^{\text{s}}|)/Y_{i,t}$) will not reflect changes in forecasting accuracy in terms of a symmetric loss function. More specifically, for positive adjustments, $d_{i,t}^{\text{APE}}$ will systematically downgrade improvements in accuracy and exaggerate degradations of accuracy (on the percentage scale). In contrast, for negative adjustments, the improvements will be exaggerated, while the errors from harmful forecasts will receive smaller weights. Since the difference in MAPEs is calculated as the sample mean of $d_{i,t}^{\text{APE}}$ (in accordance with Eq. 4.1), the comparison of forecasts using MAPE will also give a result which is biased towards underrating positive adjustments and overrating negative adjustments. Consequently, since the forecast errors arising from adjustments of different signs are penalised differently, the MAPE measure is flawed when comparing the performances of adjustments of different signs. One of the aims of the present research has therefore been to reinterpret the results of previous studies through the use of alternative measures.

A second measure based on percentage errors was also used by Franses and Legerstee [14]. In order to evaluate the accuracy of improvements, the RMSPE (root mean square percentage error) was calculated for the statistical and judgmentally adjusted forecasts, and the resulting values were then compared. Based on this measure, it was concluded that the expert adjusted forecasts were no better than the model forecasts. However, the RMSPE is also based on percentage errors, and is affected by the outliers and biases described above even more strongly.

4.3.2 Relative Errors

Another approach to obtaining scale-independent measures is based on using relative errors. The relative error (RE) is defined as

$$RE_{i,t} = e_{i,t}/e^{\mathrm{b}}_{i,t},$$

where $e_{i,t}{}^{\mathrm{b}}$ is the forecast error obtained from a benchmark method. Usually a naïve forecast is taken as the benchmark method.

Well-known measures based on relative errors include Mean Relative Absolute Error (MRAE), Median Relative Absolute Error (MdRAE), and Geometric Mean Relative Absolute Error (GMRAE):

$$\text{MRAE} = \text{mean}\left(|RE_{i,t}|\right),$$

$$\text{MdRAE} = \text{median}\left(|RE_{i,t}|\right),$$

$$\text{GMRAE} = \text{gmean}\left(|RE_{i,t}|\right),$$

where mean, median, and gmean respectively denote the sample mean, sample median, and the sample geometric mean over all possible values of i and t.

Averaging the ratios of absolute errors across individual observations overcomes the problems related to dividing by actual values. In particular, the RE-based measures are not affected by the presence of low actual values, or by the correlation between errors and actual outcomes. However, REs also have a number of limitations.

The calculation of $RE_{i,t}$ requires division by the non-zero error of the benchmark forecast $e_{i,t}{}^{\mathrm{b}}$. In the case of calculating GMRAE, it is also required that $e_{i,t} \neq 0$. The actual and forecasted demands are usually count data, which means that the forecasting errors are count data as well. With count data, the probability of a zero error of the benchmark forecast can be non-zero. Such cases must be excluded from the analysis when using relative errors. When using intermittent demand data, the use of relative errors becomes impossible due to the frequent occurrences of zero errors [18, 29].

As was pointed out by Hyndman and Koehler [20], in the case of continuous distributions, the benchmark forecast error $e_{i,t}{}^{\mathrm{b}}$ can have a positive probability density at zero, and therefore the use of MRAE can be problematic. In particular, $RE_{i,t}$ can follow a heavy-tailed distribution for which the sample mean becomes a highly inefficient estimate that is vulnerable to outliers. In addition, the distribution of $|RE_{i,t}|$ is highly skewed. At the same time, while MdRAE is highly robust, it cannot be sufficiently informative, as it is insensitive to large REs which lie in the tails of the distribution. Thus, even if the large REs are not outliers which arise from the division by relatively small benchmark errors, they still will not be taken into account when using MdRAE. Averaging the absolute REs using GMRAE is preferable to using either MRAE or MdRAE, as it provides a reliable and robust estimate and at the same time takes into account the values of REs which lie in the tails of the distribution. Also, when averaging the benchmark ratios, the geometric mean has the advantage that it produces rankings which are invariant to the choice of the benchmark (see [13]).

Fildes [10] recommends the use of the Relative Geometric Root Mean Square Error (RelGRMSE). The RelGRMSE for a particular time series i is defined as

$$\text{RelGRMSE}_i = \left(\frac{\prod_{t \in T_i} (e_{i,t})^2}{\prod_{t \in T_i} (e_{i,t}^{\text{b}})^2} \right)^{\frac{1}{2n_i}},$$

where T_i is a set containing time periods for which non-zero errors $e_{i,t}$ and $e_{i,t}{}^{\text{b}}$ are available, and n_i is the number of elements in T_i.

After obtaining the RelGRMSE for each series, Fildes [10] recommends finding the geometric mean of the RelGRMSEs across all time series, thus obtaining gmean(RelGRMSE$_i$). As Hyndman [18] pointed out, the Geometric Root Mean Square Error (GRMSE) and the Geometric Mean Absolute Error (GMAE) are identical because the square roots cancel each other in a geometric mean. Similarly, it can be shown that

$$\text{gmean}\left(\text{RelGRMSE}_i\right) = \text{GMRAE}.$$

An alternative representation of GMRAE is:

$$\text{GMRAE} = \exp\left[\frac{1}{\sum_{i=1}^{m} n_i} \sum_{i=1}^{m} \sum_{t \in T_i} \ln |RE_{i,t}| \right],$$

where m is the total number of time series, and other variables retain their previous meaning.

For the adjustments data set under consideration, only a small proportion of observations contain zero errors (about 1 %). It has been found empirically that for the given data set the log-transformed absolute REs, $\ln |RE_{i,t}|$, can be approximated adequately using a distribution which has a finite variance. In fact, even if a heavy-tailed distribution of $\ln |RE_{i,t}|$ arises, the influence of extreme cases can be eliminated based on various robustifying schemes such as trimming or Winsorizing. In contrast to APEs, the use of such schemes for $\ln |RE_{i,t}|$ is unlikely to lead to biased estimates, since the distribution of $\ln |RE_{i,t}|$ is not highly skewed.

Though GMRAE (or, equivalently, gmean(RelGRMSE$_i$)) has some desirable statistical properties and can give a reliable aggregated indication of changes in accuracy, its use can be complicated for the following two reasons. Firstly, as was mentioned previously, zero-error forecasts cannot be taken into account directly.

Secondly, in a similar way to the median, the geometric mean of absolute errors generally does not reflect changes in accuracy under standard loss functions. For instance, for a particular time series, GMAE (and, hence, GMRAE) favours methods which produce errors with heavier tailed-distributions, while for the same series RMSE (root mean square error) can suggest the opposite ranking.

The latter aspect of using GMRAE can be illustrated using the following example. Suppose that for a particular time series, method A produces errors e_t^{A} that are independent and identically distributed variables following a heavy-tailed distribution. More specifically, let e_t^{A} follow the t-distribution with $\nu = 3$ degrees of freedom: $e_t^{\text{A}} \sim t_\nu$. Also, let method B produce independent errors that follow the normal distribution: $e_t^{\text{B}} \sim N(0,3)$. Let method B be the benchmark method. It can be shown analytically that the variances for e_t^{A} and e_t^{B} are equal: $\text{Var}(e_t^{\text{A}}) = \text{Var}(e_t^{\text{B}}) = 3$. Thus, the relative RMSE (RelRMSE, the ratio of the two RMSEs) for this series is one. However, the Relative Geometric RMSE (or GMRAE) will show that method A is better than method B: GMRAE ≈ 0.69 (based on 10^6 simulated pairs of e_t^{A} and e_t^{B}). Now if, for example, $e_t^{\text{B}} \sim N(0,2.5)$, then the RelRMSE and GMRAE will be 1.10 and 0.76, respectively. This means that method B is now preferable in terms of the variance of errors, while method A is still (substantially) better in terms of the GMRAE. However, the geometric mean absolute error is rarely used when optimising predictions with the use of mathematical models. Some authors claim that the comparison based on RelRMSE can be more desirable, as in this case the criterion used for the optimisation of predictions corresponds to the evaluation criteria [9, 35].

The above example has demonstrated that even for a single time series a statistically significant improvement of GMRAE is not equivalent to a statistically significant improvement in terms of RMSE. Analogously, it can be demonstrated that the GMRAE is not indicative of changes in terms of MAE.

Thus, analogously to what was said with regard to PE-based measures, if the aim of the comparison is to choose a method that is better in terms of a linear or a quadratic loss, then GMRAE may not be sufficiently informative, or may even lead to counterintuitive conclusions.

4.3.3 Percent Better

A simple approach to compare forecasting accuracy of methods A and B is to calculate the percentage of cases when method A was closer to the actual observation than method B. This measure is known as 'Percent Better' (further abbreviated as PB) and was recommended by some authors as a fairly good indicator (see, e.g., [4, 6]). It has the advantage of being immune to outliers and is scale-independent (it can therefore be used to assess accuracy across series). In addition, it can be used for qualitative forecasts (but we will not look at this kind of forecasts in this paper). Although the measure seems to be easy to interpret, the following important limitations should be taken into account.

One problem with PB is that it does not show the magnitude of changes in accuracy [20]. Therefore, it becomes hard to assess the consequences of using one method instead of another. Moreover, as was the case for the GMRAE, we can show that if shapes of error distributions are different for different methods, PB becomes non-indicative of changes in terms of a linear or quadratic loss even for a single series.

Another problem arises when methods A and B frequently produce equal forecasts (e.g., this happens with intermittent demand data). In such situations, obtaining a PB value that is lower than 50 % is not necessarily a bad result, but without additional information we cannot draw any conclusions about the changes in accuracy. Suppose absolute errors for methods A and B can be approximated using the Poisson distribution: $|e_t^{\mathrm{A}}| \sim \mathrm{Pois}(\lambda = 1)$ and $|e_t^{\mathrm{B}}| \sim \mathrm{Pois}(\lambda = 3)$. Method A is much better than method B in terms of MAE: $E[|e_t^{\mathrm{A}}|]/E[|e_t^{\mathrm{B}}|] = 1/3$, but $P(|e_t^{\mathrm{A}}| < |e_t^{\mathrm{B}}|) \approx 0.077$. Thus, the PB is, approximately, only 7.7 % – a figure that can be misleading. For this example, even looking at 'Percent Worse' and relating it to the PB will also not give us an informative and easily interpretable indication of accuracy.

Thus, in spite of its apparent simplicity, the PB measure is often confusing and does not necessarily show changes in accuracy under linear loss. Moreover, it is not representative of the magnitude of changes and therefore it cannot ensure a complete and reliable analysis of accuracy.

4.3.4 Scaled Errors

In order to overcome the imperfections of PE-based measures, Hyndman and Koehler [20] proposed the use of the MASE (mean absolute scaled error). For the scenario when forecasts are produced from varying origins but with a constant horizon, the MASE is calculated as follows (see Appendix 1):

$$q_{i,t} = \frac{e_{i,t}}{\mathrm{MAE}_i^{\mathrm{b}}}, \quad \mathrm{MASE} = \mathrm{mean}\left(|q_{i,t}|\right),$$

where $q_{i,t}$ is the scaled error and $\mathrm{MAE}_i^{\mathrm{b}}$ is the mean absolute error (MAE) of the naïve (benchmark) forecast for series i.

Though this was not specified by Hyndman and Koehler [20], it is possible to show (see Appendix 1) that in the given scenario, the MASE is equivalent to the weighted arithmetic mean of relative MAEs, where the number of available values of $e_{i,t}$ is used as the weight:

$$\mathrm{MASE} = \frac{1}{\sum_{i=1}^{m} n_i} \sum_{i=1}^{m} n_i r_i, \quad r_i = \frac{\mathrm{MAE}_i}{\mathrm{MAE}_i^{\mathrm{b}}}, \tag{4.2}$$

where m is the total number of series, n_i is the number of available values of $e_{i,t}$ for series i, MAE_i^b is the MAE of the benchmark forecast for series i, and MAE_i is the MAE of the forecast being evaluated against the benchmark.

It is known that the arithmetic mean is not strictly appropriate for averaging observations representing relative quantities, and in such situations the geometric mean should be used instead [28]. As a result of using the arithmetic mean of MAE ratios, Eq. 4.2 introduces a bias towards overrating the accuracy of a benchmark forecasting method. In other words, the penalty for bad forecasting becomes larger than the reward for good forecasting.

To show how the MASE rewards and penalises forecasts, it can be represented as

$$\text{MASE} = 1 + \frac{1}{\sum_{i=1}^{m} n_i} \sum_{i=1}^{m} n_i \, (r_i - 1).$$

The reward for improving the benchmark MAE from A to B ($A > B$) in a series i is $R_i = n_i(1 - B/A)$, while the penalty for harming MAE by changing it from B to A is $P_i = n_i(A/B - 1)$. Since $R_i < P_i$, the reward given for improving the benchmark MAE cannot balance the penalty given for reducing the benchmark MAE by the same quantity. As a result, obtaining $\text{MASE} > 1$ does not necessarily indicate that the accuracy of the benchmark method was better on average. This leads to ambiguity in the comparison of the accuracy of forecasts.

For example, suppose that the performance of some forecasting method is compared with the performance of the naïve method across two series ($m = 2$) which contain equal numbers of forecasts and observations. For the first series, the MAE ratio is $r_1 = 1/2$, and for the second series, the MAE ratio is the opposite: $r_2 = 2/1$. The improvement in accuracy for the first series obtained using the forecasting method is the same as the reduction for the second series. However, averaging the ratios gives $\text{MASE} = ½(r_1 + r_2) = 1.25$, which indicates that the benchmark method is better. While this is a well-known point, its implications for error measures, with the potential for misleading conclusions, are widely ignored.

In addition to the above effect, the use of MASE (as for MAPE) may result in unstable estimates, as the arithmetic mean is severely influenced by extreme cases which arise from dividing by relatively small values. In this case, outliers occur when dividing by the relatively small MAEs of benchmark forecast which can appear in short series.

Some authors (e.g., [17]) recommend the use of the MAD/MEAN ratio. In contrast to the MASE, the MAD/MEAN ratio approach assumes that the forecasting errors are scaled by the mean of time series elements, instead of by the in-sample MAE of the naïve forecast. The advantage of this scheme is that it reduces the risk of dividing by a small denominator (see [21]). However, Hyndman [18] notes that the MAD/MEAN ratio assumes that the mean is stable over time, which may make it unreliable when the data exhibit trends or seasonal patterns. In Sect. 4.5, we show that both the MASE and the MAD/MEAN are prone to outliers for the data set we consider in this paper. Generally, the use of these schemes has the risk of producing unreliable estimates that are based on highly skewed left-bounded distributions.

Thus, while the use of the standard MAPE has long been known to be flawed, the newly proposed MASE also suffers from some of the same limitations, and may also lead to an unreliable interpretation of the empirical results. We therefore need a measure that does not suffer from these problems. The next section presents an improved statistic which is more suitable for comparing the accuracies of SKU-level forecasts.

4.4 Recommended Accuracy Evaluation Scheme

4.4.1 Measuring the Accuracy of Judgmental Adjustments

The recommended forecast evaluation scheme is based on averaging the relative efficiencies of adjustments across time series. The geometric mean is the correct average to use for averaging benchmark ratio results, since it gives equal weight to reciprocal relative changes [13]. Using the geometric mean of MAE ratios, it is possible to define an appropriate measure of the average relative MAE (AvgRelMAE). If the baseline statistical forecast is taken as the benchmark, then the AvgRelMAE showing how the judgmentally adjusted forecasts improve/reduce the accuracy can be found as

$$\text{AvgRelMAE} = \left(\prod_{i=1}^{m} r_i^{n_i}\right)^{1/\sum_{i=1}^{m} n_i}, \quad r_i = \frac{\text{MAE}_i^{\text{f}}}{\text{MAE}_i^{\text{s}}}, \tag{4.3}$$

where MAE_i^{s} is the MAE of the baseline statistical forecast for series i, MAE_i^{f} is the MAE of the judgmentally adjusted forecast for series i, n_i is the number of available errors of judgmentally adjusted forecasts for series i, and m is the total number of time series. This differs from the proposals of Fildes [10], who examined the behaviour of the GRMSEs of the individual relative errors.

The MAEs in Eq. 4.3 are found as

$$\text{MAE}_i^{\text{f}} = \frac{1}{n_i}\sum_{t\in T_i} \left|e_{i,t}^{\text{f}}\right|, \quad \text{MAE}_i^{\text{s}} = \frac{1}{n_i}\sum_{t\in T_i} \left|e_{i,t}^{\text{s}}\right|,$$

where $e_{i,t}^{\text{f}}$ is the error of the judgmentally adjusted forecast for period t and series i, T_i is a set containing the time periods for which $e_{i,t}^{\text{f}}$ are available, and $e_{i,t}^{\text{s}}$ is the error of the baseline statistical forecast for period t and series i.

AvgRelMAE is immediately interpretable, as it represents the average relative value of MAE adequately, and directly shows how the adjustments improve/reduce the MAE compared to the baseline statistical forecast. Obtaining AvgRelMAE < 1 means that on average $\text{MAE}_i^{\text{f}} < \text{MAE}_i^{\text{s}}$, and therefore adjustments improve the accuracy, while AvgRelMAE > 1 indicates the opposite. The average percentage improvement in MAE of forecasts is found as $(1 - \text{AvgRelMAE}) \times 100$. If required,

Eq. 4.3 can also be extended to other measures of dispersion or loss functions. For example, instead of MAE one might use the MSE (mean square error), interquartile range, or mean prediction interval length. The choice of the measure depends on the purposes of analysis. In this study, we use MAE, assuming that the penalty is proportional to the absolute error.

Equivalently, the geometric mean of MAE ratios can be found as

$$\text{AvgRelMAE} = \exp\left(\frac{1}{\sum_{i=1}^{m} n_i} \sum_{i=1}^{m} n_i \ln r_i\right).$$

Therefore, obtaining $\sum_{i=1}^{m} n_i \ln r_i < 0$ means an average improvement of accuracy, and $\sum_{i=1}^{m} n_i \ln r_i > 0$ means the opposite.

In theory, the following effect may complicate the interpretation of the AvgRelMAE value. If the distributions of errors $e_{i,t}^{\text{f}}$ and $e_{i,t}^{\text{s}}$ within a given series i have different levels of the kurtosis, then $\ln r_i$ is a biased estimate of $\ln(E|e_{i,t}^{\text{f}}|/E|e_{i,t}^{\text{s}}|)$. Thus, the indication of an improvement under linear loss given by the AvgRelMAE may be biased. In fact, if $n_i = 1$ for each i, then the AvgRelMAE becomes equivalent to the GMRAE, which has the limitations described in Sect. 4.3.2. However, our experiments have shown that the bias of $\ln r_i$ diminishes rapidly as n_i increases, becoming negligible for $n_i > 4$.

To eliminate the influence of outliers and extreme cases, the trimmed mean can be used in order to define a measure of location for the relative MAE. The trimmed AvgRelMAE for a given threshold t $(0 \le t \le 0.5)$ is calculated by excluding the $[tm]$ lowest and $[tm]$ highest values of $n_i \ln r_i$ from the calculations (square brackets indicate the integer part of tm). As was mentioned in Sect. 4.2, the optimal trim level depends on the distribution. In practice, the choice of the trim level usually remains subjective, since the distribution is unknown. Wilcox [33] wrote that 'Currently there is no way of being certain how much trimming should be done in a given situation, but the important point is that some trimming often gives substantially better results, compared to no trimming' (p. 16). Our experiments show that a 5 % level can be recommended for the AvgRelMAE measure. This level ensures high efficiency, because the underlying distribution usually does not exhibit very large departures from the normal distribution. A manual screening for outliers could also be performed in order to exclude time series with non-typical properties from the analysis.

The results described in the next section show that the robust estimates obtained using a 5 % trimming level are very close to the estimates based on the whole sample. The distribution of $n_i \ln r_i$ is more symmetrical than the distribution of either the APEs or absolute scaled errors. Therefore, the analysis of the outliers in relative MAEs can be performed more efficiently than the analysis of outliers when using the measures considered previously. Besides, we can assess the statistical significance of changes in accuracy by testing the mean of $n_i \ln r_i$ against zero.

Since the AvgRelMAE does not require scaling by actual values, it can be used in cases of low or zero actuals, as well as in cases of zero forecasting errors. Consequently, it is suitable for intermittent demand forecasts. The only limitation is that the MAEs in Eq. 4.3 should be greater than zero for all series. If zero MAEs do occur, they can be handled by the procedure that we describe below.

Thus, the advantages of the recommended accuracy evaluation scheme are that it (i) can be interpreted easily, (ii) represents the performance of the adjustments objectively (without the introduction of substantial biases or outliers), (iii) is informative and uses available information efficiently, (iv) is applicable in a wide range of settings, with minimal assumptions about the features of the data, and (v) gives rankings and indicates relative improvements that are invariant to the choice of the benchmark. Importantly, the last property can be ensured only through the use of the geometric mean. If we used a sample median or sample mean instead, this could lead to different rankings depending on the choice of the benchmark.

4.4.2 *Generalized Scheme for Measuring the Accuracy of Point Forecasts*

In general, in order to ensure a reliable evaluation of forecasting accuracy under a symmetric linear loss, we recommend using the following scheme. Suppose we want to measure the accuracy of h-step-ahead forecasts produced with some forecasting method A across m time series. Firstly, we need to select a benchmark method. This, in particular, can be the naïve method. Let n_i denote the number of periods for which both the h-step-ahead forecasts and actual observations are available for series i. Then the accuracy measurement procedure is as follows:

1. For each i in $1 \ldots m$
   (a) Calculate the relative MAE as $r_i = \frac{\text{MAE}_i^A}{\text{MAE}_i^B}$, where $\text{MAE}_i{}^A$ and $\text{MAE}_i{}^B$ denote out-of-sample h-step-ahead MAEs for method A and for the benchmark, respectively.
   (b) Calculate the weighted log relative MAE as $l_i = n_i \ln r_i$.
2. Calculate the Average Relative MAE as

$$\text{AvgRelMAE} = \exp\left(\frac{1}{\sum_{i=1}^{m} n_i} \sum_{i=1}^{m} l_i\right).$$

If there is an evidence for a non-normal distribution of l_i, use the following procedure to ensure more efficient estimates:

(a) Find the indices of l_i that correspond to the 5 % of largest and 5 % of lowest values. Let R be a set that contains the remaining indices.

(b) Calculate the trimmed version of the AvgRelMAE:

$$\text{AvgRelMAE}^{\text{trimmed}} = \exp\left(\frac{1}{\sum_{i\in R} n_i}\sum_{i\in R} l_i\right).$$

3. Assess the statistical significance of changes by testing the mean of l_i against zero. For this purpose, the Wilcoxon's one-sample signed rank test can be used (assuming that the distribution of l_i is symmetric, but not necessarily normal). If the distribution of l_i is non-symmetric, the binomial test can be used to test the median of l_i against zero. If the distribution has a negative skew then it is likely that the negative median will indicate negative mean as well.

Notes

(a) For low volume data it can be the case that $\text{MAE}_i^{\text{A}} = 0$ or $\text{MAE}_i^{\text{B}} = 0$ (or both). Essentially, MAE represents our estimate of the expected value of absolute error. But our prior knowledge suggests that the expected value of absolute error is larger than zero because for any forecasting task we assume that some level of uncertainty is present. Therefore, obtaining a zero MAE is an inadequate result and we may use some sufficiently small number instead (say $\text{MAE} = 0.001$). The extreme r_i values corresponding to such cases should then be excluded from the analysis on step 2 by setting a sufficiently large trim level. If the frequency of obtaining zero MAEs is too high (say larger than 30 %), a reliable estimation of the average relative MAE becomes unavailable, and we then have to resort to simply estimating the success rate for the MAE improvement. This can be done by calculating the number of cases when $\text{MAE}_i^{\text{A}} < \text{MAE}_i^{\text{B}}, i = 1 \ldots, m$, and then dividing this number by the total number of time series, m. Importantly, as mentioned in Sect. 4.3.3, getting a success rate that is statistically lower than 0.5 does not necessarily indicate that method A is worse than method B for count data (because of the possibility of equal MAEs); therefore the sum of ranks should be reported as well. But it is also important to keep in mind that neither the success rate nor the sum of ranks will be indicative of improvements under linear loss if sampling distribution for l_i is heavily skewed.

(b) If distribution of absolute errors is heavily skewed, the MAE, as any sample mean, becomes a very inefficient estimate of the expected value of absolute error. One simple method to improve the efficiency of the estimates while not introducing substantial bias is to use asymmetric trimming algorithms, such as those described by [1]. However, further discussions on this topic are outside the scope of our paper.

(c) If a suitable benchmark method is unavailable, we can use the sample mean of time series values instead of the benchmark MAE. The procedure then becomes similar to the MAD/MEAN ratio approach described in Sect. 4.3.4, but here the use of the geometric mean (i) ensures the correct averaging of ratios (i.e., deviations from the mean will be treated symmetrically) and (ii) gives more robust measurement results in cases when mean time series values are relatively small compared to absolute forecasting errors.

(d) In step 2, the optimal trim level depends on the shape of the distribution of l_i. Our experiments suggest that, for the distributions that are likely to be obtained, the efficiency of the trimmed mean is not highly sensitive to the choice of the trim level and any value between 2 % and 10 % gives reasonably good results. Generally, as was shown by [2], when the underlying distribution is symmetrical and heavy-tailed relative to the Gaussian, the variance of the trimmed mean is quite a lot smaller than the variance of the sample mean. Therefore, the use of the trimmed means for symmetrical distributions can be highly recommended.

4.5 Results of Empirical Evaluation

The results of applying the measures described above are shown in Table 4.3.

For the given dataset, a large number of APEs have extreme values (>100 %) which arise from low actual demand values (Fig. 4.6). Following Fildes et al. [12], we used a 2 % trim level for MAPE values. However, as noted, it is difficult to determine an appropriate trim level. As a result, the difference in APEs between the system and final forecasts has a very high dispersion and cannot be used efficiently

Table 4.3 Accuracy of adjustments according to different error measures

	Positive adjustments		Negative adjustments		All nonzero adjustments	
Error measure	Statistical forecast	Adjusted forecast	Statistical forecast	Adjusted forecast	Statistical forecast	Adjusted forecast
MAPE, % (untrimmed)	**38.85**	61.54	70.45	**45.13**	**47.88**	56.85
MAPE, % (2 % trimmed)	**30.98**	40.56	48.71	**30.12**	**34.51**	37.22
MdAPE, %	25.48	**20.65**	23.90	**17.27**	24.98	**19.98**
GMRAE	1.00	**0.93**	1.00	**0.70**	1.00	**0.86**
GMRAE (5 % trimmed)	1.00	**0.94**	1.00	**0.71**	1.00	**0.87**
MASE	**0.97**	0.97	0.95	**0.70**	0.96	**0.90**
Mean (MAD/Mean)	**0.37**	0.42	0.33	**0.24**	**0.36**	0.37
Mean (MAD/Mean) (5 % trimmed)	**0.34**	0.35	0.29	**0.21**	0.33	**0.31**
AvgRelMAE	1.00	**0.96**	1.00	**0.71**	1.00	**0.90**
AvgRelMAE (5 % trimmed)	1.00	**0.96**	1.00	**0.73**	1.00	**0.89**
Avg. improvement based on AvgRelMAE	0.00	**0.04**	0.00	**0.29**	0.00	**0.10**

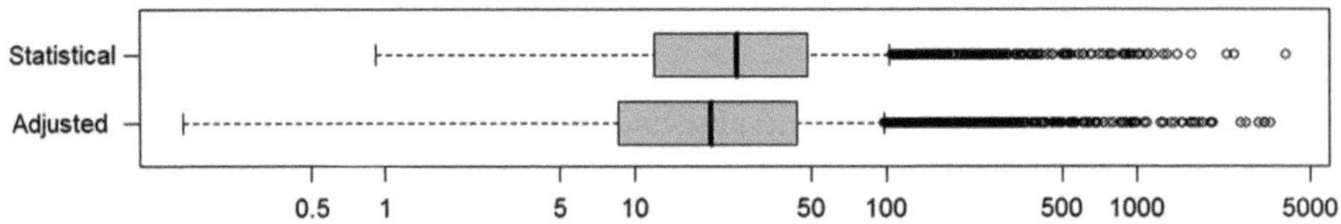

Fig. 4.6 Box-and-whisker plot for absolute percentage errors (log scale, zero-error forecasts excluded)

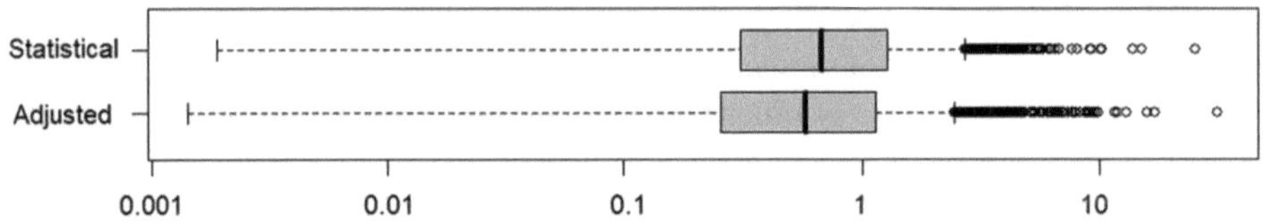

Fig. 4.7 Box-and-whisker plot for the absolute scaled errors found by the MASE scheme (log scale, zero-error forecasts excluded)

to assess improvements in accuracy. It can also be seen that the distribution of APEs is highly skewed, which means that the trimmed means cannot be considered as unbiased estimates of the location. Albeit the distribution of the APEs has a very high kurtosis, our experiments show that increasing the trim level (say from 2 % to 5 %) would substantially bias the estimates of the location of the APEs due to the extremely high skewness of the distribution. We therefore use the 2 % trimmed MAPE in this study. Also, the use of this trim level makes the measurement results comparable to the results of Fildes et al. [12].

Table 4.3 shows that the rankings based on the trimmed MAPE and MdAPE differ, suggesting different conclusions about the effectiveness of adjustments. As was explained in Sect. 4.3.1, the interpretation of PE-based measures is not straightforward. While MdAPE is resistant to outliers, it is not sufficiently informative, as it is insensitive to APEs which lie above the median. Also, PE-measures produce a biased comparison, since the improvement on the real scale within each series is correlated markedly with the actual value. Therefore, applying percentage errors in the current setting leads to ambiguous results and to confusion in their interpretation. For example, for positive adjustments, the trimmed MAPE and MdAPE suggest the opposite rankings: while the trimmed MAPE shows a substantial worsening of the final forecast due to the judgmental adjustments, the MdAPE value points in the opposite direction.

The absolute scaled errors found using the MASE scheme (as described in Sect. 4.3.4) also follow a non-symmetrical distribution and can take extremely large values (Fig. 4.7) in short series where the MAE of the naïve forecast is smaller than the error of judgmental forecast. For the adjustments data, the lengths of the series vary substantially, so the MASE is affected seriously by outliers. Figure 4.8 shows that the use of the MAD/MEAN scheme instead of the MASE does not improve the properties of the distribution of the scaled errors. Table 4.3 shows that

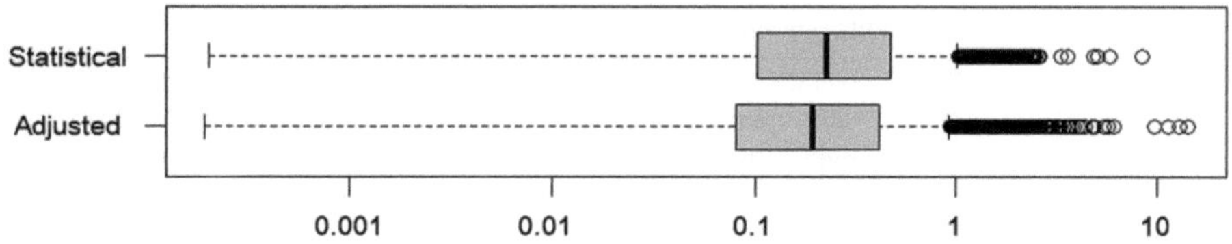

Fig. 4.8 Box-and-whisker plot for absolute scaled errors found by the MAD/MEAN scheme (log scale, zero-error forecasts excluded)

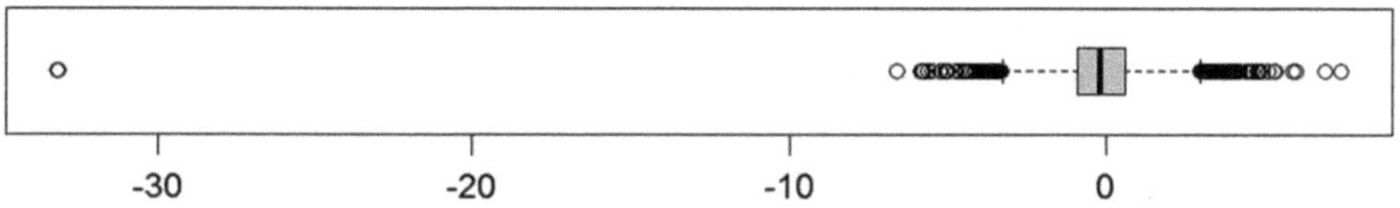

Fig. 4.9 Box-and-whisker plot for the log-transformed relative absolute errors (using the statistical forecast as the benchmark)

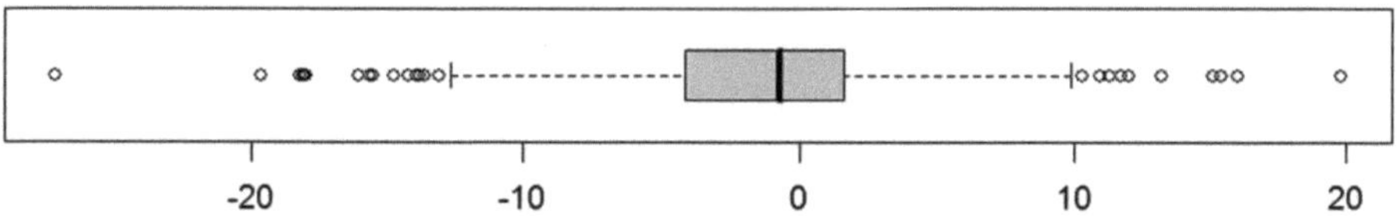

Fig. 4.10 Box-and-whisker plot for the weighted log-transformed relative MAEs ($n_i \ln r_i$)

a trimmed version of the MAD/MEAN scheme gives the opposite rankings with regard to the overall accuracy of adjustments, which indicates that this scheme is highly unstable. Moreover, with such distributions, the use of trimming for either MASE or MAD/MEAN leads to biased estimates, as was the case with MAPE.

Figure 4.9 shows that the log-transformed relative absolute errors follow a symmetric distribution and contain outliers that are easier to detect and to eliminate. Based on the shape of the underlying distribution, it seems that using a 5 % trimmed GMRAE would give a location estimate with a reasonable level of efficiency. Although the GMRAE measure is not vulnerable to outliers, its interpretation can present difficulties, for the reasons explained in Sect. 4.3.2.

Compared to the APEs and the absolute scaled errors, the log-transformed relative MAEs are not affected severely by outliers and have a more symmetrical distribution (Fig. 4.10). The AvgRelMAE can therefore serve as a more reliable indicator of changes in accuracy. At the same time, in terms of a linear loss function the AvgRelMAE scheme represents the effectiveness of adjustments adequately and gives a directly interpretable meaning.

The AvgRelMAE result shows improvements from both positive and negative adjustments, whereas according to MAPE and MASE, only negative adjustments improve the accuracy. For the whole sample, adjustments improve the MAE of statistical forecast by 10 %, on average. Positive adjustments are less accurate

Table 4.4 Results of using the binomial test to analyse the frequency of a successful adjustment

Adjustment sign	Total number of adjustments	Number of adjustments that improved forecast	p-value	Probability of a successful adjustment	95 % confidence interval for the probability of a successful adjustment	
Positive	3,394	1,815	<0.001	0.535	0.518	0.552
Negative	1,385	915	<0.001	0.661	0.635	0.686
Both	4,779	2,730	<0.001	0.571	0.557	0.585

than negative adjustments and provide only minor improvements. To assess the significance of changes in accuracy in terms of MAE, we applied the two-sided Wilcoxon test to test the mean of the weighted relative log-transformed MAEs against zero. The p-value was less than 0.01 for the set containing the adjustments of both signs, less than 0.05 for the set containing only positive adjustments, and less than $2.2 \cdot 10^{-16}$ for the set containing only negative adjustments.

To determine whether the probability of a successful adjustment is higher than 0.5, the two-sided binomial test was applied. The results are shown in Table 4.4.

Based on the p-values obtained for each sample, it can be concluded that adjustments improved the accuracy of forecasts more frequently than they reduced it. However, the probability of a successful intervention was rather low for positive adjustments.

4.6 Conclusions

The appropriate measurement of forecasting accuracy is important in many organizational settings, and is not of merely academic interest. Where an inappropriate error measure is used the consequences can be the adoption of a poor forecasting process. In addition forecasters can be rewarded or penalized (appropriately or not) for their performance and this is evaluated through the organization's choice of error measure. Due to the specific features of SKU-level demand data, many well-known error measures are not appropriate for use in evaluating the effectiveness of adjustments. This is especially true for fast-moving fashionable products. In particular, the use of percentage errors is not advisable because of the considerable proportion of low actual values, which lead to high percentage errors with no direct interpretation for practical use. Moreover, the errors corresponding to adjustments of different signs are penalised differently when using percentage errors, because the forecasting errors are correlated with both the actual demand values and the adjustment sign. As a result, measures such as MAPE and MdAPE do not provide sufficient indication of the effectiveness of adjustments, in terms of a linear loss function. Similar arguments were also found to apply to the calculation of MASE, which can also induce biases and outliers as a result of using the arithmetic mean to average relative quantities. Thus, an organization which determines its forecast improvement strategy based on an inadequate measure will misallocate its resources, and will therefore fail in its objective of improving the accuracy at the SKU level.

In order to overcome the disadvantages of existing measures, it is recommended that an average relative MAE be used which is calculated as the geometric mean of relative MAE values. This scheme allows for the objective comparison of forecasts, and is more reliable for the analysis of adjustments.

For the empirical dataset, the analysis has shown that adjustments improved accuracy in terms of the average relative MAE (AvgRelMAE) by approximately 10 %. For the same dataset, a range of well-known error measures, including MAPE, MdAPE, GMRAE, MASE, and the MAD/MEAN ratio, indicated conflicting results. The MAPE-based results suggested that, on the whole, adjustments did not improve the accuracy, while the MdAPE results showed a substantial improvement (dropping from 25 % to 20 %, approximately). The analysis using MASE and the MAD/MEAN ratio was complicated, due to a highly skewed underlying distribution, and did not allow any firm conclusions to be reached. The GMRAE showed that adjustments improved the accuracy by 13 %, a result that is close to that one obtained using the AvgRelMAE. Since analyses based on different measures can lead to different conclusions, it is important to have a clear understanding of the statistical properties of any error measure used. We have described various undesirable effects that complicate the interpretation of the well-known error measures. As an improved scheme which is appropriate for evaluating changes in accuracy under linear loss, we recommend using the AvgRelMAE. The generalisation of this scheme can be obtained straightforwardly for other loss functions as well.

One question that arises after the analysis of the accuracy of judgmental adjustments is whether or not these adjustments are systematically biased and can we improve them using some statistical calibration. A number of studies have been now conducted to address these questions (see, e.g., [7, 12, 14, 30]) and it has been found that judgmental adjustments do contain persistent systematic errors. Albeit this topic is outside the scope of the current paper, but, of course, we think that any study of procedures for the correction of judgmental forecasts should contain thorough analysis of accuracy based on appropriate and well-justified error measures.

The process by which a new error measure is developed and accepted by an organisation has not received any research attention. A case in point is intermittent demand, where service improvements can be achieved, but only by abandoning the standard error metrics and replacing them with service-level objectives [29]. When an organisation and those to whom the forecasting function reports insist on retaining MAPE or similar (as will mostly be the case), the forecaster's objective must then shift to delivering to the organisation's chosen performance measure, whilst using a more appropriate measure, such as the AvgRelMAE, to interpret what is really going on with the data. In essence, the forecaster cannot reasonably resort to using the organisation's measure and expect to achieve a cost-effective result.

Appendix 1 Alternative Representation of MASE

According to Hyndman and Koehler [20], for the scenario when forecasts are made from varying origins but with a constant horizon (here taken as one), the scaled error is defined as[1]

$$q_{i,t} = \frac{e_{i,t}}{\text{MAE}_i^{\text{b}}}, \quad \text{MAE}_i^{\text{b}} = \frac{1}{l_i - 1}\sum\nolimits_{j=2}^{l_i} \left|Y_{i,j} - Y_{i,j-1}\right|,$$

where $\text{MAE}_i{}^{\text{b}}$ is the MAE from the benchmark (naïve) method for series i, $e_{i,t}$ is the error of a forecast being evaluated against the benchmark for series i and period t, l_i is the number of elements in series i, and $Y_{i,j}$ is the actual value observed at time j for series i.

Let the mean absolute scaled error (MASE) be calculated by averaging the absolute scaled errors across time periods and time series:

$$\text{MASE} = \frac{1}{\sum\nolimits_{i=1}^{m} n_i}\sum\nolimits_{i=1}^{m}\sum\nolimits_{t\in T_i}\frac{|e_{i,t}|}{\text{MAE}_i^{\text{b}}},$$

where n_i is the number of available values of $e_{i,t}$ for series i, m is the total number of series, and T_i is a set containing time periods for which the errors $e_{i,t}$ are available for series i.

Then,

$$\begin{aligned}
\text{MASE} &= \frac{1}{\sum\nolimits_{i=1}^{m} n_i}\sum\nolimits_{i=1}^{m}\sum\nolimits_{t\in T_i}\frac{|e_{i,t}|}{\text{MAE}_i^{\text{b}}} \\
&= \frac{1}{\sum\nolimits_{i=1}^{m} n_i}\sum\nolimits_{i=1}^{m}\frac{\sum\nolimits_{t\in T_i}|e_{i,t}|}{\text{MAE}_i^{\text{b}}} \\
&= \frac{1}{\sum\nolimits_{i=1}^{m} n_i}\sum\nolimits_{i=1}^{m} n_i\frac{\frac{1}{n_i}\sum\nolimits_{t\in T_i}|e_{i,t}|}{\text{MAE}_i^{\text{b}}} \\
&= \frac{1}{\sum\nolimits_{i=1}^{m} n_i}\sum\nolimits_{i=1}^{m} n_i r_i, \quad r_i = \frac{\text{MAE}_i}{\text{MAE}_i^{\text{b}}},
\end{aligned}$$

where MAE_i is the MAE for series i for the forecast being evaluated against the benchmark.

---

[1]The formula corresponds to the software implementation described by Hyndman and Khandakar [19].

References

1. Alkhazaleh AMH, Razali AM (2010) New technique to estimate the asymmetric trimming mean. J Probab Stat 2010 http://www.hindawi.com/journals/jps/2010/739154/cta/
2. Andrews DF, Bickel PJ, Hampel FR, Huber PJ, Rogers WH, Tuckey JW (1972) Robust estimates of location. Princeton University Press, Princeton
3. Armstrong S (1985) Long-range forecasting: from crystal ball to computer. Wiley, New York
4. Armstrong JS, Collopy F (1992) Error measures for generalizing about forecasting methods: empirical comparisons. Int J Forecast 8:69–80
5. Armstrong JS, Fildes R (1995) Correspondence on the selection of error measures for comparisons among forecasting methods. J Forecast 14(1):67–71
6. Chatfield C (2001) Time-series forecasting. Chapman & Hall, Boca Raton
7. Davydenko A, Fildes R (2008) Models for product demand forecasting with the use of judgmental adjustments to statistical forecasts. Paper presented at the 28th international symposium on forecasting (ISF2008), Nice. Retrieved on 20 Sep 2013 from http://www.forecasters.org/submissions08/DAVYDENKOANDREYISF2008.pdf
8. Davydenko A, Fildes R (2013) Measuring forecasting accuracy: the case of judgmental adjustments to SKU-level demand forecasts. Int J Forecast 29(3):510–522
9. Diebold FX (1993) On the limitations of comparing mean square forecast errors: comment. J Forecast 12:641–642
10. Fildes R (1992) The evaluation of extrapolative forecasting methods. Int J Forecast 8(1):81–98
11. Fildes R, Goodwin P (2007) Against your better judgment? How organizations can improve their use of management judgment in forecasting. Interfaces 37:570–576
12. Fildes R, Goodwin P, Lawrence M, Nikolopoulos K (2009) Effective forecasting and judgmental adjustments: an empirical evaluation and strategies for improvement in supply-chain planning. Int J Forecast 25(1):3–23
13. Fleming PJ, Wallace JJ (1986) How not to lie with statistics: the correct way to summarize benchmark results. Commun ACM 29(3):218–221
14. Franses PH, Legerstee R (2010) Do experts' adjustments on model-based SKU-level forecasts improve forecast quality? J Forecast 29:331–340
15. Goodwin P, Lawton R (1999) On the asymmetry of the symmetric MAPE. Int J Forecast 4:405–408
16. Hill M, Dixon WJ (1982) Robustness in real life: a study of clinical laboratory data. Biometrics 38:377–396
17. Hoover J (2006) Measuring forecast accuracy: omissions in today's forecasting engines and demand-planning software. Foresight Int J Appl Forecast 4:32–35
18. Hyndman RJ (2006) Another look at forecast-accuracy metrics for intermittent demand. Foresight Int J Appl Forecast 4(4):43–46
19. Hyndman RJ, Khandakar Y (2008) Automatic time series forecasting: the forecast package for R. J Stat Softw 27(3)
20. Hyndman R, Koehler A (2006) Another look at measures of forecast accuracy. Int J Forecast 22(4):679–688
21. Kolassa S, Schutz W (2007) Advantages of the MAD/MEAN ratio over the MAPE. Foresight Int J Appl Forecast 6:40–43
22. Makridakis S (1993) Accuracy measures: theoretical and practical concerns. Int J Forecast 9:527–529
23. Marques CR, Neves PD, Sarmento LM (2000) Evaluating core inflation indicators. Working paper 3-00, Economics Research Department, Banco de Portugal
24. Mathews B, Diamantopoulos A (1987) Alternative indicators of forecast revision and improvement. Mark Intell 5(2):20–23
25. McCarthy TM, Davis DF, Golicic SL, Mentzer JT (2006) The evolution of sales forecasting management: a 20-year longitudinal study of forecasting practice. J Forecast 25:303–324
26. Mudholkar GS (1983) Fisher's z-transformation. Encyclopedia Stat Sci 3:130–135

27. Sanders N, Ritzman L (2004) Integrating judgmental and quantitative forecasts: methodologies for pooling marketing and operations information. Int J Oper Prod Manage 24:514–529
28. Spizman L, Weinstein M (2008) A note on utilizing the geometric mean: when, why and how the forensic economist should employ the geometric mean. J Legal Econ 15(1):43–55
29. Syntetos AA, Boylan JE (2005) The accuracy of intermittent demand estimates. Int J Forecast 21(2):303–314
30. Trapero JR, Fildes RA, Davydenko A (2011) Non-linear identification of judgmental forecasts at SKU-level. J Forecast 30(5):490–508
31. Trapero JR, Pedregal DJ, Fildes R, Weller M (2011) Analysis of judgmental adjustments in presence of promotions. Paper presented at the 31th international symposium on forecasting (ISF2011), Prague
32. Tversky A, Kahneman D (1974) Judgment under uncertainty: heuristics and biases. Science 185:1124–1130
33. Wilcox RR (1996) Statistics for the social sciences. Academic, San Diego
34. Wilcox RR (2005) Trimmed means. Encyclopedia Stat Behav Sci 4:2066–2067
35. Zellner A (1986) A tale of forecasting 1001 series: the Bayesian knight strikes again. Int J Forecast 2:491–494

Chapter 5
Forecasting Demand for Fashion Goods: A Hierarchical Bayesian Approach

Phillip M. Yelland and Xiaojing Dong

Abstract A central feature of demand for products in the fashion apparel segment is a pronounced *product life cycle*—demand for a fashion product tends to rise and fall dramatically in accordance with the rate of public of adoption. Product demands that vary in such a manner can be difficult to forecast, especially in the critical early period of a product's life, when observed demand can be a very unreliable yardstick of demand later on. This paper examines the applicability of a Bayesian forecasting model—based on one developed for use in the computer industry—to fashion products. To do so, we use an agent-based simulation to produce a collection of demand series consistent with commonly-accepted characteristics of fashion adoption. Using Markov chain Monte Carlo techniques to make predictions using the Bayesian model, we are able quantitatively to demonstrate its superior performance in this application.

5.1 Introduction

According to the US Office of Technology Assessment (1987), the apparel market in the US can be divided into three segments: (1) *fashion* products, which have a very short product life cycle, around 10 weeks, and account for approximately 35 % of the market; (2) *seasonal* products, which have a slightly longer product life cycle of around 20 weeks and account for approximately 45 % of the market; and (3) *basic* products, which do not have an obvious sales pattern and are sold throughout the

P.M. Yelland (✉)
Google Inc., 1600 Amphitheatre Parkway, Mountain View, CA 94043, USA
e-mail: phillip.yelland@gmail.com

X. Dong
Santa Clara University, 500 El Camino Real, Santa Clara, CA 95053, USA
e-mail: xdong1@scu.edu

T.-M. Choi et al. (eds.), *Intelligent Fashion Forecasting Systems: Models and Applications*, DOI 10.1007/978-3-642-39869-8_5,

year. The fashion clothing segment presents a particular challenge for demand planners: Competition is frequently fierce and profit margins volatile, supply chains span the globe and can be hard to coordinate, and the nature of demand for fashion goods themselves is (*ipso facto*) almost invariably highly labile and difficult to predict [33]. Regarding the latter, the most salient determinant of demand for fashion goods is their very pronounced product life cycle. Indeed, as Sproles [61] points out, "[f]ashions are, by definition, temporary cyclical phenomena adopted by consumers for a particular time and situation…, having stages of introduction and adoption by fashion leaders, increasing public acceptance (growth), mass conformity (maturation), and the inevitable decline and obsolescence awaiting all fashions".

This inherent variability of fashion product demand makes forecasting very difficult, especially early in a product's life cycle, when little is known about the product's ultimate level of market acceptance; demand early in a product's life may give scant indication of demand later on in the life cycle. To quote Kang [39]: "[T]he best-selling item of the last season could be the worst-selling item for the coming season". Compounding difficulties is the tendency of fashion cycles to shorten in recent years, a phenomenon Kang (ibid.) attributes to advances in media technology and the widespread availability of fashion clothing items.

Of course, appreciably short product lifecycles are not confined to the clothing industry; [67] describes a Bayesian forecasting model developed for computer components, where rapid technological development also leads to very pronounced short lifecycles. We set out to examine the suitability of a similar Bayesian forecasting model for demands in the fashion apparel segment, hypothesizing that a model which had proven effective in accomodating short product lifecycles held promise for fashion clothing forecasting, too.

In [67], assessment of the forecasting model is based on actual demand experienced by a particular manufacturer (Sun Microsystems Inc.); the use of actual series was largely a consequence of the model's use by that manufacturer. While the use of manufacturer data in that paper provides the assurance that the model has real-world applicability, in the strictest sense it establishes efficacy only for one particular firm over a particular period of time. To broaden the scope of the model in this work, we adopt a different approach: We *simulate* plausible demand series for fashion goods options under a variety of circumstances, and test the accuracy of a model derived from [67] in extrapolating them. Of course, very little would be achieved if the simulation were constructed along the same lines as the forecasting model itself, merely embodying the parameters and latent constructs used in the model. As Cook et al. [14] demonstrate, such an exercise can play a valuable rôle in validating the correctness of a model implementation, but it would hardly establish the broad applicability of the model itself. Instead, we use an *agent-based simulation* to calculate demand based upon individual purchase decisions, with simulation elements designed to drive those individual decisions in a manner consistent with paradigmatic characteristics of fashion goods and their markets.

In the interests of expositional clarity, we make to simplifications in both the simulation and forecasting model used in this chapter, concentrating predominantly on the treatment of the product life cycle. Thus regular cyclical or "seasonal" effects on demand, for example, are represented only in very rudimentary form; simulation of more complex seasonality represents no challenge, and many models of seasonality from the forecasting literature (such as seasonal dummies) may be added to the forecasting model without difficulty—see Harvey [31] or Brockwell and Davis [8] for examples.

The plan of the chapter is as follows: In the next section, we outline related work in the literature. The following section describes in detail the simulation used to generate option demands. We then introduce the forecasting model, with brief prefatory remarks about the Bayesian approach to forecasting in general. The forecasting performance of the model in respect of the simulated option demands is then appraised in comparison with that of a sophisticated benchmark forecasting method. We finish with concluding remarks.

5.2 Related Work

As Hines and Bruce [32] recount, the modern fashion apparel industry is characterized by increasingly short product life cycles, which contrast with long lead times and complicated supply chain (typically, it takes 2 years from the design and 1 year from production before a garment is sold). This has led to a proliferation of literature studying supply chain management [17], assortment planning [10], and—most saliently for our purposes—sales forecasting. The latter features studies using various probability distributions to fit the sales data and forecast the demand—Agrawal and Smith [1], for example, fit a negative binomial distribution to retail sales data. In the model recounted here, we supplement a probability distribution for sales with an explicit account of the product life cycle. This has many precedents in forecasting models for technology products—cf. [66], among many others.

We use a Bayesian approach in formulating our model to tackle another challenge often faced by forecasters in the fashion apparel industry: A very limited amount of available calibration data. Other researchers in the area have also adopted a Bayesian approach, mostly to account for the dynamic nature of demand updates as more data become available. Early inventory models that allow demand updating using a Bayesian approach include those of Dvoretzky et al. [18], Scarf [57], Iglehart [37], Murray and Silver [47], Azoury and Miller [5], Azoury [4], and Miller [44]. More recently, Iyer and Bergen [38] model a Quick Response apparel supply contract, allowing the demand distribution to be updated in a Bayesian fashion using early sales data. The demand process in this model is assumed to follow a normal distribution. Other recent studies adopt a two-stage demand process for a fashion product. Gurnani and Tang [30], for example, allow a retailer to place two orders before the selling season. They derive an optimal ordering policy, while allowing the first-stage demand to be updated via a Bayesian method. In a similar setup, Choi et al. [11] use a newsvendor model in a two-stage context using Bayesian information updating. Other examples include [19] and [12], to name a few.

Besides information updating, the model in this chapter illustrates that the Bayesian approach can also be applied using a *hierarchical prior*, so as to obtain forecasts for a single item with only a small amount of historical sales information by "borrowing" information from similar items. This feature of the Bayesian approach is widely adopted in the Marketing and Economics literature (see Ansari et al. [2], Narayanan and Manchanda [48], and Dong et al. [16], for example). A seminal paper in Marketing is [55], where a hierarchical Bayesian framework is adopted to analyze model parameters that are related to individual customers' responses to shopping coupons. In this study, each customer makes a limited number of observed purchases, and individual level inference is not feasible using classical statistics. The hierarchical Bayesian approach, on the other hand, calculates individual level inferences by combining population level parameter estimates with the individual level data—essentially borrowing information from the rest of the population. Rossi et al. [56] present a detailed discussion of hierarchical Bayesian methods.

As indicated in Sect. 5.1, to apply our method in an empirical context, we adopt an agent-based approach to simulate demand data. In general methodological terms, agent-based simulation investigates aggregate level phenomena by simulating the behaviors of individual agents [53]. This approach allows a proper account to be made of complexity in the data generation process while also being tractable. It has been widely adopted across multiple fields, including organizational science [13], supply chain management [64] and Marketing [28]. North et al. [49], give an account of Procter & Gamble's successful application of agent-based simulation to improve revenue. Related to our study, agent-based simulation has also been applied to investigate the diffusion of innovation—cf. for example Schwoon [59], Delre et al. [15], Schenk et al. [58], and Kiesling et al. [40]. Our own agent-based simulation is described in the next section.

5.3 Data Simulation

Our simulation of demand for fashion products over time is based on the parallels—noted by Sproles [61] among others—between fashion goods lifecycles and the more general process of innovation adoption.[1] To this end, we adapt Rand and Rust's [53] simulation of innovation adoption. This starts with a set of *agents*, indexed $1, \ldots, N$, whose communication patterns take the form of a so-called *small-world network* after Watts and Strogatz [65]. The network fixes for each agent i a set of *neighbors*, $\texttt{Neighbors}_i$, comprising those agents which are in direct communication with agent i. We simulate the actions of this set of agents over periods $t = 1, \ldots, T$.[2] In each period t, agent i may elect to purchase the

[1] A full summary of the notation in the paper, and a description of the probability distributions used is provided in the appendices.

[2] For concreteness's sake, we will frequently regard one period as 1 day, though we use the term "period" throughout to emphasize the generality of the framework.

product—an event we denote $\texttt{purch}_{it}$. In the interests of simplicity, we assume that each agent purchases the product once. Furthermore, only a subset of the agents—the product's "potential market", $\texttt{Market} \subseteq \{1, \ldots, N\}$—will *ever* purchase the product. In each period, therefore, agent i's probability of purchase is non-zero only if $i \in \texttt{Market}$ and $i \notin \texttt{Purch}_{t-1}$.[3] We abbreviate this conjunction—informally, agent i's membership of the product's potential market in period t—as $\texttt{pot}_{it}$. When the simulation begins, each agent enters into $\texttt{Market}$ independently,[4] each with the same product-specific probability r. Following a paradigm expressed in models of innovation diffusion dating from (at least) Bass [6], we assume that such purchases are motivated by either: (a) an *exogenous* influence, which stems from the promotional activities through mass-marketing channels, such as advertising, or (b) an *endogenous* influence, resulting from communication with neighboring agents who have already purchased the product. The event $\texttt{purch-ex}_{it}$ denotes agent i's *ex*ogenously-motivated purchase in period t, and $\texttt{purch-end}_{it}$ similarly denotes an *end*ogenously-motivated purchase. Since a purchase may arise exogenously or endogenously, the event $\texttt{purch}_{it}$ is the conjunction of these events, so that $\texttt{purch}_{it} = \texttt{purch-ex}_{it} \vee \texttt{purch-end}_{it}$.

Provided that agent i is in the product's potential market in period t, the probability of s/he making an exogenously-motivated purchase in period t is determined by a parameter p_i associated with agent i and a seasonal effect associated with t. As adumbrated in Sect. 5.1, to keep things simple, the simulation incorporates only one seasonal effect—a "day-of-the-week" effect that distinguishes every 7th period with a 50 % increase in sales. Thus we have:

$$p(\texttt{purch-ex}_{it} | \texttt{pot}_{it}) = \min[(1 + 0.5\texttt{S}_t)p_i, 1], \tag{5.1}$$

where $\texttt{S}_t$ is an indicator variable picking out every 7th period:

$$\texttt{S}_t = \begin{cases} 1 & \text{if } t \bmod 7 = 0, \\ 0 & \text{otherwise.} \end{cases} \tag{5.2}$$

The probability of an endogenously-motivated purchase by agent i in period t (conditional on membership of the potential market in t) depends on another agent-specific parameter, q_i, along with the seasonal effect and the fraction of agent i's neighbors who have already purchased the product:

$$p(\texttt{purch-end}_{it} | \texttt{pot}_{it}) = \min\left[(1+0.5\texttt{S}_t)q_i \frac{|\texttt{Neighbors}_i \cap \texttt{Purch}_{t-1}|}{|\texttt{Neighbors}_i|}, 1\right]. \tag{5.3}$$

---

[3]For technical convenience, we take $\texttt{Purch}_0$ to be the empty set.

[4]Throughout this section, events are assumed (conditionally) independent unless the contrary is noted.

At the outset of the simulation for a particular product, parameters p_i and q_i for each agent i are sampled from the (compound) beta distributions listed below. We use an alternate (and arguably more intuitive) parameterization, $\text{Beta}(\mu, \sigma^2)$, of the beta distribution in terms of its mean μ and variance σ^2, where it is required that $\sigma^2 < \mu(1-\mu)$; the more conventional parameters α and β can be recovered as $\mu\nu$ and $(1-\mu)\nu$ resp., for $\nu = \mu(1-\mu)/\sigma^2 - 1$. In addition, we use the shorthand $x \sim \{v_1, v_2, \ldots, v_n\}$ to indicate that value of the random variable x is drawn randomly from the set $\{v_1, v_2, \ldots, v_n\}$. Then:

$$p_i \sim \text{Beta}(\mu_p, \mu_p/2), \text{ where } \mu_p \sim \{0.00035, 0.0005, 0.001, 0.005, 0.01, 0.02\}, \tag{5.4}$$

$$q_i \sim \text{Beta}(\mu_q, \mu_q/2), \text{ where } \mu_q \sim \{0.05, 0.1, 0.2, 0.4, 0.5\}, \tag{5.5}$$

Simulating a demand series over periods $1, \ldots, T$ involves the following:

1. Initialize the agent-specific values p_i and q_i according to the distributions given in (5.4) and (5.5) resp. Compute $\mathtt{Market}$ according to r, set $\mathtt{Purch}_0$ to $\emptyset$ and $\mathtt{pot}_{i1}$ iff $i \in \mathtt{Market}$.

   For each time period t:

2. Independently for each agent i such that $\mathtt{pot}_{it}$[5]:

   (a) Draw a uniformly-distributed random variable $\mathtt{u{-}exo}_{it} \sim \text{Unif}(0, 1)$. Assert event $\mathtt{purch{-}ex}_{it}$ iff $\mathtt{u{-}exo}_{it} < p(\mathtt{purch{-}ex}_{it} | \mathtt{pot}_{it})$, the latter term being defined in Eq. (5.1).
   (b) Draw another random variable $\mathtt{u{-}endo}_{it} \sim \text{Unif}(0, 1)$ and assert $\mathtt{purch{-}end}_{it}$ iff $\mathtt{u{-}endo}_{it} < p(\mathtt{purch{-}end}_{it} | \mathtt{pot}_{it})$ from Eq. (5.3).
   (c) Assert $\mathtt{purch}_{it}$ iff $\mathtt{purch{-}ex}_{it}$ or $\mathtt{purch{-}end}_{it}$ is true.

3. Let $\mathtt{Purch}_{t+1} = \mathtt{Purch}_t \cup \{i \in 1, \ldots, N \mid \mathtt{purch}_{it}\}$.
4. Simulated demand, y_t, for the product in period t, is $\sum_{i=1}^{N} \mathcal{I}(\mathtt{purch}_{it})$, where $\mathcal{I}(\mathtt{purch}_{it})$ is 1 if $\mathtt{purch}_{it}$ is true, and 0 otherwise.

Repeating the simulation procedure a number of times produces a collection of possible trajectories for product demand over time. We took a sample of 50 such series, each of 100 periods in length, for use in our forecasting exercises; nine typical sample members appear in Fig. 5.1. In next section, we describe the Bayesian model proposed for extrapolating these series.

5.4 Forecasting Model

Before describing the details of forecasting model itself, we outline in general terms how Bayesian methods are particularly appropriate when forecasting demand for fashion goods.

[5]i.e. $i \in \mathtt{Market}$ and $i \notin \mathtt{Purch}_{t-1}$.

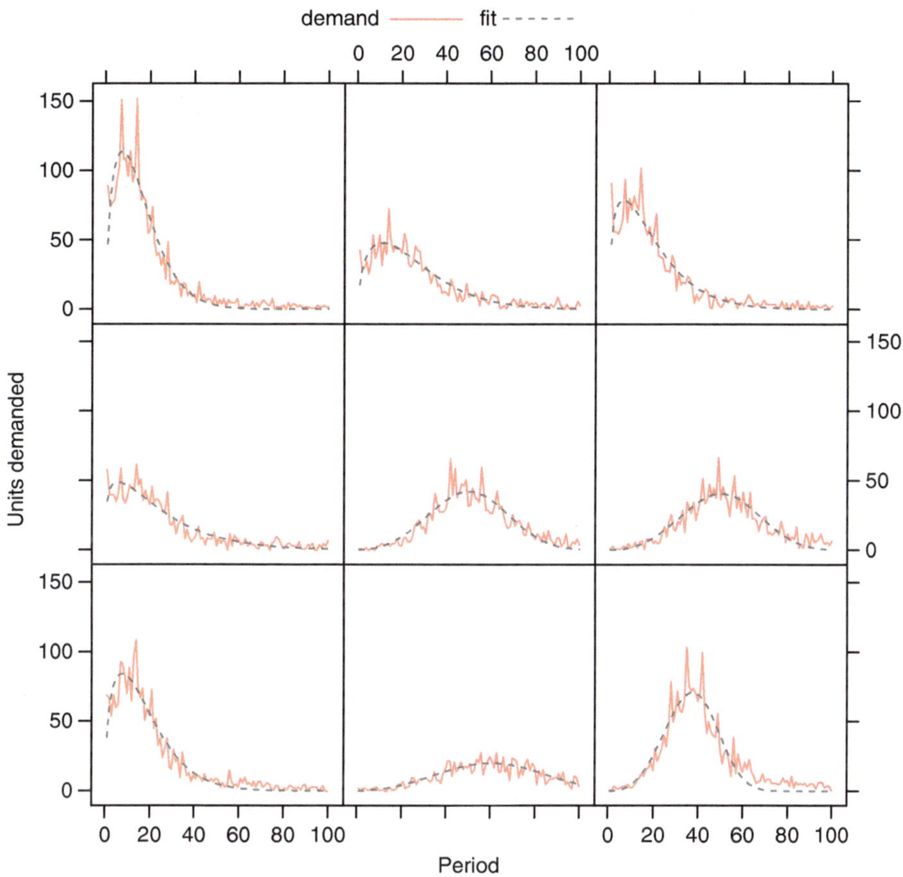

Fig. 5.1 Sample simulated product demands (*solid lines*), and corresponding fitted Weibull curves (*dotted lines*). Note the variability of the overall shape of the demand series and of the peak demand in each case

5.4.1 Bayesian Forecasting

In the conventional forecasting situation examined in the literature, a suitably long time series of observed values—$\boldsymbol{y} = (y_t, \ldots, y_T)$, say—is presented for extrapolation, and (restricting the discussion to a single period forecast horizon for simplicity) the task of the forecaster is to predict the value of the value of the series after h further periods, y_{T+h}. In the demand forecasting exercise examined here, however, short product life cycles mean that individual products frequently lack sufficient observed demand values to support reliable extrapolation. In this application, therefore, input to the forecasting process consists not only of previous demands for a particular product, but also of observed demands for *other* similar products, too—even products that are no longer available. Thus the data takes the form of a collection of series, $\boldsymbol{y}_1, \ldots, \boldsymbol{y}_J$, of potentially differing lengths (some of which may be zero), so that for $j = 1, \ldots, J$, $\boldsymbol{y}_j = (y_{j1}, \ldots, y_{jT_j})$. The aim is to forecast $y_{l\,T_l+h}$, for some chosen product l.

The objective of the model presented in this section is a statistical representation of such a collection of demand series using a set of unobserved quantities. This latter set—which we denote in the abstract by the vector $\boldsymbol{\theta}$—contains the model parameters, and may also contain the values of latent variables or processes. It is assumed that the representation in terms of $\boldsymbol{\theta}$ is sufficiently detailed that all the elements of the series are conditionally independent given $\boldsymbol{\theta}$, i.e.: [6]

$$p(\boldsymbol{y}_1, \ldots, \boldsymbol{y}_J|\boldsymbol{\theta}) = \prod_{j=1}^{J}\prod_{t=1}^{T_j} p(y_{jt}|\boldsymbol{\theta}). \tag{5.6}$$

A Bayesian forecast of $y_{l\,T_l+h}$ rests on its *posterior predictive distribution.* The latter is simply the conditional distribution of $y_{l\,T_l+h}$ given the historical demands, $p(y_{l\,T_l+h}|\boldsymbol{y}_1, \ldots, \boldsymbol{y}_J)$. The conditional independence property of the model expressed in Eq. (5.6) is pivotal to the derivation of this distribution, since on the assumption that $y_{l\,T_l+h}$ is also well-represented by $\boldsymbol{\theta}$, it should be conditionally independent of the historical demands, just as the historical demands were conditionally independent of each other:

$$p(y_{l\,T_l+h}, \boldsymbol{y}_1, \ldots, \boldsymbol{y}_J|\boldsymbol{\theta}) = p(y_{l\,T_l+h}|\boldsymbol{\theta})p(\boldsymbol{y}_1, \ldots, \boldsymbol{y}_J|\boldsymbol{\theta}). \tag{5.7}$$

Now it is easy to show that with the provision of a prior distribution for $\boldsymbol{\theta}$, $p(\boldsymbol{\theta})$, the posterior predictive distribution may be expressed as:

$$p(y_{l\,T_l+h}|\boldsymbol{y}_1, \ldots, \boldsymbol{y}_J) = \int p(y_{l\,T_l+h}|\boldsymbol{\theta})p(\boldsymbol{\theta}|\boldsymbol{y}_1, \ldots, \boldsymbol{y}_J)d\boldsymbol{\theta} \tag{5.8}$$

$$\propto \int p(y_{l\,T_l+h}|\boldsymbol{\theta})p(\boldsymbol{y}_1, \ldots, \boldsymbol{y}_J|\boldsymbol{\theta})p(\boldsymbol{\theta})d\boldsymbol{\theta}. \tag{5.9}$$

Note that the second factor in the integral on the right hand side of Eq. (5.8) is the posterior distribution of $\boldsymbol{\theta}$ given the observed data, $\boldsymbol{y}_1, \ldots, \boldsymbol{y}_J$. As many treatments of Bayesian statistics illustrate ([7,24], for example), provided that the observed data is sufficiently informative, even if $p(\boldsymbol{\theta})$ is diffuse or non-informative for elements of $\boldsymbol{\theta}$, the posterior distribution will be sharp enough to yield reasonably precise predictions for $y_{l\,T_l+h}$ in Eq. (5.8). This is an advantage in applications such as this, where very little prior information is available in advance of the model's deployment.

[6] Since some of the T_j may be zero, we adopt the convention that for any expression $\bullet$, $\prod_{j=1}^{0} \bullet = 1$.:

We also note that given a mechanism—such as the Markov chain Monte Carlo (*MCMC*) simulator described in Sect. 5.5—for drawing samples from the posterior distribution of $\boldsymbol{\theta}$, the right hand side of Eq. (5.8) shows how one may sample from the posterior predictive distribution by drawing a value $\tilde{\boldsymbol{\theta}}$ from the posterior distribution $p(\boldsymbol{\theta} \mid \boldsymbol{y}_1, \ldots, \boldsymbol{y}_J)$ and then drawing one from the conditional distribution $p(y_{l\,T_l+h} \mid \tilde{\boldsymbol{\theta}})$. The resulting sample may then be used to characterize the posterior predictive distribution for $y_{l\,T_l+h}$ in Eq. (5.8), yielding (amongst other quantities) a point forecast for $y_{l\,T_l+h}$.

To allow for some variation in demand patterns between products, we adopt a so-called *hierarchical* or *multilevel* prior [22,23] in the model. This may be thought of abstractly as dividing $\boldsymbol{\theta}$ into two collections of sub-vectors: A collection $\boldsymbol{\zeta} = (\zeta_1, \ldots, \zeta_J)$ of parameter vectors associated with products, and a single vector $\boldsymbol{\vartheta}$ of common "population-level" parameters. The prior for $\boldsymbol{\theta}$ as a whole is expressed by defining the priors for the product-level parameters in terms of the values of the population-level parameters, while the population-level parameters receive their own free-standing priors. This means that in Eq. (5.9):

$$p(\boldsymbol{\theta}) = \left\{ \prod_{j=1}^{J} p(\zeta_j \mid \boldsymbol{\vartheta}) \right\} p(\boldsymbol{\vartheta}). \tag{5.10}$$

Using common parameters at the population level allows us to pool information about typical patterns of demand, and the product-level parameters capture the heterogeneity exhibited by the particular products (see [23], for a general discussion).

5.4.2 *Use of the Weibull Curve*

Like the forecasting model in [67], the model in this paper incorporates an explicit representation of the product's life cycle. The representation used in this model is derived from the *Weibull distribution*, following a precedent established by Sharif and Islam [60] and Moe and Fader [45], who use the Weibull in the analysis of innovation diffusion and new product adoption, respectively.[7]

In Moe and Fader's [45] model, use of a Weibull curve to describe the time to first purchase of a new product has theoretical appeal, deriving from the Weibull distribution's origins in the analysis of events that occur after a period of random duration [43]. Observe, however, that the Weibull distribution plays no explicit rôle in the data generating process described in Sect. 5.3, and given the intricacies of the simulation, a foundational argument the use of the Weibull curve to describe it is difficult to make. Thus the application of the Weibull curve here follows Sharif and Islam's [60] more pragmatic approach—as both they (and in fact Moe and

[7]For a comprehensive survey of analytical models of product life cycles, see Mahajan et al. [42].

Fader) observe, the Weibull curve brings an appealing combination of parsimony and flexibility to the description of life cycles. By way of justification for this pragmatic approach, an informal indication of how well the Weibull curve—with only two parameters—captures the trend in the simulated product demands can be gauged from Fig. 5.1, where (appropriately scaled) Weibull curves have been fitted to the sample series.

5.4.3 Determinants of Product Demand

Returning to the discussion of Sect. 5.4.1, the first step in making concrete the general model of Eq. (5.6), is to specify the conditional distribution $p(y_{jt}|\boldsymbol{\theta})$ of unit demand for product j in period t. Since product demand in any time period is a discrete, non-negative quantity, it is natural to represent it as a Poisson distribution with a time-varying mean. The latter is the product of three random quantities: (1) a product-specific quantity, γ_j, that depends on the potential market for the product, (2) a discrete-time stochastic process that captures the product's life cycle, λ_{jt}, and (3) a factor ς_{jt} associated with seasonal effects. Thus:

$$y_{jt} \sim \text{Pois}(\gamma_j \lambda_{jt} \varsigma_{jt}). \tag{5.11}$$

5.4.4 Scale Factor

Filling out the specification in Eq. (5.11), we must provide a prior for the scale factor γ_j. Since this quantity is necessarily positive, its prior is a left-truncated normal distribution whose location and scale parameters are shared with other products; these shared (hyper-) parameters are themselves given non-informative priors:

$$\gamma_j \sim \text{N}_{[0,\infty)}(\mu_\gamma, \sigma_\gamma^2), \quad p(\mu_\gamma) \propto 1, \quad p(\sigma_\gamma) \propto \mathcal{I}(\sigma_\gamma > 0). \tag{5.12}$$

5.4.5 Life Cycle Curve

Following the plan set out in Sect. 5.4.3, the quantity λ_{jt} in Eq. (5.11), which traces the evolution of demand over the life cycle of an product, is determined by a suitably parameterized Weibull probability density function (*PDF*) at t:

$$\lambda_{jt} = \text{Weib}(t|\alpha_j, \delta_j). \tag{5.13}$$

In the conventional parameterization of the Weibull curve, the value of the Weibull PDF at t is equal to $(\eta/k)(t/k)^{\eta-1}e^{-(t/k)^\eta}$, where η and k are (positive) parameters of the distribution. To help the convergence of the MCMC simulator described in Sect. 5.5, and as an aid to interpretability, we use an alternate parameterization of the Weibull in Eq. (5.13), indexed by α_j and δ_j, which are respectively the 20th percentile of the distribution and the difference between its 95th and 20th percentiles.[8] A little algebraic manipulation yields conventional Weibull parameters η_j and k_j corresponding to α_j and δ_j, so that:

$$\text{Weib}(t|\alpha_j,\delta_j) = \frac{\eta_j}{k_j}\left(\frac{t}{k_j}\right)^{\eta_j-1} e^{-(t/k_j)^{\eta_j}},$$
$$\text{where } \eta_j = \frac{2.6}{\log(\alpha_j+\delta_j)-\log(\alpha_j)},\; k_j = \frac{\alpha_j}{0.22^{1/\eta_j}}. \quad (5.14)$$

Completing the specification of λ_{jt} given by Eqs. (5.13) and (5.14) requires that we provide prior distributions for the part-specific parameters α_j and δ_j. As with γ_j, the priors for both of these parameters are hierarchical, incorporating information garnered from the demand for other products. Treating the case of α_j in detail (the treatment of δ_j is analogous): Since α_j must be positive in Eq. (5.14), it is drawn (like γ_j) from a normal distribution, truncated on the left at 0.[9] The location and scale parameters, μ_α and σ_α, resp. of this truncated normal distribution are common to all parts, and have non-informative priors. In symbols:

$$\alpha_j \sim \text{N}_{[0,\infty)}(\mu_\alpha,\sigma_\alpha^2), \quad p(\mu_\alpha)\propto 1, \quad p(\sigma_\alpha)\propto \mathcal{I}(\sigma_\alpha>0). \quad (5.15)$$

5.4.6 Seasonal Effects

The representation of seasonal effects in the model mirrors that used in the simulation (Sect. 5.3).[10] Thus demand is modulated by an product-specific multiple ω_j of the indicator variable s_t from Eq. (5.2) (Fig. 5.2). To complete the specification, ω_j is drawn from a normal distribution with pooled hyperparameters:

$$\varsigma_{jt} = 1+\omega_j \text{s}_t, \quad \omega_j \sim \text{N}(\mu_\omega,\sigma_\omega^2), \quad p(\mu_\omega)\propto 1, \quad p(\sigma_\omega)\propto \mathcal{I}(\sigma_\omega>0). \quad (5.16)$$

[8]We use the difference between the 20th and 95th percentiles rather than the 95th percentile itself because α_j and δ_j might reasonably be considered a priori independent, making for easier specification of the model prior.

[9]Strictly speaking, truncation on the left should be at a point slightly greater than 0, but the technical elision is of no practical consequence.

[10]In this respect, we depart from the precept set out in the introduction requiring us to disassociate the simulation and forecasting model. However, since we do not regard seasonal effects as a defining characteristic of demand for fashion goods (to which life cycle effects are most pivotal),

Product demand

$$y_{jt} \sim \text{Pois}(\gamma_j \lambda_{jt} \varsigma_{jt})$$

Life cycle curve

$$\lambda_{jt} = \text{Weib}(t|\alpha_j, \delta_j), \quad \alpha_j \sim \text{N}_{[0,\infty)}(\mu_\alpha, \sigma_\alpha^2), \quad \delta_j \sim \text{N}_{[0,\infty)}(\mu_\delta, \sigma_\delta^2)$$

Scale

$$\gamma_j \sim \text{N}_{[0,\infty)}(\mu_\gamma, \sigma_\gamma^2)$$

Seasonal effects

$$\varsigma_{jt} = 1 + \omega_j \text{S}_t, \quad \omega_j \sim \text{N}(\mu_\omega, \sigma_\omega^2)$$

Fig. 5.2 Model summary: Unless otherwise stated, location parameters of the form $\mu_\circ$ and scale parameters $\sigma_\circ$ have non-informative priors $p(\mu_\circ) \propto 1$ and $p(\sigma_\circ) \propto \mathcal{I}(\sigma_\circ > 0)$, respectively. Indexes j and t range over products and periods, resp.

5.5 Estimation

This section discusses the procedure used to approximate the posterior distributions of the model parameters, and summarizes the approximate posteriors produced with product demands simulated as described in Sect. 5.3.

5.5.1 Metropolized Gibbs Sampler

As is commonly the case in modern applied Bayesian statistics, estimation of posterior distributions for the parameters of the model described in the previous section is carried out using a Markov chain Monte Carlo simulator—specifically, an adaptation of the *Gibbs sampler* known variously as the *Metropolized-* or the *Metropolis-within-*Gibbs sampler [54, p. 392]. Schematic descriptions of the Gibbs sampling scheme now abound in the literature—see [27, Chap. 1], for example; briefly, beginning with starting values for the parameters of the model, such a simulator constructs a Markov chain whose states converge to a dependent sample from the joint posterior of those parameters. Each transition in this Markov chain involves drawing a new value of one of the parameters from its posterior distribution conditional on the current value of the other parameters and the observed data. The *Metropolized* Gibbs sampler—first proposed by Müller [46]—adopts the same

and since alternative approaches to seasonal modeling would be unnecessarily cumbersome here, we consider such a lapse justified.

step-by-step sampling scheme as the ordinary Gibbs sampler, but *Metropolis-Hastings sampling* (also discussed by Gilks et al.) is used to sample approximately from the conditional distributions (by accepting or rejecting so-called *proposed values*) for those steps where sampling directly from the conditional distribution is problematic. The individual steps of this particular sampler are described below. Many of the direct sampling steps rely on standard results concerning conjugate updating in Bayesian analysis, which may be found in texts such as [7] or [24]. Where Metropolis-Hastings sampling is used, proposed values are generated using Gilks et al.'s [26] *adaptive rejection Metropolis sampling (ARMS)* procedure, as implemented in the R package `dlm` [52].

In the following, each step is introduced by the conditional distribution from which a sample is to be drawn. Variables of which the sampled quantity is conditionally independent are omitted from the conditioning set. In the interests of brevity, draws are specified only for α_j and σ_α; samples for δ_j and σ_δ are generated in an analogous manner. We abbreviate $\boldsymbol{y}_j = (y_{j1}, \ldots, y_{jT_j})$.

$\gamma_j \mid \boldsymbol{y}_j, \alpha_j, \delta_j, \mu_\gamma, \sigma_\gamma, \omega_j$

The kernel of the full conditional distribution is given by the expression:

$$\left[\prod_{t=1}^{T_j} \text{Pois}(y_{jt}|\gamma_j\lambda_{jt}\varsigma_{jt})\right] \times \text{N}_{[0,\infty)}(\gamma_j|\mu_\gamma, \sigma_\gamma^2),$$

where λ_{jt} and ς_{jt} are the quantities determined by α_j, δ_j and ω_j in Eqs. (5.13) and (5.16) resp. Sampling is carried out using the ARMS procedure.

$\alpha_j \mid \boldsymbol{y}_j, \gamma_j, \delta_j, \mu_\alpha, \sigma_\alpha, \omega_j$

The full conditional is proportional to the expression:

$$\left[\prod_{t=1}^{T_j} \text{Pois}(y_{jt}|\gamma_j\lambda_{jt}\varsigma_{jt})\right] \times \text{N}_{[0,\infty)}(\alpha_j|\mu_\alpha, \sigma_\alpha^2).$$

This is also sampled using ARMS.

$\mu_\alpha \mid \alpha_1, \ldots, \alpha_J, \sigma_\alpha$

Sampling is carried out using a device due to Griffiths [29]: Specifically, for $l \in 1, \ldots, J$, let:

$$\tilde{\alpha}_l = \mu_\alpha + \sigma_\alpha\ \Phi^{-1}\left[\frac{\Phi\left(\frac{\alpha_l - \mu_\alpha}{\sigma_\alpha}\right) - \Phi\left(\frac{-\mu_\alpha}{\sigma_\alpha}\right)}{1 - \Phi\left(\frac{-\mu_\alpha}{\sigma_\alpha}\right)}\right], \tag{5.17}$$

where $\Phi(\cdot)$ denotes the standard normal cumulative distribution function.

Then as Griffiths demonstrates, supposing that $\tilde{\alpha}_l \sim \mathrm{N}(\mu_\alpha, \sigma_\alpha^2)$ and drawing from the conditional distribution $\mu_\alpha \mid \tilde{\alpha}_1, \ldots, \tilde{\alpha}_J, \sigma_\alpha$ (a straightforward application of semi-conjugate updating with a non-informative prior) is equivalent to drawing from $\mu_\alpha \mid \alpha_1, \ldots, \alpha_J, \sigma_\alpha$ given that $\alpha_l \sim \mathrm{N}_{[0,\infty)}(\mu_\alpha, \sigma_\alpha^2)$.

$\sigma_\alpha \mid \alpha_1, \ldots, \alpha_J, \mu_\alpha$

Again, using Griffiths's device, draw from $\sigma_\alpha \mid \tilde{\alpha}_1, \ldots, \tilde{\alpha}_J$, given that $\tilde{\alpha}_j \sim \mathrm{N}(\mu_\alpha, \sigma_\alpha^2)$, where $\tilde{\alpha}_j$ is defined in Eq. (5.17).

$\omega_j \mid \mathbf{y}_j, \gamma_j, \alpha_j, \delta_j, \mu_\omega, \sigma_\omega$

Another ARMS step, with kernel:

$$\left[\prod_{t=1}^{T_j} \mathrm{Pois}(y_{jt}|\gamma_j \lambda_{jt}[1 + \omega_j \mathsf{S}_t])\right] \times \mathrm{N}(\omega_j|\mu_\omega, {\sigma_\omega}^2).$$

5.5.2 *Posterior Estimates and Diagnostics*

Figure 5.3 (inspired by similar figures on e.g. p. 351 of [23]) illustrates the results of estimating the model with the simulated product demands. Here the Gibbs sampler was run in a single chain for 6,000 iterations, with samples from the first 1,500 discarded; no thinning of the remaining samples was performed.

On the left of the Figure are displayed posterior distributions for the quantities associated with a random selection of products ("prd."- 7, 25, 18 and 40), as well as population-level parameters. Parameters α_j, δ_j and γ_j are summarized for the selected products, and the fitted value of y_{jt} in the fifth period is displayed as "y.5". Also shown are the population-level location parameters μ_α, μ_δ and μ_γ (labeled respectively "m.a", "m.d", "m.g" and "m.w"), as well as scale parameters σ_α, σ_δ, σ_γ and σ_ω (similarly labeled "s.a", etc.). Each posterior distribution is summarized graphically by a condensed box-and-whisker plot,[11] with the distribution's mean and (parenthesized) standard deviation given numerically.

The right-hand side of the Figure plots Geweke's [25] convergence diagnostic for each of the quantities in question. Derived from a comparison of the first and last segments of the Markov chain associated with a quantity, Geweke's statistic z has an asymptotically standard normal distribution if the chain is stationary (i.e. convergence has occurred). On the diagram, values of z are plotted on the 5th and 95th percentiles of the standard normal distribution. The plots indicate that

[11]"Boxes" delimit the interquartile range of the distributions, and "whiskers" extend 1.5 times the interquartile range from the ends of the boxes—see Tukey [62] for further details.

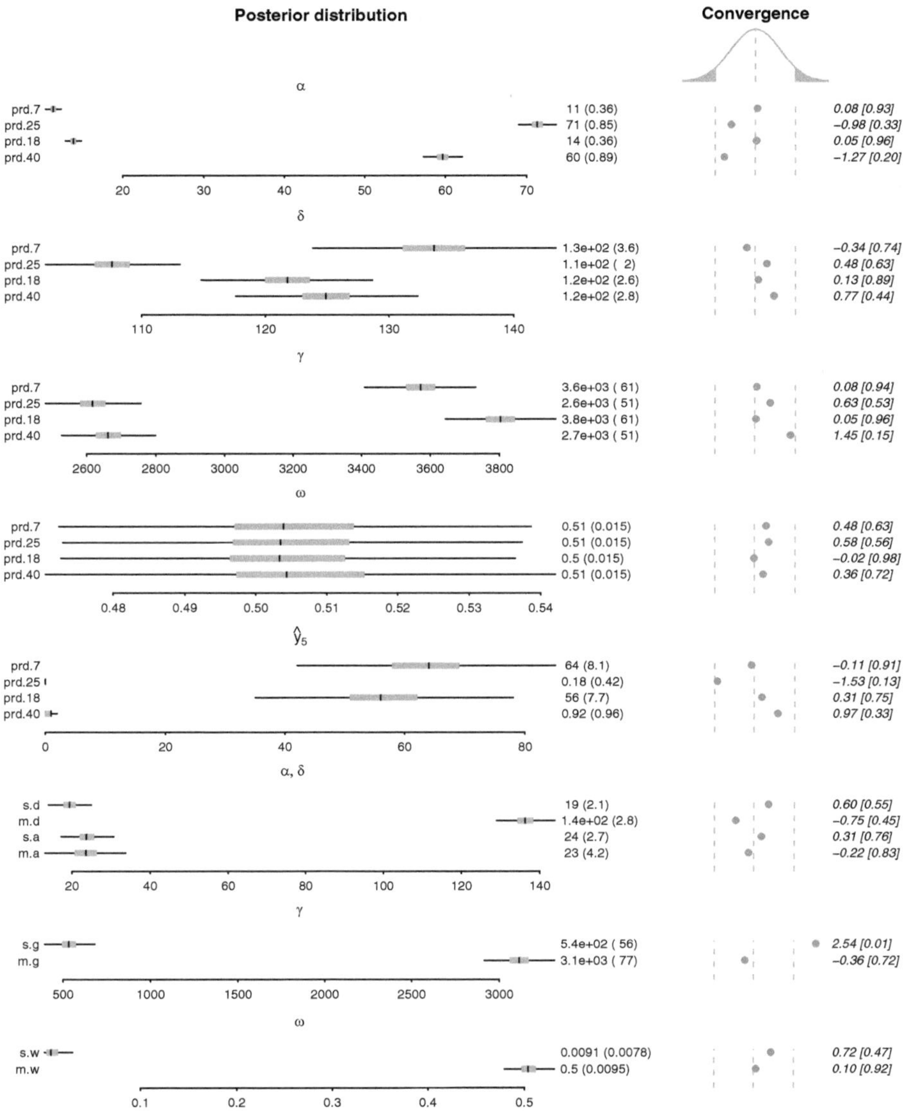

Fig. 5.3 Posterior distributions and convergence diagnostics for model fit to full sample of simulated demand series: On the *left* are interquartile ranges and 1.5×interquartile ranges of quantities associated with selected products (prd.-) and hyperparameters, together with the mean and standard deviation of the corresponding distribution. On the *right* are values of Geweke's convergence statistic; all but one of the values lie between the 5th and 95th percentiles of the standard normal distribution (statistic values and p-values appear on the far *right*), so convergence is reasonably assured

convergence has been achieved—note that with 28 quantities displayed, we would expect between 2 and 3 values of z to fall outside of the percentile bounds even with convergence.

5.6 Testing Forecast Performance

The test the efficacy of the model described in the foregoing, we used it to forecast demand for the sample of product demand series simulated using the framework described in Sect. 5.3. As Armstrong [3] points out, an objective assessment of new forecasting method requires a *benchmark* method against which to compare its performance. In this exercise, our benchmark method was the `ets` function found in the "`forecast`" R package of Hyndman and Khandakar [34]. The `ets` function embodies the forecasting framework developed by Hyndman et al. [36] which—as its authors point out—has been proven to deliver consistently superior forecast performance when applied to a wide variety of time series. Furthermore, the `ets` function is capable of producing forecasts in a largely automatic fashion (though its behavior may be affected by parameter settings). Thus while the `ets` function—unlike the hierarchical Bayesian method described in this paper—is not tailored specifically to the forecasting of fashion goods demand, it promises in its rôle as a benchmark method to furnish reasonable performance with minimal effort.

Our testing procedure was as follows:

1. Reserve 25 out of the 50 simulated demand series from Sect. 5.3 to calibrate the Bayesian forecasting model.
2. Truncate all of the remaining 25 series after k periods, where k takes successive values from 4 to 92 in increments of 8 (i.e. 4, 12, 20, etc.).
3. Using the hierarchical Bayes model and the benchmark `ets` function in turn, for each value of k, and each truncated series $\boldsymbol{s}_i = (s_{i1}, \ldots, s_{ik})$, produce two forecasts $\hat{s}^{\mathtt{hb}}_{i,k+h}$ and $\hat{s}^{\mathtt{ets}}_{i,k+h}$ of demand h periods after the point of truncation, where h ranges from 1 to $100 - k$ (since all of the simulated series are of length 100 periods).

   Forecasting with the Bayesian model involves subjecting both the 25 reserved demand series as well the 25 truncated series to the procedure set out in Sect. 5.4.1, using the MCMC simulator described in Sect. 5.5.1 to produce a sample from the posterior predictive distribution for $s_{i,k+h}$, and taking the median of this sample as the point forecast.

   The `ets` function did not use the calibration series, but we found that to produce reasonable forecasts with the function at longer horizons (i.e. h in excess of 20 or so), it was necessary to provide some hints to its automatic model selection algorithm, constraining it to look for models with *damped, additive trends* [21,36].
4. Subtracting the predicted value for $s_{i,k+h}$ from its actual value in the untruncated series produces two forecast errors. To derive *scale-free* expressions of forecast

error (in the sense of [35]), these were expressed as a percentage of the mean value of the untruncated series,[12] yielding quantities $\epsilon_{i,k+h}^{\texttt{hb}}$ and $\epsilon_{i,k+h}^{\texttt{ets}}$.

5. Finally, overall performance metrics for each method for each value of k and h were calculated by taking means of the absolute values of the scale free errors across all of the truncated series—thus $\bar{\epsilon}_{k+h}^{\texttt{hb}} = \sum_{i=1}^{25} \epsilon_{i,k+h}^{\texttt{hb}}$ and $\bar{\epsilon}_{k+h}^{\texttt{ets}} = \sum_{i=1}^{25} \epsilon_{i,k+h}^{\texttt{ets}}$.

Figure 5.4 plots the forecast metrics calculated in step 5 for all values of k (the number of periods observed before forecasting). It is evident that in this application, the Bayesian model proposed here offers substantially better forecast performance, particularly early in the product lifecycle, where the calibration data comprised by the reserved demand series is especially advantageous.[13]

5.7 Conclusions

We set out to establish the effectiveness of a Bayesian forecasting model based on a general formulation of the product life cycle in application to fashion clothing goods. The last section demonstrates that the forecasting performance of the proposed model certainly compares favorably with that of a benchmark method when applied to simulated fashion product demand series. Of course, a caveat attaches to this demonstration, in that our data is simulated; though we have been careful to derive the simulation from a generally-accepted model of consumer behavior with regard to fashion products, this is provides only a provisional assurance that the simulated series match the actual series encountered by a particular retailer or manufacturer.[14] Nonetheless, the archetypical features of the simulated data implies that the forecasting model is probably at least partially applicable in any given situation in practice, though it may require some adaptation.

Certainly, as suggested in Sect. 5.1, many elaborations of both the simulation and the forecasting model—to accommodate more realistic seasonal effects, for example—are reasonably straightforward. Yelland [67], for instance, illustrates the incorporation of a latent autoregressive process to account for serially-correlated departures of demand from a strict life cycle model. And as also shown in [67], a

[12]This is a modification of the more common *mean absolute percentage error* (MAPE) metric; since the values in the forecast series vary significantly over lifecycle of the corresponding product, the MAPE is apt to distort performance assessment by unduly inflating small absolute errors at either end of the lifecycle.

[13]Note that the comparatively poor performance of the `ets` function here should not be construed as general criticism, but rather as affirmation of the contention that the proposed model is far better suited to the type of series encountered in this context than is a general-purpose forecasting tool.

[14]In this respect, the situation here is the obverse of that in [67], where efficacy for a particular manufacturer's demand series was demonstrated, but more general applicability remained something of an open question.

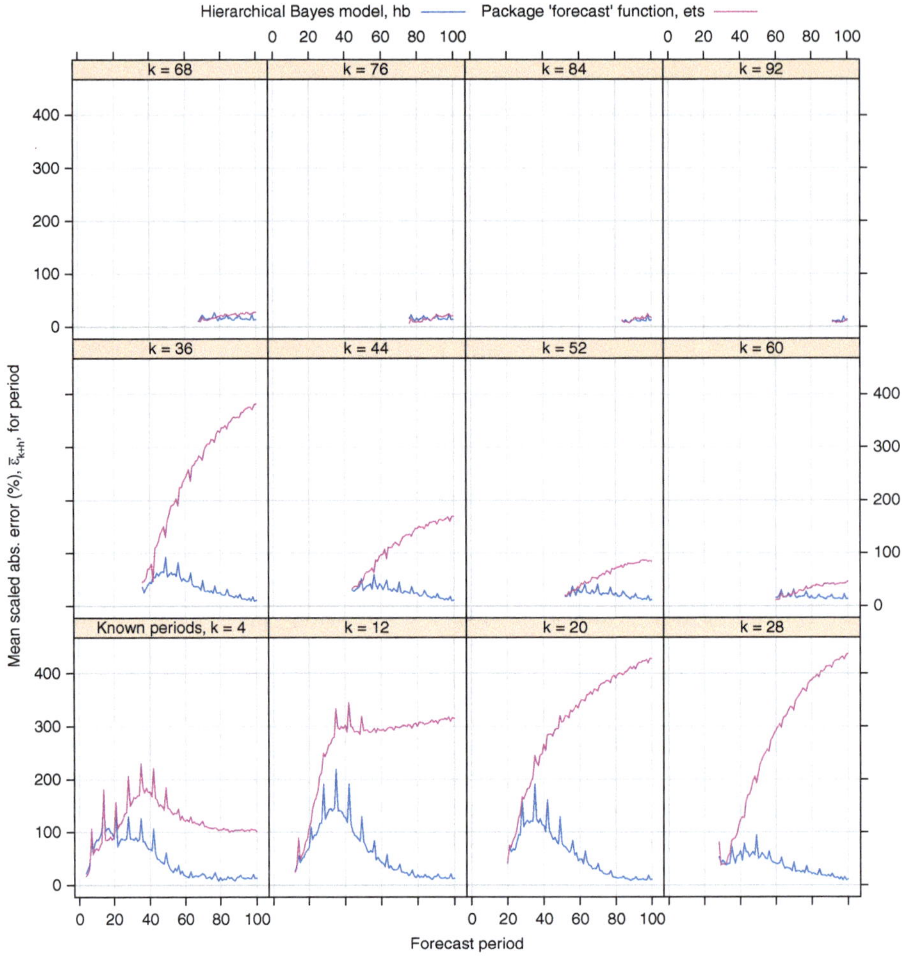

Fig. 5.4 Forecast performance of the model and benchmark

more elaborate hierarchical Bayesian model can be used to forecast demand for ancillary items, such as configurations or parts, that are correlated with product demand. And the related system documented in [68] uses substantive Bayesian priors to predict life cycle demands in a situation where—unlike the forecasting test of Sect. 5.6—comparable products are unavailable for calibration. The Bayesian framework may also be employed to address another problem Bruce and Daly [9] observe is often encountered in supply chain management for fashion retailing, viz., the availability of timely sales data that is only approximate and/or provisional. With a Bayesian model, revised forecasts can be produced by treating early sales data as *soft evidence*, known only with uncertainty—see e.g. [50, 51, 63] for details of methods for updating Bayesian models with soft evidence.

With regard to applying our work in an industry setting, as we suggest in Sect. 5.1, recent developments in the fashion industry are highly favorable to a life cycle based Bayesian model such as the one described here: First, as Hines and Bruce [32] indicate, increasing globalization of the industry—driven by the dismantling of tarrif barriers, improvements in transportation and communication technology, competitive pressures militating in favor of low-cost off-shore manufacturing and the rise of geographically-dispersed design and manufacturing hubs in Europe and the Far East—has made relatively long lead times a reality in many sectors of the industry. Effectively addressing such lead times necessitates relatively long-term forecasts, in which product life cycles are frequently a significant factor. Second, as competitive pressures accelerate the trend towards "fast fashion" and "quick response" [39] even in low-cost retail lines, updates to forecasts prior to and during the selling season are becoming the norm[15]; Bayesian forecasting of the sort demonstrated here is perfectly suited to producing such updates. We would also be interested in establishing the broader viability of the use of agent-based simulation models as a means of calibrating the efficacy of different forecasting models a priori. Agent-based simulation is already a proven approach to operations planning for supply chains (see [20], for example), but to our knowledge, the use of agent-based simulation to compare forecasting models is an area of research still to be explored. With its continuing protean changes in sourcing and retailing arrangements, the fashion industry constitutes an ideal venue for such work.

Appendices

Appendix A. Notation

Notation	Meaning
	Indexes
$i \in \{1, \ldots, N\}$	Indexes ranging over agents.
$t \in \{1, \ldots, T\}$	Index ranging over planning periods.
	Simulation
$\texttt{Neighbors}_i$	The neighbors of agent i.
$\texttt{Market}$	The potential market for a given product.
$\texttt{Purch}_t$	Set of agents who have purchased the product by time t.
$\texttt{pot}_{it}$	Agent i has a non-zero probability of purchase in period t.

(continued)

[15]Hines and Bruce [32] point out that "fast fashion" retailers such as Zara and Primark publish revised forecasts on a weekly basis.

Notation	Meaning
$\texttt{purch-ex}_{it}, \texttt{purch-end}_{it}$	An ex-, resp. endogenously-motivated purchase by agent i in period t.
$\texttt{purch}_{it}$	A purchase (endo- or exogenously motivated) by agent i in period t.
$\texttt{S}_t$	"Saturday" indicator.
p_i, q_i	Parameter governing resp. ex-, endogenously-motivated purchases by agent i.
$\texttt{u-exo}_{it}, \texttt{u-endo}_{it}$	Random variable simulating ex-, endogenous period t purchase by agent i.
y_t	Simulated product demand during period t.
	Forecasting
$j \in \{1, \ldots, J\}$	Indexes ranging over similar products involved in forecast formulation.
T_j	Number of periods that demand for product j has been observed.
$\boldsymbol{y}_j = (y_{j1}, \ldots, y_{jT_j})$	Observed demand for product j.
$l \in \{1, \ldots, J\}$	Index of product for which forecast is to be produced.
h	Forecast horizon.
$y_{l\,T_l+h}$	Demand to be forecast.
$\boldsymbol{\theta}, \boldsymbol{\zeta}, \boldsymbol{\vartheta}$	Vectors of unobserved quantities in a generic forecast model.
	Model (see also summary on p. 81)
$\mu_\theta, \sigma_\theta$	Parameters (usually mean and std. dev., resp.) of prior distribution for generic parameter θ.
γ_j	Scale factor associated with potential market for product j.
λ_{jt}	Stochastic process describing the life cycle of product j, delineating a Weibull curve.
α_j	20th percentile of the Weibull distribution representing product j's life cycle.
δ_j	Difference between 95th and 20th percentiles of the Weibull distribution representing the product j's life cycle.
ς_{jt}	Demand variation produced by day of the week effect.

(continued)

Notation	Meaning
	Testing
s_i	Simulated demand series, truncated for testing.
k	The period after which simulated demand series was truncated.
$\hat{s}^{\texttt{ets}}_{i,k+h}, \hat{s}^{\texttt{hb}}_{i,k+h}$	Forecast value for simulated demand series s_i produced by benchmark `ets` function and proposed Bayesian model, resp.
$\epsilon^{\texttt{ets}}_{i,k+h}, \epsilon^{\texttt{hb}}_{i,k+h}$	Scale-free errors for benchmark and model forecasts.

Appendix B. Standard Probability Distributions

Below we list the probability distributions used in the paper, along with their standard parameterizations. For further details, see e.g. [41].

Distribution	Description	Density/mass function
$\text{Beta}(\alpha, \beta)$	Beta distribution with shape parameters α and β.	$\text{Beta}(x\|\alpha, \beta) = \frac{\Gamma(\alpha+\beta)}{\Gamma(\alpha)\Gamma(\beta)} x^{\alpha-1}(1-x)^{\beta-1}$, $x \in [0, 1]$
$\text{Pois}(\lambda)$	Poisson distribution with parameter λ.	$\text{Pois}(x\|\lambda) = \frac{1}{x!}\lambda^x \exp(-\lambda)$, $x = 0, 1, \ldots$
$\text{Weib}(\lambda, k)$	Weibull distribution with shape λ and scale k.	$\text{Weib}(x\|\lambda, k) = \lambda k^{-\lambda}\theta^{-1+\lambda} e^{-\left(\frac{\theta}{k}\right)^{\lambda}}$, $x \geq 0$
$\text{N}(\mu, \sigma^2)$	Normal distribution with mean μ and standard deviation σ.	$\text{N}(x\|\mu,\sigma^2) = \frac{1}{\sqrt{2\pi}\sigma} \exp\left[-\frac{1}{2\sigma^2}(x-\mu)^2\right]$
$\text{N}_{[0,\infty)}(\mu, \sigma^2)$	The normal distribution $\text{N}(\mu, \sigma^2)$, truncated on the left at 0.	$\text{N}_{[0,\infty)}(x\|\mu, \sigma^2) = 2\text{N}(x\|\mu,\sigma^2)$, $x \geq 0$
$\text{Inv-}\chi^2(\nu)$	The inverse chi-squared distribution with ν degrees of freedom.	$\text{Inv-}\chi^2(x\|\nu) = \frac{2^{-\nu/2}}{\Gamma(\nu/2)} x^{-(\nu/2+1)} \exp[-1/(2x)]$, $x > 0$

References

1. Agrawal N, Smith SA (1996) Estimating negative binomial demand for retail inventory management with unobservable lost sales. Nav Res Logist 43(6):839–861
2. Ansari A, Jedidi K, Jagpal S (2000) A hierarchical Bayesian methodology for treating heterogeneity in structural equation models. Mark Sci 19(4):328–347
3. Armstrong JM (2001) Standards and practices for forecasting. In: Armstrong JM (ed) Principles of forecasting: a handbook for researchers and practitioners. Kluwer, Norwell, pp 171–192
4. Azoury KS (1985) Bayesian solution to dynamic inventory models under unknown demand distribution. Manag Sci 31:1150–1160
5. Azoury KS, Miller BS (1984) A comparison of the optimal levels of Bayesian and non-Bayesian inventory models. Manag Sci 30:993–1003
6. Bass F (1969) A new product growth model for consumer durables. Manag Sci 15:215–227
7. Bernardo JM, Smith AFM (1994) Bayesian theory. Wiley, Hoboken
8. Brockwell PJ, Davis RA (2002) Introduction to time series and forecasting, 2nd edn. Springer, New York
9. Bruce M, Daly L (2007) Challenges of fashion buying and merchandising. In: Hines T, Bruce M (eds) Fashion marketing: contemporary issues, 2nd edn. Elsevier, Oxford, pp 54–69. Chapter 3
10. Caro F, Gallien J (2007) Dynamic assortment with demand learning for seasonal consumer goods. Manag Sci 53(2):276–292
11. Choi TM, Li D, Yan HM (2003) Optimal two-stage ordering policy with Bayesian information updating. J Oper Res Soc 54(8):846–859
12. Choi TM, Li D, Yan HM (2006) Quick response policy with Bayesian information updates. Eur J Oper Res 170(3):788–808
13. Cohen MD, March JG, Olsen JP (1972) A garbage can model of organizational choice. Adm Sci Q 17:1–25
14. Cook SR, Gelman A, Rubin DB (2006) Validation of software for Bayesian models using posteior quantiles. J Comput Graph Stat 15(3):675–692
15. Delre SA, Jager W, Bijmolt THA, Janssen MA (2007) Targeting and timing promotional activities: an agent-based model for the takeoff of new products. J Bus Res 60(8):826–835
16. Dong X, Manchanda P, Chintagunta PK (2009) Quantifying the benefits of individual-level targeting in the presence of firm strategic behavior. J Mark Res 9(3):301–337
17. Donohue KL (2000) Efficient supply contracts for fashion goods with forecast updating and two production modes. Manag Sci 46(11):1397–1411
18. Dvoretzky A, Kiefer J, Wolfowitz J (1952) The inventory problem: case of known distribution of demand. Econometrica 20:187–222
19. Eppen GD, Iyer AV (1997) Improved fashion buying with Bayesian updating. Oper Res 45(6):805–819
20. Fox MS, Barbuceanu M, Teigen R (2000) Agent-oriented supply-chain management. Int J Flex Manuf Syst 12:165–188
21. Gardner ES, McKenzie E (1989) Seasonal exponential smoothing with damped trends. Manag Sci 35(3):372–376
22. Gelman A (2006) Prior distributions for variance parameters in hierarchical models. Bayesian Anal 1(3):515–533
23. Gelman A, Hill J (2006) Data analysis using regression and multilevel/hierarchical models. Cambridge University Press, New York
24. Gelman A, Carlin J, Stern H, Rubin D (2003) Bayesian data analysis, 2nd edn. Chapman & Hall/CRC, Boca Raton
25. Geweke J (1992) Evaluating the accuracy of sampling-based approaches to calculating posterior moments. In: Bernardo JM, Berger JO, Dawid AP, Smith AFM (eds) Bayesian statistics, vol 4. Clarendon, Wotton-under-Edge/Gloucestershire, pp 169–193

26. Gilks WR, Best NG, Tan KKC (1995) Adaptive rejection Metropolis sampling within Gibbs sampling. Appl Stat 44:455–472. (Corr: Neal, R.M. 1997 vol 46 pp 541–542)
27. Gilks WR, Richardson S, Spiegelhalter DJ (1996) Markov chain Monte Carlo in practice. Chapman & Hall, Boca Raton
28. Goldenberg J, Han S, Lehmann DR, Hong JW (2009) The role of hubs in the adoption process. J Mark 73(2):1–13
29. Griffiths W (2004) A Gibbs sampler for the parameters of a truncated multivariate normal distribution. In: Becker R, Hum S (eds) Contemporary issues in economics and econometrics: theory and application, Edward Elgar, Cheltenham/Northampton, pp 75–91
30. Gurnani H, Tang C (1999) Note: optimal ordering decisions with uncertain cost and demand forecast updating. Manag Sci 45(10):1456–1462
31. Harvey AC (1989) Forecasting, structural time series models and the Kalman filter. Cambridge University Press, Cambridge
32. Hines T, Bruce M (2007) Fashion marketing. Elsevier, Oxford
33. Hunter NA, Valentino P (1995) Quick response—ten years later. Int J Cloth Sci Technol 7: 30–40
34. Hyndman RJ, Khandakar Y (2008) Automatic time series forecasting: the forecast package for R. J Stat Softw 27(3):1–22. http://www.jstatsoft.org/v27/i03
35. Hyndman RJ, Koehler AB (2006) Another look at measures of forecast accuracy. Int J Forecast 22:679–688
36. Hyndman RJ, Koehler AB, Snyder RD, Grose S (2002) A state space framework for automatic forecasting using exponential smoothing methods. Int J Forecast 18(3):439–454
37. Iglehart D (1964) The dynamic inventory problem with unknown demand distribution. Manag Sci 10:429–440
38. Iyer A, Bergen ME (1997) Quick response in manufacturer-retailer channels. Manag Sci 43(4):559–570
39. Kang KY (1999) Development of an assortment-planning model for fashion-sensitive products. PhD thesis, Virginia Polytechnic Institute and State University
40. Kiesling E, Gunther M, Stummer C, Wakolbinger LM (2009) An agent-based simulation model for the market diffusion of a second generation biofuel. In: Winter simulation conference, Austin
41. Krishnamoorthy K (2006) Handbook of statistical distributions with applications. Statistics: a series of textbooks and monographs. Chapman and Hall/CRC, Boca Raton
42. Mahajan V, Muller E, Wind Y (eds) (2000) New-product diffusion models. Kluwer, Norwell
43. McCool JI (2012) Using the Weibull distribution: reliability, modeling, and inference. Wiley, Hoboken
44. Miller B (1986) Scarf's state reduction method, flexibility and a dependent demand inventory model. Oper Res 34(1):83–90
45. Moe WW, Fader PS (2002) Using advance purchase orders to forecast new product sales. Mark Sci 21(3):347–364
46. Müller P (1991) A generic approach to posterior integration and Gibbs sampling. Technical report 91-09, Department of Statistics, Purdue University
47. Murray GR Jr, Silver EA (1966) A Bayesian analysis of the style goods inventory problem. Manag Sci 12(11):785–797
48. Narayanan S, Manchanda P (2009) Heterogeneous learning and the targeting of marketing communication for new products. Mark Sci 28(3):424–441
49. North MJ, Macal CM, St Aubin J, Thimmapuram P, Bragen M, Hahn J (2010) Multi-scale agent-based consumer market modeling. Complexity 15(5):37–47
50. Pan R, Peng Y, Ding Z (2006) Belief update in Bayesian networks using uncertain evidence. In: International conference on tools with artificial intelligence, ICTAI, Washington, DC, pp 441–444
51. Pearl J (1988) Probabilistic reasoning in intelligent systems: networks of plausible inference. Morgan Kaufmann, San Mateo

52. Petris G (2010) dlm: Bayesian and likelihood analysis of dynamic linear models. http://cran.r-project.org/web/packages/dlm/index.html
53. Rand W, Rust RT (2011) Agent-based modeling in marketing: guidelines for rigor. Int J Res Mark 28(3):181–183
54. Robert CP, Casella G (2005) Monte Carlo statistical methods, 2nd edn. Springer, New York
55. Rossi PE, McCulloch RE, Allenby GM (1996) The value of purchase history data in target marketing. Mark Sci 15(4):321–340
56. Rossi PE, Allenby GM, McCulloch RE (2005) Bayesian statistics and marketing. Wiley, Hoboken
57. Scarf H (1959) Bayes solutions of the statistical inventory problem. Ann Math Stat 30(2): 490–508
58. Schenk TA, Loffler G, Rauh J (2007) Agent-based simulation of consumer behavior in grocery shopping on a regional level. J Bus Res 60(8):894–903
59. Schwoon M (2006) Simulating the adoption of fuel cell vehicles. J Evol Econ 16(4):435–472
60. Sharif MN, Islam MN (1980) The Weibull distribution as a general model for forecasting technological change. Technol Forecast Soc Change 18:247–256
61. Sproles GB (1981) Analyzing fashion life cycles: principles and perspectives. J Mark 45: 116–124
62. Tukey J (1977) Exploratory data analysis. Addison-Wesley, Reading
63. Valtorta M, Young-Gyun K, Vomlel J (2002) Soft evidential update for probabilistic multiagent systems. Int J Approx Reason 29:71–106
64. Walsh W, Wellman M (1999) Modeling supply chains formation in multi-agent systems. In: IJCAI-99 workshop agent-mediated electronic commerce, Stockholm
65. Watts DJ, Strogatz SH (1998) Collective dynamics of ‘small-world’ networks. Nature 393: 409–410
66. Wu DS, Kempf KG, Atan MO, Aytac B, Shirodkar SA, Mishra A (2010) Improving new product forecasting at Intel corporation. Interfaces 40(5):385–396
67. Yelland PM (2010) Bayesian forecasting of parts demand. Int J Forecast 26(2):374–396
68. Yelland PM, Kim S, Stratulate R (2010) A Bayesian model for sales forecasting at Sun Microsystems. Interfaces 40:118–129

Chapter 6
Forecasting Fashion Store Reservations: Booking Horizon Forecasting with Dynamic Updating

Alwin Haensel

Abstract A highly accurate demand forecast is fundamental to the success of any booking management model. As often required in practice and theory, we aim to forecast the accumulated booking curve as well as the number of expected reservations for each day in the booking horizon. To reduce the high dimensionality of this problem, we apply singular value decomposition on the historical booking profiles. The forecast of the remaining part of the booking horizon is dynamically adjusted to the earlier observations using the penalized least squares and the historical proportion method. Our proposed updating procedure considers the correlation and dynamics of bookings within the booking horizon and between successive product instances. The approach is tested on simulated demand data and shows a significant improvement in forecast accuracy.

Keywords Demand forecasting • Dynamic forecast updating • Dimension reduction • Penalized least squares • Time series • Booking control • Revenue management

6.1 Introduction

In this chapter we study the challenge of accurate booking horizon forecasting in an application to fashion shop reservations. It is common practice at luxury and high-end fashion shops that customers make reservations. This is done in order to create an exclusive shopping event for the customer, which comprises a pleasant personal atmosphere, space in the shop, no queuing, full attention of the staff and all items instantly available. So the general problem is a booking management (BM) problem.

A. Haensel (✉)
Haensel AMS, Berlin, Germany
e-mail: alwin.haensel@lri.fr; alwin@haensel-ams.com

T.-M. Choi et al. (eds.), *Intelligent Fashion Forecasting Systems: Models and Applications*, DOI 10.1007/978-3-642-39869-8_6,

BM can be investigated from two directions: First, from a planning perspective, i.e., minimizing staffing and operational costs while ensuring certain service levels or output requirements, which highly depend on the uncertain demand. Second, from a revenue management (RM) perspective, i.e., maximizing the obtainable revenue or profit by an optimal selection of customers to accept for bookings. RM methods are used to control the booking process in many sectors, such as the airline, hotel and car rental industry. A brief introduction to models and topics of RM is given in [12] and a research review is presented in [2], who review 221 papers and five books and provide with it a very comprehensive overview of revenue management developments in research. At the heart of every BM model always lies a demand forecast, whose accuracy is crucial for the success of the model. Pölt [9] estimates for the airline industry that a 20 % increase in forecast accuracy can be translated in a 1 % increase in revenue generated by the underlying RM system. Van Ryzin [13] and Zeni [18] argue that new models of demand forecasts are needed to adjust to the new market situation with more competition. Besides the choice of the forecasting model and its adjustment to the demand time series, there are three important steps to include into the forecasting process. The first step is data unconstraining. It is important to note that sales figures are usually not equal to the real demand. This follows from capacity restrictions, booking control actions and the existence of competitors. Second, the customers' choice behavior has to be considered. A variety of product offers from a company or its competitors influence the customers' purchasing decision and thus the demand. Different approaches to model the customer' choice behavior are presented in [11, 14] and [4]. The third point and the one on which this paper focuses is the dynamic updating of forecasts when new information becomes available. As shown in [8] the forecast accuracy can be improved by updating, especially when the time series is trended. In case of fashion products, and therefore also for the shopping demand, the dependency of customer decisions due to IN-factors of collections and designs, special events or offers give additional hope for benefits from forecast updating. Intensive research on forecast updating is done in the context of call centers. A significant correlation between within-day (morning, midday, evening) call arrivals is found. Models are proposed to forecast not only the call volume for future days, but also the updating of expected call volumes for future time periods within the day. In [16] a multiplicative Gaussian time series model, with a Bayesian Markov chain Monte Carlo algorithm for parameter estimation and forecasting, is proposed. Shen and Huang [10] suggest a competitive updating method which requires less computation time. Their method consists of a dimensionality reduction of the forecasting problem and a penalized least square procedure to adjust the time series forecast to observed realizations. Haensel and Koole [5] adapt the ideas of [10] for call center forecasting to the RM context of hotel reservation forecasting. The equivalence to the within-day periods for which the forecast is updated is the booking horizon in the hotel RM setting. In contrast to the call center case, booking horizons for different product instances are overlapping and correlated in their booking pattern and behavior. Another important difference is the level of forecast data. The call volume in call centers is generally very large, compared to often small demand numbers in the revenue management case. In RM problems a forecast on disaggregated level is required, since booking control actions are applied daily and on product level. In this chapter we apply the methods of [5] to the fashion shop booking problem. Both BM problems, i.e., for the fashion shops or hotels, are actually very similar from a modeling perspective and this gives rise to possible significant potential of the proposed forecast updating approach.

This paper is organized as follows. First, in Sect. 6.2, we introduce and analyze the data. Next, in Sect. 6.3, the forecasting methods are explained, followed by the introduction of the forecast updating procedure and methods in Sect. 6.4. Finally, in Sect. 6.5, numerical results are presented before we conclude our findings in Sect. 6.6.

6.2 Data

For our forecasting analysis we are working with simulated reservation data and we consider three datasets with different correlation patterns within the booking horizon, the datasets are denoted by A, B and C. To better illustrate the method, we will restrict this analysis to a fixed day of week (DOW) as the arrival day at the store, i.e., our reservation product. This separation of the forecasting problem into DOWs is widely common in practice, since reservation patterns and volumes vary significantly for different arrival DOWs, compare for a discussion with [15] on hotel reservations. The product is repeated every week, so each week corresponds to a product instance. Further, each instance has a booking horizon of 4 weeks, 28 days, with day 28 corresponding to the arrival day at the store. All datasets are given in form of a $n \times m$ demand data matrix X, with $n = 200$ product instances (as rows) and their associated $m = 28$ booking horizon days (as columns). In our case, the product instances correspond to the successive arrival weeks of our store shopping products for a fixed DOW. For clarity, the $X_{i,j}$ entry denotes the demand for product instance i (arrival week i) at the jth day in the booking horizon.

The demand data is generated as follows: The mean demands of the four booking horizon weeks are: 20 customers in week 1, the beginning of the booking horizon, 40 customers in week 2, 50 customers in week 3 and 70 customers in week 4, the week prior to the shopping day. The mean weekly demand itself is the sum of three components: seasonality s (corresponding for 30 %), trend d (corresponding for 20 %) and random component r (corresponding for 50 %). The weekly seasonality index s is shown in Fig. 6.1. We observe four peaks, corresponding to spring, summer, autumn and the Christmas period. January is considered to be the lowest demand season. The trend index d for all instances are shown in Fig. 6.2, it is increasing until instance 91 with a global maximum of 1.6 and afterwards decreasing to a minimum of 0.91 at the last instance 200. Note that we will test our forecast techniques on the last 50 instances, so on the down sloping part. The random component is modeled by a multivariate normal distribution with the mean $\mu_w^{(r)} = 0.5\mu_w$, i.e., 50 % of the mean week demands, and the standard deviation in

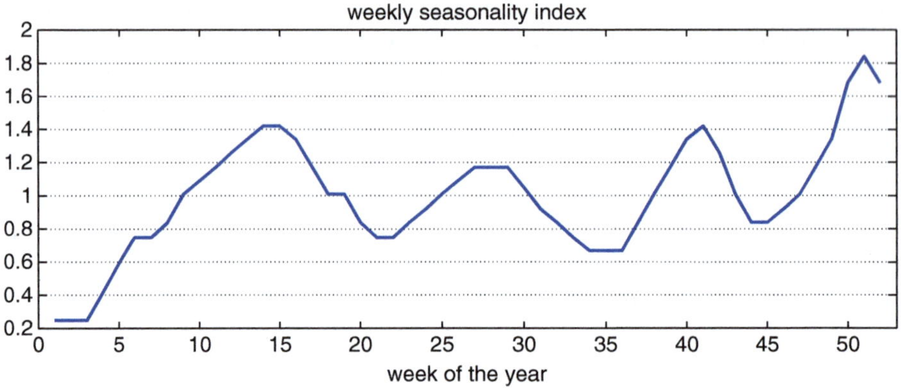

Fig. 6.1 Seasonality index

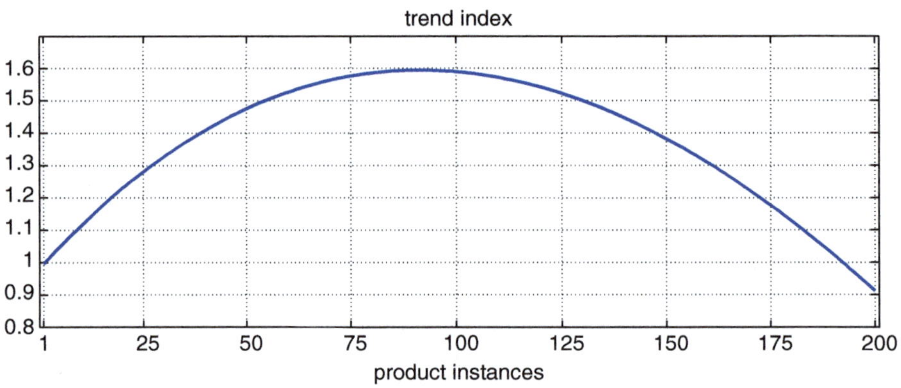

Fig. 6.2 Trend index

week w is set to $\sigma_w^{(r)} = \sqrt(0.2\mu_w^{(r)})$. The remainder component also contains the correlation between demand within the booking horizon. Our three datasets differ only in the correlation matrix $\mathbb{C}$ on the mean week demands, given by

$$\mathbb{C}_A = \begin{pmatrix} 1.0 & 0.8 & 0.7 & 0.7 \\ 0.8 & 1.0 & 0.8 & 0.7 \\ 0.7 & 0.8 & 1.0 & 0.8 \\ 0.7 & 0.7 & 0.8 & 1.0 \end{pmatrix}, \quad \mathbb{C}_B = \begin{pmatrix} 1.0 & 0.6 & 0.5 & 0.4 \\ 0.6 & 1.0 & 0.6 & 0.5 \\ 0.5 & 0.6 & 1.0 & 0.5 \\ 0.4 & 0.5 & 0.5 & 1.0 \end{pmatrix},$$

$$\mathbb{C}_C = \begin{pmatrix} 1.0 & 0.7 & -0.3 & -0.5 \\ 0.7 & 1.0 & 0.0 & -0.4 \\ -0.3 & 0.0 & 1.0 & 0.8 \\ -0.5 & -0.4 & 0.8 & 1.0 \end{pmatrix}.$$

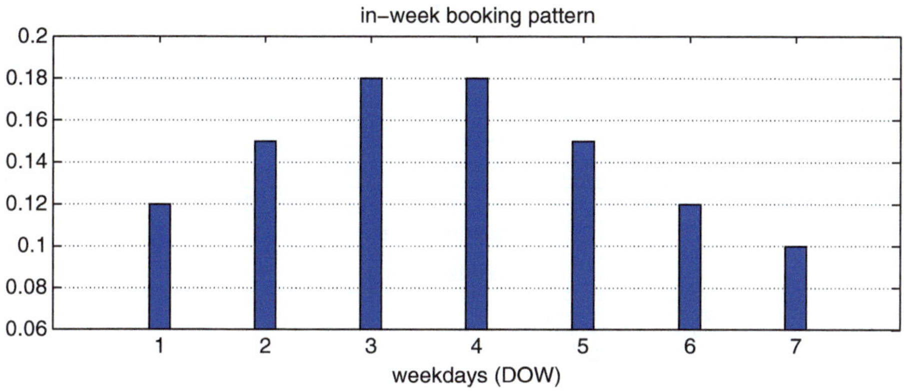

Fig. 6.3 In-week booking intensity

$\mathbb{C}_{i,j}$ denotes the correlation between demand for week i and week j. Dataset A and B have positive correlations between demands at different booking weeks, only dataset A has higher correlation coefficients. In dataset C we have a mixed correlation structure, with positive correlation between week 1 and 2 as well as week 3 and 4, but a negative correlation between the first and the second half of the booking horizon. The covariance matrix $\mathbb{V}$ is then simply given by

$$\mathbb{V}_{i,j} = \mathbb{C}_{i,j} \cdot \sigma_i^{(r)} \cdot \sigma_j^{(r)}$$

The actual final daily demand is following a Poisson distribution with mean equal to the corresponding realized week demand times π_t, the booking intensity index for the corresponding day t. The booking pattern is the same for all booking weeks and is shown in Fig. 6.3.

Concluding, the demand for product instance i, at weekday t in booking week w is given by

$$x_{i,t+(w-1)7} \sim Poisson\left(\pi_t \left(s_{(i \, mod \, 52)}\mu_w^{(s)} + d_i \mu_w^{(d)} + r_w\right)\right) \quad (6.1)$$
$$\text{with } r \sim N(\mu^{(r)}, \mathbb{V})$$

with $\mu_w^{(s)} = 0.3\mu_w$ denoting the seasonal part of the mean booking week demand denoted by μ_w, respectively $\mu_w^{(d)} = 0.2\mu_w$ and $\mu_w^{(r)} = 0.5\mu_w$ denote the corresponding mean trend and random remainder levels.

In the remainder we will only work on the generated demand data without any knowledge on how it was generated.

In forecasting research and practice it is common to work on accumulated demand, i.e., booking curves, rather than on individual demand per booking day. However, we see three reasons for using the latter. First, if additional, usually administration, work is required to process reservations, the second visualization form

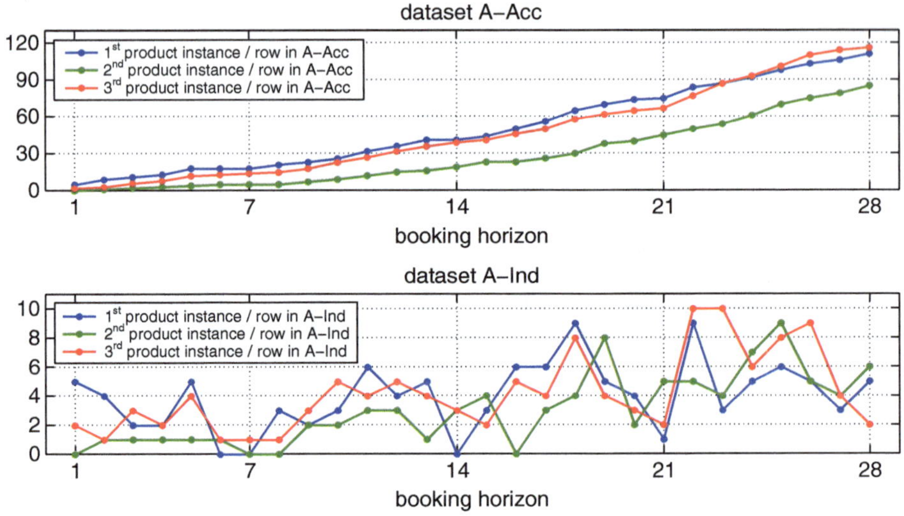

Fig. 6.4 Example plot of first three product instances/first three rows of A-Acc and A-Ind

provides important input for the workforce planning. Second, since reservations are received at daily level, users often prefer to compare actuals and forecasted values also on daily level. Third, as also stated in [13], the current major direction in revenue management research is to incorporate customer choice behavior under offered alternatives. Thus, it is more important to know the expected customer group demand per individual booking day rather than the aggregated totals. We will work with both visualizations of the booking process, using "Acc" and "Ind" to abbreviate the accumulated and individual reservations respectively. Hence, we obtain six datasets on the three regions: A-Acc, A-Ind, B-Acc, B-Ind, C-Acc and C-Ind.

The first 146 product instances/rows of X are used for data analysis, testing and parameter estimation. The last 50 instances/rows of X are used in Sect. 6.5 for evaluation of the proposed forecast updating methods. There is a gap of 4 weeks between the estimation and evaluation sample, caused by the time structure in the dataset: At arrival of product i, the realization of the first booking horizon week of product instance $i + 3$ is known. The booking behavior of the first three instances in A-Acc and A-Ind, i.e., rows of X, are shown in Fig. 6.4. The total aggregated numbers of reservations received per product instances for all datasets are shown in Fig. 6.5. Note that the time between the product instances, 1 week, is much smaller than the booking horizon of 4 weeks. The mean and variance of the booking behaviors within the booking horizon for all datasets are shown in Fig. 6.6. We observe that the variance is not constant (heteroscedasticity) and that the variance is greater than the mean (overdispersion). In order to stabilize and reduce the variance, we will work on the logarithmic transformed data. Let x denote the number of demand. Set $y = \log(x + 1)$, one is added because the dataset contains many

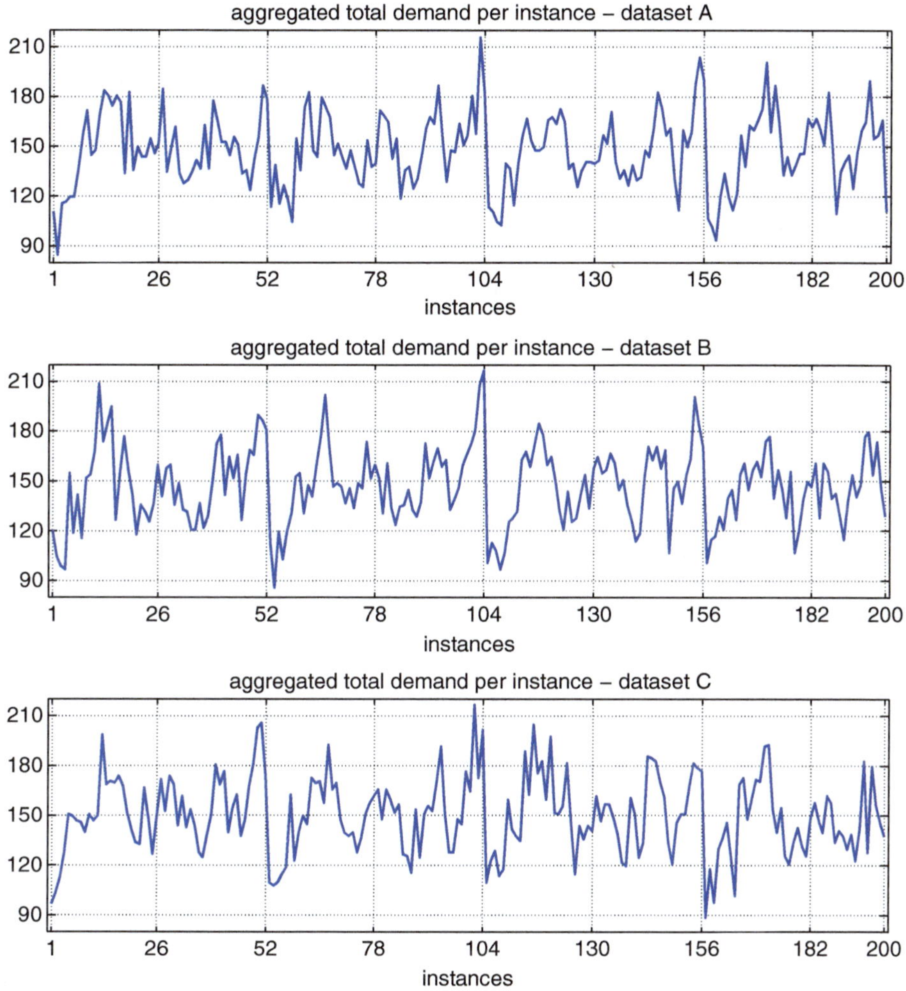

Fig. 6.5 Total aggregated reservations per product instances for all three datasets

booking days with zero reservations. The forecast of y is denoted by $\hat{y}$ and the forecast of x is then given by $\hat{x} = \exp(\hat{y}) - 1$. The following forecasting methods are working on the transformed data, and the forecast error analysis in Sect. 6.5 is made on the back transformed data.

An important property in the data structure is the shifted realization time, which means that parts of different product instances are realized at the same time. For example, suppose we select a product instance i, i.e., the ith row in X, and consider the corresponding time as the current time. All information up to instance i plus the first 3 weeks of the booking horizon of the following instance $i + 1$, the first 2 weeks of $i + 2$ and the first week of instance $i + 3$ are known at our current

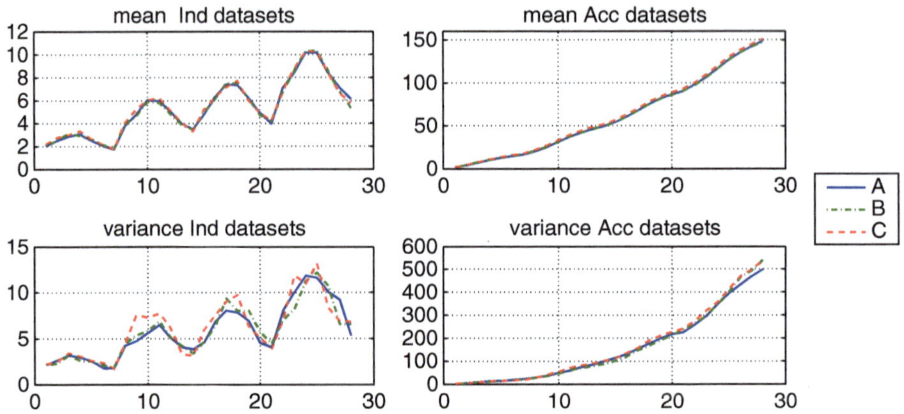

Fig. 6.6 Mean and variance of the booking process of all datasets

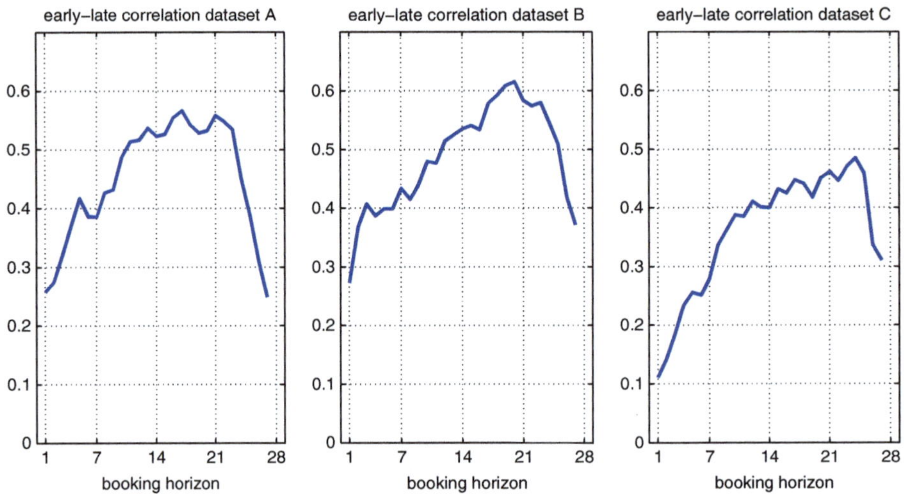

Fig. 6.7 Correlation coefficients $C(k)$ for early-late booking split days $k = 1, \ldots, 27$

time. In other words, fixing an arrival week in our data set as a time point enables us to know the demand realization for the first 3 weeks of the booking horizon for the next-week-arrival product. The same is true for the in-2-weeks arrival and in-3-weeks arrival products, where we know the realization of the first two and first week of the booking horizon, respectively. This research is concerned with the question of how to update demand forecasts when the realizations of earlier time stages in the booking horizon become known. Therefore we analyze the correlation between demands at different moments in the booking horizon.

In Fig. 6.7, the correlation coefficients between early (long in advance) and late reservations (close to arrival at the store) are plotted as a function of the day in the

Table 6.1 Correlation $C(\cdot,\cdot)$ of aggregated demands between specific booking weeks

Dataset	$C(w_1, w_2)$	$C(w_1, w_{2,3,4})$	$C(w_2, w_3)$	$C(w_2, w_{3,4})$	$C(w_3, w_4)$	$C(w_{1,2,3}, w_4)$
A	0.32	0.39	0.34	0.48	0.45	0.56
B	0.25	0.43	0.34	0.43	0.52	0.58
C	0.26	0.28	0.37	0.38	0.47	0.46

booking horizon that is the frontier between early and late. The correlation function for split day k is defined on the accumulated dataset X by

$$C(k) = corr\ (X_{\cdot,k}, (X_{\cdot,28} - X_{\cdot,k})) \qquad k = 1, \ldots, 27, \tag{6.2}$$

where $corr(a, b)$ is a function returning the linear correlation coefficient between the vectors a and b. The general correlation curve is similar for all three datasets. The correlation analysis is made on the raw demand data, i.e., including seasonality and trend pattern. The results are different from what we would expect with the knowledge of the input correlation matrix of the random component. This also illustrates how important an advanced time series data analysis is in order to gain a good understanding of the underlying process. Coming back to our data, we observe very similar patterns for dataset A and B, with B having slightly higher values. Dataset C has generally lower correlation values, but shows a very steep increase towards day 14. Consequently, the benefit of dynamic forecast updating is assumed to be most beneficial for the dataset A and B.

Now consider the correlation between bookings in different weeks. Define $w_i = \{7(i-1)+1, \ldots, 7(i-1)+7\}$, the set of days in week i. The correlation function defined on booking weeks w_i and w_j and a dataset X consisting of individual reservations per booking day, is given by

$$C(w_i, w_j) = corr\left(\sum_{d \in w_i} X_{\cdot,d}, \sum_{d \in w_j} X_{\cdot,d}\right). \tag{6.3}$$

The correlations are shown in Table 6.1. Multiple subscripts represent the aggregation over multiple weeks, e.g., $w_{1,2,3}$ stands for the aggregated reservations made in week 1, 2 and 3. It illustrates again the dependence between early and late bookings.

6.3 Forecasting Method

The data matrix X contains all demands per product instance and day in the booking horizon. Our aim is to forecast the number of future demands to expect for the forthcoming product instances in the next 4 weeks. The forecast is chosen to work on individual numbers of reservations per booking day ("Ind" datasets) as well as on the accumulated reservations ("Acc" datasets). Each product instance (the arrival week) has a booking horizon of $m = 28$ days. The ith row of X, $x_i = (x_{i,1}, \ldots, x_{i,m})^{\mathrm{T}}$, represents all reservations per day in the booking horizon of instance i. As in [10] and [5], we are applying singular value decomposition (SVD) to reduce the forecasting dimension. The procedure works as follows:

We are interested in computing a small number of base vectors $f_1, \ldots, f_K$ with which the time series $\{x_t\}$ can be reasonably well approximated. The decomposition is given by

$$x_i = \gamma_{i,1} f_1 + \cdots + \gamma_{i,K} f_K + \epsilon_i \qquad i = 1, \ldots, n, \tag{6.4}$$

where $\gamma \in \mathbb{R}^{n \times K}$ is the weight matrix, $f_1, \ldots, f_K \in \mathbb{R}^m$ are the base vectors and $\epsilon_1, \ldots \epsilon_n \in \mathbb{R}^m$ are the error terms. We suppose that the $x_i's$ can be well approximated by a linear approximation of the base vectors, so that the error terms are reasonably small. This leads to the following optimization problem

$$\min_{\substack{\gamma_{1,1}, \ldots, \gamma_{n,K} \\ f_1, \ldots, f_K}} \sum_{i=1}^{n} \|\epsilon_i\|, \tag{6.5}$$

for a fixed value K. This problem can be solved by applying SVD to matrix X as follows. Matrix X can be rewritten as

$$X = USV^{\mathrm{T}}, \tag{6.6}$$

where S is a $m \times m$ diagonal matrix, U and V are orthogonal matrices with dimension $n \times m$ and $m \times m$ respectively. The diagonal elements of S are in decreasing order and nonnegative, $s_1 \geq \cdots \geq s_r > 0$, with $r = \mathit{rank}\ (X)$ and $s_k = 0$ for all $r + 1 \leq k \leq m$. From (6.6) we follow now

$$x_i = s_1 u_{i,1} v_1 + \cdots + s_r u_{i,r} v_r, \tag{6.7}$$

where v_k denotes the kth column of matrix V. Hence, the K-dimensional approximation is obtained by keeping the largest K singular values ($K < r$), since S is ordered decreasingly the largest are equivalent with the first K values,

$$x_i \approx s_1 u_{i,1} v_i + \cdots + s_K u_{i,K} v_K. \tag{6.8}$$

Setting now $\gamma_{i,k} := s_k u_{i,k}$ and $f_k := v_k$, for all $i = 1, \ldots, n$ and $k = 1, \ldots, K$, we have found an optimal solution of (6.5). The mean squared estimation error (MSEE) of product instance i and fixed K is computed by

$$\mathrm{MSEE}_i = \frac{1}{m} \sum_{j=1}^{m} \left(x_{i,j} - \Big(\sum_{k=1}^{K} \gamma_{i,k} f_k \Big)_j \right)^2. \tag{6.9}$$

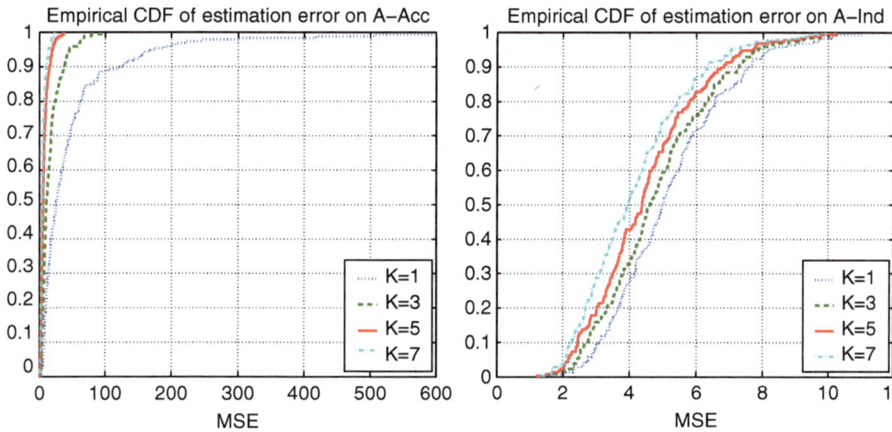

Fig. 6.8 Empirical distribution function of mean squared estimation errors for different numbers of base vectors K

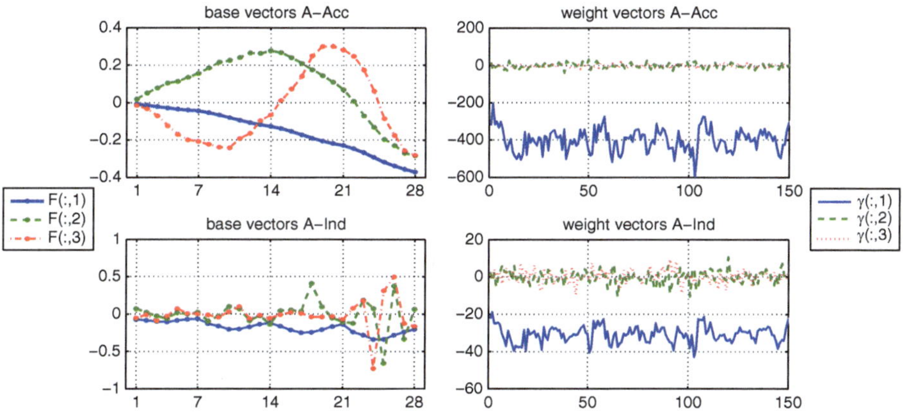

Fig. 6.9 Base vectors f_k and weights $\gamma_{i,k}$ for $K = 3$

Figure 6.8 shows the empirical distribution function of the MSEE, computed over the first 130 product instances, for different values of K. We find reasonably small errors for $K = 3$. These values are still outperformed by $K = 5$ or 7, but for computational reasons we try to keep the dimension small. In the numerical results, where we use $K = 3$ and 5, we will see that $K = 3$ will produce reasonably good forecasting results. The resulting three base vectors in the case of $K = 3$ and their weights computed over the first 130 instances of the datasets A-Acc and A-Ind are shown in Fig. 6.9. The base vectors represent the data characteristics in decreasing importance, i.e., the first base vector in A-Ind represents the strong weekly pattern and the first base vector in A-Acc represent the general increasing booking curve pattern. In fact, base vector f_1 in A-Acc is negative and decreasing, but since the corresponding weights time series γ_1 takes negative values, the represented booking pattern is increasing. Remember that the singular value decomposition is applied to the transformed data, when comparing with Fig. 6.6. The forecasting method will work on the time series of $\gamma_{i,k}$ values. The base vectors $f_1, \ldots, f_K$ are calculated on the historical data and are kept fixed during the forecasting process. Due to the construction of the weights series $\gamma_1, \ldots, \gamma_K$ out of the columns of U, we have that vectors γ_k and γ_l are orthogonal for $k \neq l$. Hence the cross correlation between different weight series can be assumed to be small.

We initially choose as a forecasting method the univariate exponential smoothing with trend and seasonality, i.e., the Holt-Winters (HW) method developed by Holt [6] and Winters [17]. Holt-Winters is a commonly used method in similar problems, and in practice known to be reasonably accurate, robust and easy to implement. Two seasonal models, additive and multiplicative, are distinguished and both are tested on the three datasets. The Additive Holt-Winters (AHW) h-step ahead forecast of $\gamma_{i+h,k}$, for fixed $k = 1, \ldots, K$ is

$$\hat{\gamma}_{i+h,k}^{AHW} = a(i) + h \cdot b(i) + c\big((i+h) \bmod p\big), \tag{6.10}$$

where $a(i)$, $b(i)$ and $c(i)$ are given by

$$\begin{aligned} a(i) &= \alpha \cdot \big(\gamma_{i,k} - c(i-p)\big) + (1-\alpha) \cdot \big(a(i-1) + b(i-1)\big), \\ b(i) &= \beta \cdot \big(a(i) - a(i-1)\big) + (1-\beta) \cdot b(i-1), \\ c(i) &= \delta \cdot \big(\gamma_{i,k} - a(i)\big) + (1-\delta) \cdot c(i-p). \end{aligned}$$

In contrast, the Multiplicative Holt-Winters (MHW) h-step ahead forecast of $\gamma_{i+h,k}$ is

$$\hat{\gamma}_{i+h,k}^{MHW} = \Big(a(i) + h \cdot b(i)\Big) \cdot c\big((i+h) \bmod p\big), \tag{6.11}$$

where $a(i)$, $b(i)$ and $c(i)$ are computed by

$$\begin{aligned} a(i) &= \alpha \cdot \frac{\gamma_{i,k}}{c(i-p)} + (1-\alpha) \cdot \big(a(i-1) + b(i-1)\big), \\ b(i) &= \beta \cdot \big(a(i) - a(i-1)\big) + (1-\beta) \cdot b(i-1), \\ c(i) &= \delta \cdot \frac{\gamma_{i,k}}{a(i)} + (1-\delta) \cdot c(i-p). \end{aligned}$$

The period length is 1 year and because the product instances are weekly $p = 52$. The initial values of a, b and c are derived from a simple decomposition in trend and seasonal component using moving averages (averaging for each time unit over all periods). The decomposition is performed by the R function Decompose from the R-stats library. Optimal α, β and δ values are found by minimizing the squared one-step prediction error, evaluated over historical values. Since the weights

Table 6.2 Holt-Winters mean squared errors between the actual and forecasted $\gamma_{\cdot,k}$

Dataset	ϵ_1 AHW	ϵ_2 AHW	ϵ_3 AHW	ϵ_1 MHW	ϵ_2 MHW	ϵ_3 MHW
A-Ind	0.59	0.69	0.65	0.59	1.00	4.32
A-Acc	1.13	1.01	0.52	1.13	4,895.85	2.27

time series γ_k take negative and positive values, a positive constant is added in the MHW calculation to ensure positivity and subtracted from the forecasts before being processed further. The Holt-Winters forecast for both seasonal models, of the future booking horizon $\hat{x}_{i+h}^{HW} = (\hat{x}_{i+h,1}^{HW}, \ldots, \hat{x}_{i+h,m}^{HW})$ is computed by

$$\hat{x}_{i+h}^{HW} = \hat{\gamma}_{i+h,1}^{HW} \cdot f_1 + \cdots + \hat{\gamma}_{i+h,K}^{HW} \cdot f_K. \tag{6.12}$$

The forecast accuracy for both seasonal models is tested on the sample of 30 1–4 step/weeks ahead forecasts, starting at instance 100 (within the estimation sample) and computed on the A dataset. The mean squared errors between the actual γ_k and forecasted $\hat{\gamma}_k^{HW}$ are shown in Table 6.2 and abbreviated with ϵ_k, for k $= 1, 2, 3$. The additive seasonal model clearly outperforms the multiplicative, as one would expect with the knowledge on how we generated the data. We will further continue only with the additive seasonal model for the Holt-Winters forecasting method.

Our second forecasting approach is to decompose the γ time series into seasonal, trend and remainder components and to apply an auto-regressive (AR) time series model on the remainder. The additive seasonal models seem to give a good approximation. Therefore we apply a decomposition procedure based on LOESS, i.e., local polynomial regression fitting, as described by Cleveland et al. [3]. The decomposition is performed by the R function STL (seasonal decomposition of time series by loess) from the R-stats library. The γ time series are separately decomposed into additive seasonal, trend and remainder components, see Fig. 6.10 for the case of dataset A-Acc and $K = 3$. The decomposition equation is

$$\gamma_{i,k} = s_{i,k} + d_{i,k} + r_{i,k} \qquad \text{for all } i = 1, \ldots, n \text{ and } k = 1, \ldots, K, \tag{6.13}$$

where s denotes the seasonal, d the trend and r the remainder component of the time series γ.

The auto-regressive model of $r_{\cdot,k}$ of order p is given by

$$r_{i,k} = \nu_k + a_1 \cdot r_{i-1,k} + \cdots + a_p \cdot r_{i-p,k} + u_{i,k}, \qquad k = 1, \ldots, K, \tag{6.14}$$

where $a_1, \ldots, a_p \in \mathbb{R}$ represents fixed coefficients, u_k a zero mean white noise process and ν_k the intercept. When μ_k denotes the mean of $r_{\cdot,k}$, the intercept is defined as $\nu_k = (1 - \sum_{t=1}^{p} a_t)\mu_k$. Let $\hat{r}_{i,k}$ denote the forecast of $r_{i,k}$, the h-step ahead forecast of the weights time series γ_k at instance i is then computed by

$$\hat{\gamma}_{i+h,k}^{AR} = s_{i+h,k} + d_{i+h,k} + \hat{r}_{i+h,k} \tag{6.15}$$

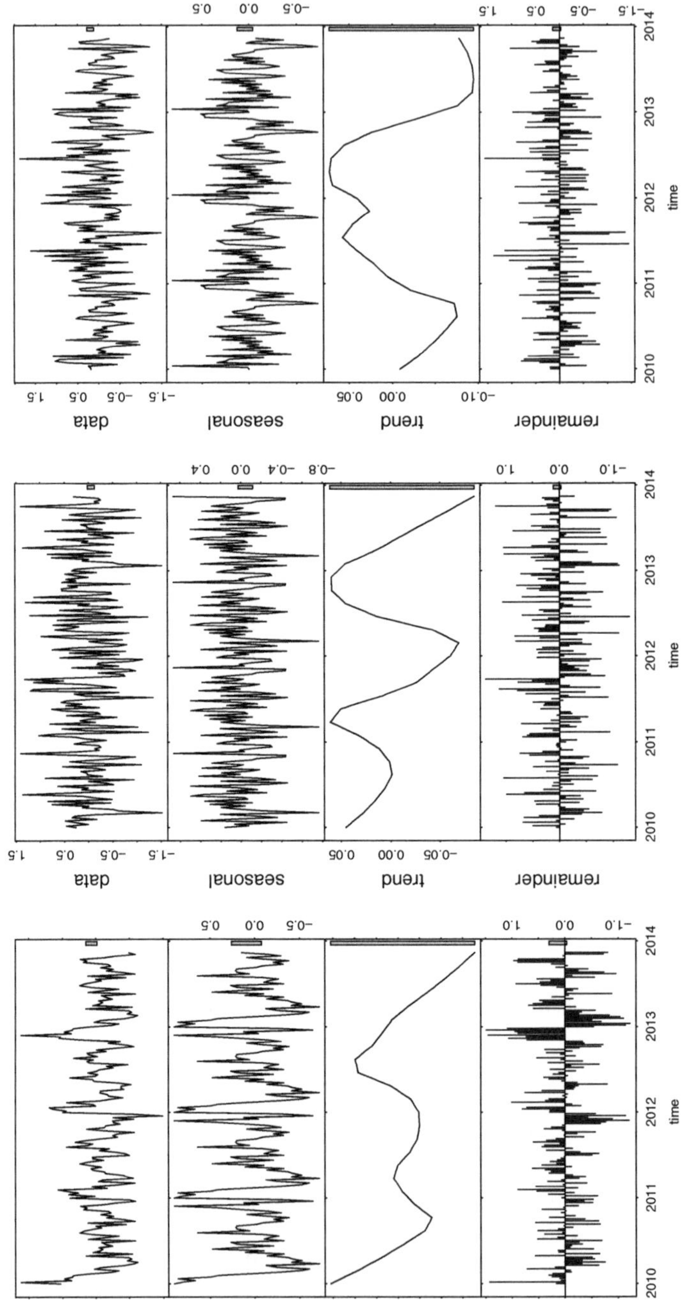

Fig. 6.10 Decomposition of γ time series of the dataset A-Acc into seasonal, trend and remainder for $K = 3$

Table 6.3 AR and VAR mean squared errors between the actual and forecasted $\gamma_{\cdot,k}$

Dataset	ϵ_1 VAR	ϵ_2 VAR	ϵ_3 VAR	ϵ_1 AR	ϵ_2 AR	ϵ_3 AR
A-Ind	0.53	0.36	0.50	0.54	0.36	0.50
A-Acc	1.13	0.65	0.16	1.19	0.66	0.16

where the trend component d is computed by a linear extrapolation of the last five known trend values $d_{i-4,k}, \ldots, d_{i,k}$ and the respective seasonal components s are obtained from the LOESS decomposition. The Akaike Information Criterion (AIC) is used to find the optimal model order p. We test the AIC for orders $p = 0, \ldots, 6$ on all datasets. The AIC results were generally the best for $p = 1$ and we will continue to use the AR(1) model for all six datasets. A further interesting observation is that the dependency, measured by the pairwise correlation coefficients, among the remainder $r_{\cdot,k}$ time series after the decomposition slightly increases compared to the dependency between the original weights series $\gamma_{\cdot,k}$. Therefore, we will compare the univariate AR(1) model with the vector auto-regressive (VAR) model, see [7] and [1], on the joint remainder time series r. The VAR(1) model of the remainder $r(i) = (r_{i,1}, \ldots, r_{i,3})$ has the following form

$$r(i) = \nu + A \cdot r(i-1) + u_i, \tag{6.16}$$

where $A \in \mathbb{R}^{K \times K}$ represents a fixed coefficient matrix, u a zero mean white noise process and ν the intercept. When μ denotes the mean of r, the intercept is equivalently defined as $\nu = (I - A)\mu$. Let $\hat{r} = (\hat{r}_{i,1}, \ldots, \hat{r}_{i,K})$ denote the VAR forecast of r, the h-step ahead forecast of the weights time series γ at instance i is equivalent to the AR forecast computed by

$$\hat{\gamma}^{VAR}_{i+h,k} = s_{i+h,k} + d_{i+h,k} + \hat{r}_{i+h,k} \qquad \text{for all } k = 1, \ldots, K, \tag{6.17}$$

where the trend component d is again computed by a linear extrapolation of the last five known trend values. As in the comparison of both HW models, the forecast accuracy of the AR and the VAR forecast is tested on the sample of 30 1 till 4 step ahead forecast, starting at instance 100 and computed on the A dataset. The mean squared forecast errors ϵ_k in the weights time series γ_k are shown in Table 6.3. Both forecasts generate roughly the same forecast errors, but a closer look shows that the VAR produces slightly smaller errors. It is of more interest to compare the accuracy results of the Holt-Winters with the auto-regression forecasts, i.e., Table 6.2 with Table 6.3. The combination of seasonal-trend decomposition and auto-regression forecasts on the remainder increases the forecast accuracy. In the remainder of the paper, we will work with the VAR(1) model as the second forecasting method as opposed to the AHW. The VAR forecast of the future booking horizon $\hat{x}^{VAR}_{i+h} = (\hat{x}^{VAR}_{i+h,1}, \ldots, \hat{x}^{VAR}_{i+h,m})$ is obtained by

$$\hat{x}^{VAR}_{i+h} = \hat{\gamma}^{VAR}_{i+h,1} \cdot f_1 + \cdots + \hat{\gamma}^{VAR}_{i+h,K} \cdot f_K. \tag{6.18}$$

6.4 Forecast Updating

With the previously described method, the forecaster is able to compute a forecast of an entire booking horizon, i.e., a forecast of the accumulated booking curve or the estimated incoming reservations for each day in the booking horizon. The forecasting methods work only on completed booking horizons. This means that we are not updating a forecast for future weeks when the realization of week 1, 2 or 3 become known. Furthermore, the information of the booking realizations for 1, 2 or 3 weeks prior to the forecast date are not used in the computation, because their booking horizon is not completed yet.

Therefore we propose the following general updating procedure, which includes one of the forthcoming updating methods. The procedure is as follows:

1. Forecast the next booking horizon based on data of all completed product instances (of which all realizations are known).
2. If realizations of the forecasted booking process are known, update the future part of the horizon accordingly.
3. If a further forecast is required, regard the forecasted (and updated) horizon as completed and go back to 1.

The application of the procedure to our datasets (being at arrival of product instance i) is as follows:

1. A one week ahead forecast of the complete booking horizon for instance $i+1$ (the next week arrival) is generated based on data of all completed booking horizons (instances $1, \ldots, i$). Realizations of the first 3 weeks in the booking horizon are already known and the forecast of reservations in the last week for instance $i+1$ are adjusted based on this.
2. The adjusted forecast of $i+1$ is further regarded as the completed booking horizon of instance $i+1$.
3. A one week ahead forecast of the complete booking horizon for instance $i+2$ is computed based on the data of all instances $1, \ldots, i+1$. Realizations of the first 2 weeks are already known and the forecast for the last 2 weeks of the booking horizon is adjusted.
4. The adjusted forecast of $i+2$ is further regarded as the completed booking horizon of instance $i+2$.
5. A one week ahead forecast of the complete booking horizon for instance $i+3$ is computed based on the data of all instances $1, \ldots, i+2$. The realization of the first week is already known and the forecast for the following 3 weeks is adjusted.
6. The adjusted forecast of $i+3$ is further regarded as the completed booking horizon of instance $i+3$.
7. Finally, a one week ahead forecast of the complete booking horizon for instance $i+4$ is computed based on the data of all instances $1, \ldots, i+3$. Because we are considering a booking horizon of 4 weeks, no bookings for this instance are known and the forecast can not be adjusted.

In the following we will discuss two forecast updating methods, as described in [10] and [5].

Let us concentrate on instance $i + 1$, the forecast of (6.12) or (6.18) can be written as

$$\hat{x}_{i+1} = F\hat{\gamma}_{i+1}, \tag{6.19}$$

where $F = (f_1, \ldots, f_K)$ denotes a $m \times K$ matrix formed by the base vectors and $\hat{\gamma}_{i+1} = (\hat{\gamma}_{i+1,1}, \ldots, \hat{\gamma}_{i+1,K})^{\mathrm{T}}$ represents a column vector. Let the superscript a denote that we only consider the first a columns of a matrix or components of a vector. When x_{i+1}^a becomes known, we can compute the forecast error ϵ_{i+1}^a by

$$\epsilon_{i+1}^a = x_{i+1}^a - \hat{x}_{i+1}^a = x_{i+1}^a - F^a\hat{\gamma}_{i+1}. \tag{6.20}$$

The direct least squares (LS) method would now try to solve the problem

$$\hat{\gamma}_{i+1}^{LS} = \operatorname{argmin}_{\hat{\gamma}_{i+1}} \left\| \epsilon_{i+1}^a \right\|^2, \tag{6.21}$$

to find the γ_{i+1} values for which the forecast of the first a days fits the actual bookings x_{i+1}^a best. The LS solution can be obtained by

$$\hat{\gamma}_{i+1}^{LS} = \left((F^a)^{\mathrm{T}} F^a\right)^{-1} (F^a)^{\mathrm{T}} x_{i+1}^a. \tag{6.22}$$

To uniquely define $\hat{\gamma}_{i+1}^{LS}$, we need of course that $a \geq K$. In our case $K = 3$ or 5, the booking horizon is further in days and the forecast updates are made weekly, $a = 7, 14$ and 21. The idea is to apply the solution of (6.21) in (6.19) to obtain the direct least squares forecast update $\hat{x}_{i+1}^{LS}$ by

$$\hat{x}_{i+1}^{LS} = F\hat{\gamma}_{i+1}^{LS}. \tag{6.23}$$

Clearly this is a very volatile updating method and the forecast update will not be too reliable for small a values compared to m, length of the whole booking horizon. Therefore we suggest the penalized least squares method (PLS), which works as the LS method but it penalizes large deviations from the original time series (TS) forecast. The optimization problem (6.21) is altered with the parameter λ to

$$\hat{\gamma}_{i+1}^{PLS} = \operatorname{argmin}_{\hat{\gamma}_{i+1}} \left\| \epsilon_{i+1}^a \right\|^2 + \lambda \left\| \hat{\gamma}_{i+1} - \hat{\gamma}_{i+1}^{TS} \right\|^2, \tag{6.24}$$

where $\hat{\gamma}^{TS}$ denotes the original time series forecast. We observe that if $\lambda = 0$, $\hat{\gamma}^{PLS} = \hat{\gamma}^{LS}$, and for $\lambda \to \infty$, $\hat{\gamma}^{PLS} = \hat{\gamma}^{TS}$. As shown in [10], the PLS updated forecast can be computed with

$$\hat{\gamma}_{i+1}^{PLS} = \left((F^a)^{\mathrm{T}} F^a + \lambda I\right)^{-1} \left((F^a)^{\mathrm{T}} x_{i+1}^a + \lambda \hat{\gamma}_{i+1}^{TS}\right). \tag{6.25}$$

And finally, the PLS updated forecast of the future booking horizon $\hat{x}_{i+1}^{PLS}$ is obtained by

$$\hat{x}_{i+1}^{PLS} = \hat{\gamma}_{i+1,1}^{PLS} f_1 + \cdots + \hat{\gamma}_{i+1,K}^{PLS} f_K. \tag{6.26}$$

One other more intuitive updating approach is the historical proportion (HP) method. The accuracy of the forecast is simply computed by the ratio of already observed realization and their forecasted values. Suppose we are at updating point a, i.e., realizations of the first a days in the booking horizon are known. The ratio R is given by

$$R = \frac{\sum_{j=1}^{a} x_{i+1,j}}{\sum_{j=1}^{a} \hat{x}_{i+1,j}}, \tag{6.27}$$

keeping in mind that $\hat{x}_{i+1}$ denotes the time series based forecast of x_{i+1}. The HP updated forecast for the remaining booking days is the with R scaled $\hat{x}_{i+1}$,

$$\hat{x}_{i+1,j}^{\text{HP}} = R \cdot \hat{x}_{i+1,j} \qquad j = a+1, \ldots, m. \tag{6.28}$$

In the following section we will compare the PLS and HP updating method with the forecast results that are not updated.

6.5 Numerical Results

In this section we will compare all combinations of the additive Holt-Winters and the vector auto-regressive forecasts with the two previously proposed updating methods penalized least squares and historical proportion, as well as with the not updated forecasts (NU). The number behind the abbreviation of the forecasting method (AHW or VAR) denotes the number of base vectors K used in the singular value decomposition. In our test case we are working with $K = 3$ or 5. The evaluation set consists of the last 50 instances, i.e., arrival weeks, of our six datasets (instances 150–200). As measures of forecast accuracy the mean squared error (MSE) and the mean week relative absolute error (MWRAE) are computed for the four booking horizon weeks, similar to [5]. The squared error (SE) and the week relative absolute error (WRAE) are defined for instance i and weeks $w = 1, \ldots, 4$ by

$$\text{SE}(i, w=1) = \sum_{k=1}^{7} (x_{i,k} - \hat{x}_{i,k})^2 \quad \text{WRAE}(i, w=1) = \frac{|\sum_{k=1}^{7} x_{i,k} - \sum_{k=1}^{7} \hat{x}_{i,k}|}{\sum_{k=1}^{7} x_{i,k}}$$

$$\text{SE}(i, w=2) = \sum_{k=8}^{14} (x_{i,k} - \hat{x}_{i,k})^2 \quad \text{WRAE}(i, w=2) = \frac{|\sum_{k=8}^{14} x_{i,k} - \sum_{k=8}^{14} \hat{x}_{i,k}|}{\sum_{k=8}^{14} x_{i,k}}$$

Table 6.4 λ parameter for PLS updating methods, respectively for dataset and booking week

Forecast	Dataset	λ_1	λ_2	λ_3	Dataset	λ_1	λ_2	λ_3
VAR 3	A-Acc	0.0664	0.2045	0.1936	A-Ind	5.6378	1.9223	0.5701
VAR 5		2.4043	0.0410	0.0000		1.4960	0.0000	0.0000
AHW 3		0.0312	0.0319	0.0902		0.1648	0.4409	0.0000
AHW 5		0.0168	0.0059	0.0059		2.1228	0.4719	0.0000
VAR 3	B-Acc	0.0357	0.0508	0.1326	B-Ind	0.0000	0.4660	0.7135
VAR 5		2.0210	0.0098	0.0419		0.3863	0.2445	0.6018
AHW 3		1.2319	0.0386	0.0871		0.0000	1.3042	0.3101
AHW 5		0.4375	0.0149	0.0146		0.0950	2.3321	0.1856
VAR 3	C-Acc	0.0175	0.0571	0.0707	C-Ind	0.3207	1.5848	0.3370
VAR 5		0.0051	0.0209	0.0187		0.5337	3.3194	0.3170
AHW 3		2.0827	0.0252	0.0170		1.0071	0.2106	0.1070
AHW 5		2.0284	0.0076	0.0039		0.1524	0.2145	0.0927

$$\text{SE}(i, w=3) = \sum_{k=15}^{21} (x_{i,k} - \hat{x}_{i,k})^2 \quad \text{WRAE}(i, w=3) = \frac{|\sum_{k=15}^{21} x_{i,k} - \sum_{k=15}^{21} \hat{x}_{i,k}|}{\sum_{k=15}^{21} x_{i,k}}$$

$$\text{SE}(i, w=4) = \sum_{k=22}^{28} (x_{i,k} - \hat{x}_{i,k})^2 \quad \text{WRAE}(i, w=4) = \frac{|\sum_{k=22}^{28} x_{i,k} - \sum_{k=22}^{28} \hat{x}_{i,k}|}{\sum_{k=22}^{28} x_{i,k}}.$$

The MSE and the MWRAE are computed by averaging the SE and WRAE over our 50 evaluation instances. The MSE gives insight into the accuracy on daily level, while the MWRAE provides the proportional absolute difference in week totals. The optimal λ parameter for the PLS are found by minimizing the MSE updating error at the last 46 instances of the testing and estimation sample (instances 100 till 146), see Table 6.4 for the final values. λ_1, λ_2 and λ_3 are respectively used in the updating in booking horizon weeks 1, 2 and 3.

The best forecast and updating method combinations for each dataset, which minimize the forecast error per booking horizon week, are given in Table 6.5. All generated MSE and MWRAE error results are shown in Table 6.6, the smallest errors for dataset and booking week combination are highlighted by an asterisk (*).

For the MSE we find in weeks 3 and 4 the smallest values for the PLS updated forecasts, except for the C-Ind dataset in week 4, there the VAR 3 PLS value exceeds the VAR 3 NU value by 2, which only corresponds to an increase of 3 %. We also observe that the VAR outperforms the AHW forecast on the last booking weeks 3 and 4 completely, also on the weeks 1 and 2, except fot A-Acc and C-Acc, but here we find again only a small increase of the MSE compared to the best VAR forecast. At first glance at Table 6.5 in the MWRAE area, the PLS updating is still the best, but with less dominance compared to the MSE part. With a closer look at Table 6.6, we find that the PLS error values are very close to the best performing methods;

Table 6.5 Best forecast and updating methods respectively to minimization of MSE or MWRAE per booking week and dataset, *mult* indicates that more than two combinations have the smallest value

	MSE			
Dataset	First week	Second week	Third week	Fourth week
A-Ind	VAR 3 all	VAR 3 NU, PLS	VAR 3 PLS	VAR 3 PLS
A-Acc	AHW 3 NU	VAR 3 PLS	VAR 5 PLS	VAR 3 PLS
B-Ind	VAR 3 HP, AHW 3 NU	VAR 3, AHW 5 NU	VAR 3 PLS	VAR 3 PLS
B-Acc	VAR 3 HP	VAR 3 PLS	VAR 3 PLS	VAR 5 PLS
C-Ind	VAR 3 NU, PLS	VAR 3 NU	VAR 3 NU, PLS	VAR 3 NU
C-Acc	VAR 3 HP	AHW 3 NU	VAR 3 PLS	VAR 5 PLS
	MWRAE			
	First week	Second week	Third week	Fourth week
A-Ind	Mult	Mult	AHW 5 NU	AHW 3 NU
A-Acc	VAR 3 NU	VAR 3 PLS	VAR 5 PLS	Mult
B-Ind	VAR 3, 5 HP	AHW 3 NU	Mult	VAR 3, 5 PLS
B-Acc	All VAR	VAR 3 PLS	VAR, AHW 3 PLS	VAR, AHW 5 PLS
C-Ind	Mult	VAR 3 NU	Mult	VAR 3 NU
C-Acc	VAR 3 HP	Mult	VAR 5 PLS	VAR, AHW 5 PLS

compare for example the VAR 3 PLS values for A-Ind and C-Ind with the best performing methods. Note that approximately 89 % of all bookings are made within this last 3 weeks of the booking horizon and 67 % within the last two booking weeks and still 39 % in the last booking week. Therefore a forecast accuracy increase in the later part of the booking horizon is much more important than in the early stages. Comparing the two forecasting methods additive Holt-Winters and vector auto-regression, we observe that the mean values of the VAR outperform the AHW forecast. This shows that the correlation between the base vectors should not be neglected. The results of the different updating methods are graphically illustrated in Fig. 6.11, for one instance of the evaluation set for datasets A-Ind and A-Acc and base forecast VAR 3.

For practitioners, the accurate forecast of the overall number of reservations is as important as the forecast of the booking curve or individual reservations per booking day. The total relative absolute error (TRAE) for "Ind" datasets is then defined by

$$\mathrm{TRAE}(i) = \frac{|\sum_{k=1}^{28} \hat{x}_{i,k} - \sum_{k=1}^{28} x_{i,k}|}{\sum_{k=1}^{28} x_{i,k}}.$$

In case of accumulated "Acc" datasets the TRAE is simply computed by the last column values

$$\mathrm{TRAE}(i) = \frac{|\hat{x}_{i,28} - x_{i,28}|}{x_{i,28}}.$$

Table 6.6 Mean squared errors (MSE) and mean week relative absolute errors (MWRAE) for all datasets and forecast combinations – the asterisk highlights the smallest errors for each dataset and booking week combination

			MSE				MWRAE			
			First week	Second week	Third week	Fourth week	First week	Second week	Third week	Fourth week
A-Ind	VAR 3	NU	19*	40*	41	78	0.20*	0.18*	0.15	0.13
		PLS	19*	40*	40*	75*	0.21	0.18*	0.14	0.13
		HP	19*	80	53	95	0.21	0.39	0.22	0.19
	VAR 5	NU	21	42	41	77	0.20*	0.18*	0.13*	0.13
		PLS	20	43	53	81	0.20*	0.18*	0.22	0.16
		HP	21	92	55	99	0.20*	0.40	0.22	0.21
	AHW 3	NU	20	42	41	78	0.20*	0.18*	0.15	0.12*
		PLS	20	44	42	82	0.21	0.24	0.17	0.17
		HP	20	59	49	95	0.21	0.28	0.21	0.19
	AHW 5	NU	79	51	44	79	0.25	0.19	0.15	0.13
		PLS	22	44	42	81	0.20*	0.22	0.17	0.16
		HP	22	62	49	97	0.20*	0.29	0.21	0.2
A-Acc	VAR 3	NU	144	518	1,091	1,954	0.24*	0.15	0.13	0.11
		PLS	151	275*	427	704*	0.29	0.11*	0.08	0.06*
		HP	168	22,866	13,488	17,543	0.32	0.65	0.31	0.25
	VAR 5	NU	151	545	1,194	2,814	0.28	0.15	0.13	0.13
		PLS	145	638	381*	777	0.27	0.18	0.07*	0.06*
		HP	151	22,891	14,554	17,727	0.28	0.67	0.32	0.26
	AHW 3	NU	132*	463	1,011	1,869	0.29	0.15	0.12	0.11
		PLS	136	323	606	894	0.30	0.12	0.09	0.07
		HP	136	8,575	4,793	14,447	0.30	0.46	0.23	0.22
	AHW 5	NU	133	455	1,011	1,824	0.29	0.15	0.12	0.10
		PLS	140	345	732	723	0.30	0.13	0.09	0.06*
		HP	140	8,320	5,407	13,945	0.30	0.47	0.24	0.22

(continued)

Table 6.6 (continued)

			MSE				MWRAE			
			First week	Second week	Third week	Fourth week	First week	Second week	Third week	Fourth week
B-Ind	VAR 3	NU	20	39*	48	67	0.22	0.17	0.16	0.15
		PLS	21	82	47*	66*	0.23	0.38	0.15*	0.14*
		HP	19*	96	56	74	0.20*	0.47	0.20	0.17
	VAR 5	NU	20	41	49	67	0.21	0.16	0.15*	0.15
		PLS	20	43	50	67	0.22	0.18	0.17	0.14*
		HP	20	102	55	74	0.20*	0.48	0.20	0.17
	AHW 3	NU	19*	38	49	68	0.21	0.16*	0.16	0.15
		PLS	21	82	50	70	0.25	0.38	0.18	0.16
		HP	21	57	54	71	0.25	0.35	0.20	0.17
	AHW 5	NU	20	39*	49	69	0.21	0.17	0.15*	0.16
		PLS	23	53	51	70	0.25	0.23	0.18	0.16
		HP	23	59	53	73	0.25	0.34	0.19	0.17
B-Acc	VAR 3	NU	74	286	769	1,743	0.22*	0.13	0.12	0.11
		PLS	73	177*	287*	695	0.22*	0.09*	0.06*	0.06
		HP	69*	3,634	3,010	4,247	0.22*	0.41	0.22	0.16
	VAR 5	NU	78	311	774	1,725	0.22*	0.14	0.12	0.10
		PLS	73	261	693	475*	0.22*	0.12	0.10	0.05*
		HP	70	3,789	3,150	5,162	0.22*	0.42	0.22	0.17
	AHW 3	NU	89	282	805	2,129	0.23	0.12	0.12	0.12
		PLS	128	323	313	776	0.30	0.14	0.06*	0.06
		HP	128	6,138	5,662	7,790	0.30	0.50	0.28	0.21
	AHW 5	NU	95	295	788	1,882	0.23	0.13	0.12	0.11
		PLS	132	407	703	550	0.29	0.16	0.10	0.05*
		HP	132	6,028	5,649	7,163	0.29	0.51	0.28	0.19

C-Ind	VAR 3	NU	22*	45*	46*	64*	0.22*	0.19*	0.15*	0.18*
		PLS	22*	47	46*	66	0.22*	0.20	0.15*	0.19
		HP	24	60	58	79	0.23	0.30	0.24	0.23
	VAR 5	NU	24	46	47	65	0.23	0.20	0.15*	0.19
		PLS	24	47	47	68	0.22*	0.20	0.15*	0.20
		HP	25	65	61	86	0.26	0.33	0.25	0.24
	AHW 3	NU	23	47	48	66	0.22*	0.20	0.16	0.19
		PLS	24	48	51	70	0.29	0.22	0.20	0.20
		HP	24	61	66	83	0.29	0.30	0.29	0.24
	AHW 5	NU	24	50	47	68	0.22*	0.20	0.16	0.19
		PLS	28	52	52	74	0.27	0.21	0.20	0.22
		HP	28	71	65	87	0.27	0.35	0.28	0.23
C-Acc	VAR 3	NU	108	375	815	1,992	0.29	0.14*	0.10	0.10
		PLS	120	380	357*	1,283	0.31	0.14*	0.07	0.08
		HP	102*	3,237	3,755	7,122	0.27*	0.36	0.24	0.21
	VAR 5	NU	116	476	881	1,930	0.29	0.17	0.11	0.10
		PLS	127	461	438	895*	0.32	0.15	0.06*	0.07*
		HP	114	3,765	4,269	6,820	0.29	0.36	0.25	0.21
	AHW 3	NU	117	368*	754	1,586	0.28	0.14*	0.10	0.10
		PLS	143	530	502	1,519	0.30	0.18	0.08	0.09
		HP	143	5,646	4,140	8,645	0.30	0.47	0.23	0.21
	AHW 5	NU	120	380	790	1,559	0.28	0.14*	0.10	0.10
		PLS	138	655	745	964	0.29	0.20	0.08	0.07*
		HP	138	6,352	4,497	9,138	0.29	0.48	0.24	0.21

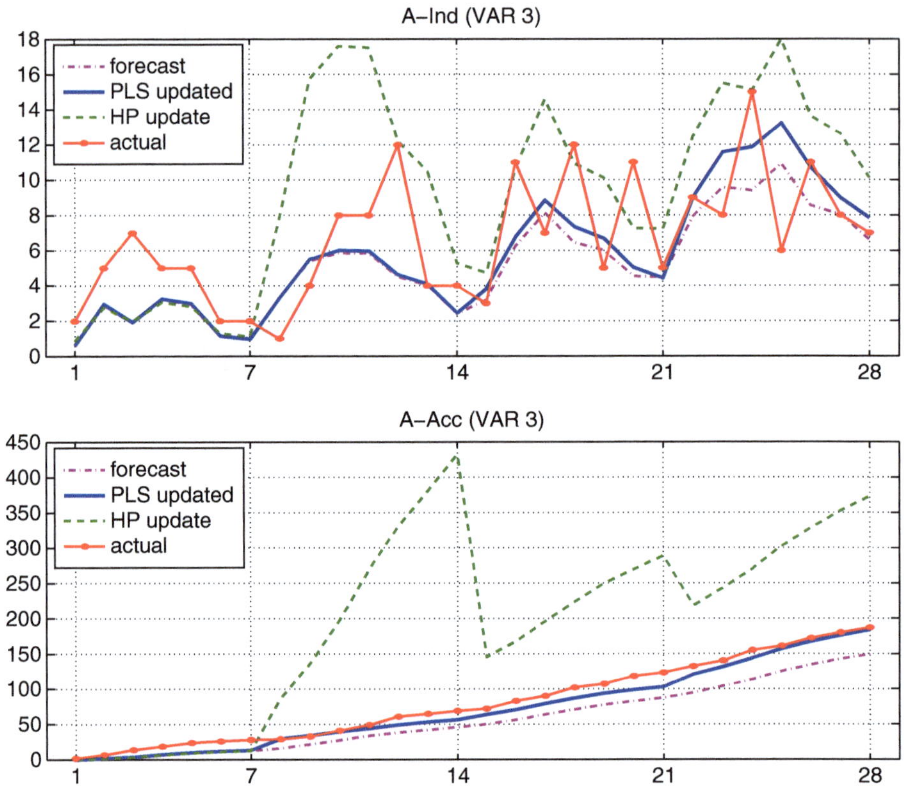

Fig. 6.11 Example of reservation actuals vs. updated and not updated forecasts for one instance of datasets A-Acc and A-Ind

Table 6.7 Mean and median of total relative absolute error (TRAE) for all updating methods and datasets with VAR 3 as base forecast

	Mean TRAE			Median TRAE		
Dataset	NU	PLS	HP	NU	PLS	HP
A-Ind	0.1265	0.1037	0.1438	0.1255	0.1050	0.1242
B-Ind	0.0965	0.1148	0.1331	0.0887	0.0882	0.1239
C-Ind	0.0876	0.0760	0.1361	0.0666	0.0647	0.0996
A-Acc	0.1159	0.0517	0.2961	0.1114	0.0392	0.1821
B-Acc	0.1092	0.0428	0.1877	0.0944	0.0354	0.1481
C-Acc	0.0931	0.0487	0.2013	0.0657	0.0397	0.1458

In Table 6.7 the different mean and median TRAE values are shown for all datasets and updating methods applied to a VAR 3 forecast. The PLS is outperforming the not updating, except for B-Ind, and HP updating in all cases. Further, the TRAE for datasets of the same region is always minimized on the accumulated dataset. Two interesting observations are: First, the HP updating is never better than not updating, and second that PLS updating on "Ind" datasets results in lower TRAE than not updating on "Acc" datasets, except for B-Ind. The accuracy increase is very large on the "Acc" datasets with 55 % in average.

6.6 Conclusion

In this chapter we have analyzed forecast updating methods using simulated demand data. The datasets contain a significant correlation between early and late bookings. Consequently not updating the demand forecast when early realizations in the booking horizon become available means ignoring important information that can dramatically affect the end result. But, also for datasets with low correlation between early and late bookings (dataset C) we observe a significant accuracy increase by updating. The forecast updating is performed dynamically when new demand realizations become available, in our case weekly. The initial forecast results are then updated using either the penalized least squares (PLS) or the historical proportion method. In the case of a multi step ahead forecast, the base forecast produces multiple one step ahead forecasts on historical data and previous updated forecasts. We find that dynamic updating reservation forecasts using PLS is very beneficial in most situations with low and high correlation between different parts of the booking horizon, and is never significantly harmful compared to not updating. Also computationally the method is very fast and therefore feasible for use by practitioners in larger forecasting problems. Singular value decomposition is applied to reduce the dimensionality of the forecasting problem and the results show its effectiveness. As base forecasts we use a multivariate vector autoregressive model and a univariate Holt-Winters model on the reduced forecasting problem. The results show that the VAR on a small scale outperforms the AHW. Thus, the dependency between base vectors after the SVD should generally not be ignored. In addition, an increase of base vectors from 3 to 5 generally does not result in significant lower error values. Overall, the VAR 3 forecast method seems to be the best base forecast for our datasets.

So far in this study we have assumed the demand to be independent for different products, i.e., weekdays, time slot within the day, reservations possibilities at different stores/branches. In reality a reservation decision depends crucially on the offered alternatives. Therefore the application of updating methods to choice based demand forecasts should also be investigated. Further testing on actual fashion shop reservation data as well as extended simulation tests are necessary to better quantify the expected forecast accuracy increase in real world applications. A straightforward extension of the proposed approach would be to include the dimension of time slots during the day into the forecasting procedure as well as multiple stores. Finally, another interesting direction for further research would be to investigate the impact of the customer information event, i.e., when potential customers are informed by the store about new product arrivals, on the booking behavior and possible adjustments to the forecasting updating procedure.

References

1. Box GEP, Jenkins GM, Reinsel GC (1994) Time series analysis: forecasting and control, 3rd edn. Prentice Hall, Englewood Cliffs
2. Chiang WC, Chen JCH, Xu X (2007) An overview of research on revenue management: current issues and future research. Int J Revenue Manag 1(1):97–128
3. Cleveland RB, Cleveland WS, McRae JE, Terpenning I (1990) STL: a seasonal-trend decomposition procedure based on loess. J Off Stat 6(1):3–73
4. Haensel A, Koole GM (2011) Estimating unconstrained demand rate functions using customer choice sets. J Revenue Pricing Manag 10(5):438–454
5. Haensel A, Koole GM (2011) Booking Horizon forecasting with dynamic updating: a case study on hotel reservation data. Int J Forecast 27(3):942–960
6. Holt CC (1957) Forecasting seasonals and trends by exponentially weighted moving averages. ONR Research Memorandum Carnigie Institute 52
7. Lütkepohl H (2005) New introduction to multiple time series analysis. Springer, Berlin
8. O'Connor M, Remus W, Griggs K (2000) Does updating judgmental forecasts improve forecast accuracy? Int J Forecast 16:101–109
9. Pölt S (1998) Forecasting is difficult, especially if it refers to the future. In: AGIFORS – reservations and yield management study group meeting proceedings, Prague
10. Shen H, Huang JZ (2008) Interday forecasting and intraday updating of call center arrivals. Manuf Serv Oper Manag 10(3):391–410
11. Talluri KT, Van Ryzin GR (2004) Revenue management under a general discrete choice model of customer behavior. Manag Sci 50(1):15–33
12. Talluri KT, Van Ryzin GR (2004) The theory and practice of revenue management. Springer, New York
13. Van Ryzin GR (2005) Future of revenue management – models of demand. J Revenue Pricing Manag 4(2):204–210
14. Van Ryzin GR, Vulcano G (2012) An expectation-maximization algorithm to estimate a general class of non-parametric choice models. Working paper
15. Weatherford LR, Kimes SE (2003) A comparison of forecasting methods for hotel revenue management. Int J Forecast 19:401–415
16. Weinberg J, Brown LD, Stroud JR (2007) Bayesian forecasting of an inhomogeneous poisson process with applications to call center data. J Am Stat Assoc 102(480):1185–1198. Applications and case studies
17. Winters PR (1960) Forecasting sales by exponentially weighted moving averages. Manag Sci 6:324–342
18. Zeni RH (2007) Can we really look to the past to forecast future demand? J Revenue Pricing Manag 6(4):312–314

Part III
Intelligent Fashion Forecasting: Applications and Analysis

Chapter 7
Fuzzy Forecast Combining for Apparel Demand Forecasting

Murat Kaya, Engin Yeşil, M. Furkan Dodurka, and Sarven Sıradağ

Abstract In this chapter, we present a novel approach for apparel demand forecasting that constitutes a main ingredient for a decision support system we designed. Our contribution is twofold. First, we develop a method that generates forecasts based on the inherent seasonal demand pattern at product category level. This pattern is identified by estimating lost sales and the effects of special events and pricing on demand. The method also allows easy integration of product managers' qualitative information on factors that may affect demand. Second, we develop a fuzzy forecast combiner. The combiner calculates the final forecast using a weighted average of forecasts generated by independent methods. Combination weights are adaptive in the sense that the weights of the better-performing methods are increased over time. Forecast combination operations employ fuzzy logic. We illustrate our approach with a simulation study that uses data from a Turkish apparel firm.

7.1 Introduction

The ultimate goal of supply chain management is having the right product at the right location at the right time. While challenging in general, this goal is particularly difficult to achieve in the apparel industry due mainly to unpredictable

M. Kaya (✉)
Faculty of Engineering and Natural Sciences, Sabanci University, Istanbul 34956, Turkey
e-mail: mkaya@sabanciuniv.edu

E. Yeşil • M.F. Dodurka
Faculty of Electrical and Electronics Engineering, Department of Control Engineering, Istanbul Technical University, Maslak, TR-34469 Istanbul, Turkey
e-mail: yesileng@itu.edu.tr; furkan.dodurka@getron.com

S. Sıradağ
Getron Bilişim Hizmetleri A.Ş, Yıldız Teknik Üniversitesi Davutpaşa Kampüsü, Teknopark Binası B1 Blok, Esenler, 34220 Istanbul, Turkey
e-mail: sarven.siradag@getron.com

T.-M. Choi et al. (eds.), *Intelligent Fashion Forecasting Systems: Models and Applications*, DOI 10.1007/978-3-642-39869-8_7,

consumer demand, short product life cycles, extremely high product variety and long supply lead times. In fact, most firms acknowledge the impossibility of accurately forecasting apparel demand, especially the demand for high-fashion products. Rather than conducting long-range forecasting, successful apparel firms are investing in Quick Response (QR) capabilities that allow them to react to observed demand changes quickly [19, 28].

Although supply–demand mismatches may be impossible to avoid, their adverse effects can be mitigated through smart use of information. Thanks to widespread use of point-of-sale systems, most apparel retailers readily have access to sales and inventory data. However, there is still a shortage of practical quantitative models that use this data effectively [29]. To this end, we developed a decision support system that aids managers with the following three decisions which may help apparel firms match supply and demand across stores:

- **Repeat production** decisions for products that are highly demanded. Relevant parameters include unit cost, profit margin, production lead time, production lot size and remaining season length.
- **Discount** (markdown) decisions for products that are poorly demanded. Relevant parameters include unit cost, profit margin, demand curve (that indicates reaction to price change) and remaining season length.
- **Transshipment** decisions for products that are running out of stock in some store but having excess inventory in some other. Relevant parameters include store capacities, transshipment capacity and transshipment cost.

The core task of our decision support system is to compare the current inventory levels with the expected demand in the remaining of the selling season. This requires generating demand forecasts *for each SKU (defined as a particular color-size combination of a garment style) at each store for the upcoming weeks.* This task is difficult for a number of reasons:

- **Fickle consumer taste:** New fashion trends are created and spread around the globe very quickly thanks to the media and the Internet.
- **Lack of historical data:** Most apparel products are new designs, for which no historical demand data exists. For this reason, firms often generate forecasts at higher levels, such as style or category level, and/or use data from similar past products.
- **High number of similar styles:** To satisfy consumer needs, apparel firms offer a high number of somewhat similar garment styles. These products steal demand from each other, and it is difficult to know in advance which styles will be more popular than others.
- **Granularity of the forecasting unit**: The weekly sales of an SKU in one store may be quite low, often zero. Such sparse data may result in small fractional forecasts (such as 0.45 units) for which even rounding up or down makes a big difference.

- **Lost sales:** Traditionally, stores record sales using POS systems. Demand that is not satisfied (lost sales) or satisfied with some other product (substitution) is not recorded. The proportion of lost sales can be high due to relatively low store inventory levels per SKU.
- **Pricing:** Demand can be quite price sensitive especially for non-fashion apparel products. Firms discount prices heavily throughout the season to boost sales, causing wide swings in demand.
- **Seasonality and systematic events:** Demand for most apparel products has inherent seasonality. Seasonality is also shaped by systematic events that occur regularly in the same week of every year. These include special days such as the New Year's Day, Valentine's Day and Fathers' Day, and regular sales periods.
- **Unsystematic events:** One-time events such as social or weather-related events, or irregularly-repeating events may affect apparel demand significantly.
- **Competitor actions:** Demand is shaped not only by the actions of the firm itself but also by the product design, pricing, promotion and store location decisions of its competitors.

This chapter presents a forecasting approach that addresses some of these issues. Our contribution is twofold. First, we develop a forecasting method, *Seasonal Pattern Based Forecasting*, that is particularly suitable to use in the apparel industry. This method generates forecasts based on the seasonal pattern in product category demand. The method uncovers the seasonal demand pattern by estimating lost sales, and the effects of special events and pricing on demand. It also allows practical integration of judgmental input from product managers. The method is similar to Product-Life-Cycle-Based forecasting (PLCB) approach which is known to be effective for short-lifecycle products. Burruss and Kuettnerr [5], for example, report using PLCB method to forecast the demand for Hewlett Packard's (HP) inkjet printers.

Our second contribution is the development of a *fuzzy forecast combiner* that combines the forecasts generated by different methods using adaptive weights and fuzzy logic. We illustrate the use of this combiner through a simulation study that uses real sales data from a Turkish apparel firm. In the simulation, the combiner combines the forecasts of three methods, one of them being the Seasonal Pattern Based forecasting method we developed. We observe the combined forecast to be considerably more accurate than the three individual methods, as well as several other alternative methods.

Combined forecasts are used widely in forecasting diverse phenomena including football game outcome, electric demand, gross national product, market volatility, meteorological data, political risks and city populations [8]. The M-Competition forecasting competitions have repeatedly found combined forecasts to perform better than each of the individual forecasts [22]. Academic literature on forecast combining initiated with the seminal work of Bates and Granger [4]. These authors combined two forecasts by choosing combination weights that minimize the total mean squared error of the combined forecast. Granger and Newbold [18] discuss different methods to determine combination weights. Clemen [8] provides a review and an annotated bibliography of related research in the first 20 years of this research stream. Timmermann's [32] comprehensive survey focuses on the theoretical aspects of forecast combinations. As Timmermann states, simple combinations such as arithmetic averages or weights based on mean squared errors often perform better than more sophisticated schemes that depend on the variance-covariance matrix of forecast errors. This finding is supported by Winkler and Makridakis's [33] time series analysis, as well as Stock and Watson's [30] extensive comparison of 49 forecasting methods using 215 US macroeconomic time series. Practitioners also value forecast combining. Collopy and Armstrong's [9] survey finds 83 % of expert forecasters to believe that combining the results from individual forecasting methods leads to better forecasts. Other important references on forecast combining include Newbold and Granger [25], Granger [17] and Armstrong [2].

The accuracy of different forecasting methods change over time as demand characteristics of a product evolves. One method that provides accurate forecasts in the initial weeks of the sales season may cease to do so towards the end of season. Similarly, methods that make good forecasts during relatively stable demand conditions may fail when demand fluctuates. For this reason, our forecast combiner updates the combination weights of the methods periodically based on the methods' relative forecast error performance. The use of adaptive (time-varying) weights is supported in the literature [32]. Eliott and Timmermann [12], Zellner et al. [38] and Deutsch [11] are among the works that consider time-varying combination weights. Chan et al. [6] uses quality control techniques to determine when to update the combination weights.

Our forecast combiner determines the combination weights using fuzzy logic. We preferred to use a fuzzy approach because we do not want to be too strict with the definition of forecast accuracy. After all, what constitutes "good", "bad" or "slightly good" forecast accuracy is subjective matter. The theory of fuzzy sets [36] proposed by Zadeh has achieved a great success in various fields [7, 21, 24, 34]. One of the basic aims of fuzzy sets and fuzzy logic is to offer a computational framework for representation of knowledge and inference in an environment of imprecision and uncertainty. Fuzzy logic is effective in such environments, when the solutions need not be precise and/or it is acceptable for a conclusion to have a dispositional rather than categorical validity [37]. Since there are so many real world applications which fit these conditions, especially in the realm of knowledge-based systems for decision-making, fuzzy logic has been used as a solution for various problems.

The following section explains the seasonal pattern based (SPB) forecasting method that we developed. Section 7.3 discusses our fuzzy forecast combination approach in detail. Section 7.4 provides the results of a simulation study where we use the forecast combiner to combine forecasts from three different methods, one of them being the SPB method that is explained in Sect. 7.3. Section 7.5 provides our concluding remarks.

7.2 Seasonal Pattern Based (SPB) Forecasting

This section presents "Seasonal Pattern Based (SPB) Forecasting" method, which is a novel method we developed for apparel forecasting. The method is based on identifying a repeating seasonal demand pattern for a product category. In Sect. 7.2.1, we explain how the seasonal demand pattern is uncovered using a six-step procedure that removes the effects of stockouts, price changes and certain unsystematic events from past sales data. Then, in Sects. 7.2.2 and 7.2.3, we outline how this seasonal pattern is prepared for forecasting, and used in generating demand forecasts.

7.2.1 *Illustration of the Six-Step Procedure to Uncover True Seasonal Pattern*

Figure 7.1 summarizes the six-step procedure to obtain the seasonal demand pattern from past sales data. In the following paragraphs, we illustrate the procedure using

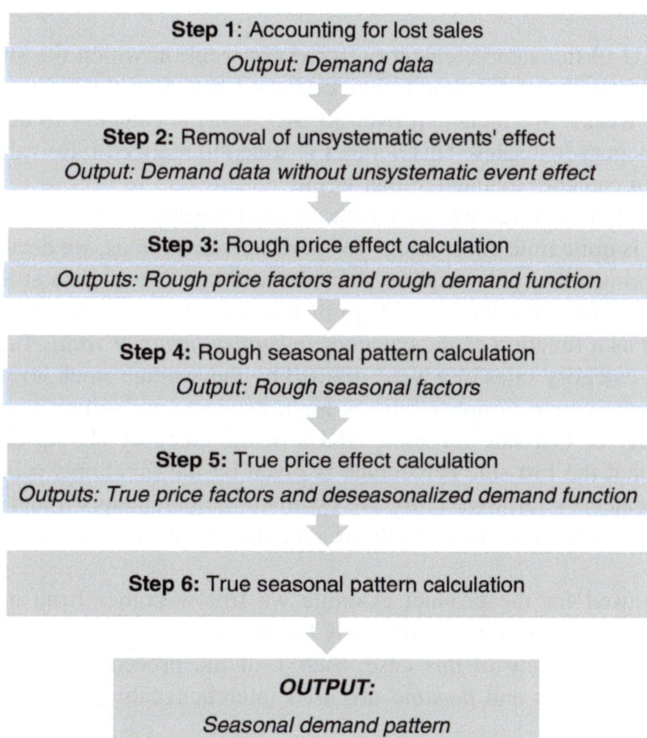

Fig. 7.1 The six steps to construct the seasonal demand pattern

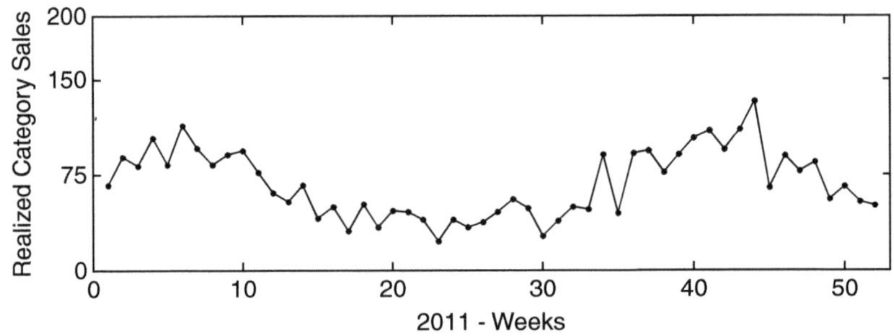

Fig. 7.2 Weekly sales of sample product category in 2011

the sales data of a particular slim-fit men's shirt category from a Turkish Apparel firm as an example. Figure 7.2 presents the weekly sales of this product category at a particular store in year 2011. A seasonal length of one year is used because the product is sold throughout the year.

7.2.1.1 Step 1: Accounting for Lost Sales

For each SKU of the sample category, for every week in which the stock level is zero, we estimate the realized and unmet demand based on the sales quantities of the previous weeks. We then sum over all SKUs of the category to determine the estimated category lost sales. This number is added to realized sales value to obtain an estimate of category demand in that week.

This procedure requires working with detailed weekly stock level data of each SKU, which is quite time consuming. To speed up calculations, we developed a fast heuristic approach that only requires the sales and stock level data at the category level. We conjecture that the percentage of lost sales for the category can roughly be estimated as a function of the category *inventory turnover ratio*. Turnover ratio is defined as category sales in a week divided by the average stock level during the week. In weeks where turnover ratio is high, products are selling fast and hence the probability of lost sale for some SKUs of the category should also be high. We assume that the lost sale percentage is given by the function $y = ae^{bx}$ where x denotes the category turnover ratio. We estimate the parameters a and b using the SKU-level lost sale quantities which are calculated with the aforementioned first method.

The data used for the product example we follow comes from a large store where inventory levels are usually high for all SKUs in the category. Because lost sales would be few in this case, Step 1 of the procedure is ignored. As a result, the terms *sales* and *demand* are used interchangeably in references to the example.

7.2.1.2 Step 2: Removal Unsystematic Event Effect

Certain special events strongly affect the demand for apparel products not only in the week they occur, but in the preceding and following weeks as well. For example, the demand in weeks that follow sales periods can be weaker than normal. Based on their regularity, these events can be categorized into systematic and unsystematic events. Our procedure handles these two categories differently, as explained below.

- **Systematic events:** These are the events that occur regularly in the same week of every year. Examples include special days such as the New Year's Day, Valentine's Day and Fathers' Day, and regular sales periods. Our procedure does not remove the effects of these events on product demand because these events constitute a natural component of the seasonal demand pattern. The two religious holidays (Ramadan Festival, and Feast of Sacrifice) present a special challenge because they are observed according to the lunar calendar. That is, their dates shift back 10–11 days every year. We developed a separate procedure to estimate these Festivals' effects on demand in related weeks.
- **Unsystematic events:** These are the events that will not repeat regularly in the same week of every year. Examples include one-time sales events, and social or weather-related events that cause store closings. The effects of unsystematic events need to be eliminated from data as they distort the underlying seasonal demand pattern. To this end, we replace the data of weeks that contain such events with a 3-week moving average demand value.

The following four steps (steps 3–6) of the procedure aims to remove the price effect on demand. This, however, is a difficult process because of the interdependency between the price effect and the seasonality effect: The same sales price leads to different demand values at different weeks of the year. To decouple the effects of price and seasonality, we use a *double-pass approach* as summarized below:

- **The first (rough) pass:** In Step 3, we ignore seasonality and obtain the rough price effect. Then, in Step 4 we remove the price effect from demand data, and obtain the rough seasonal pattern. Using this, we deseasonalize the demand data of Step 2.
- **The second pass:** In Step 5, we recalculate the price effect (the true price effect), this time using the rough deseasonalized data from the first pass. Finally, in Step 6, we obtain the true seasonal pattern by removing the true price effect from the demand data of Step 2.

7.2.1.3 Step 3: Rough Price Effect Calculation

In this step, we ignore seasonality in data and estimate a rough demand curve that illustrates the relation between price and weekly average demand. The firm changes product prices frequently throughout the year to stimulate demand. We calculate average weekly sales achieved for each price point that the firm uses.

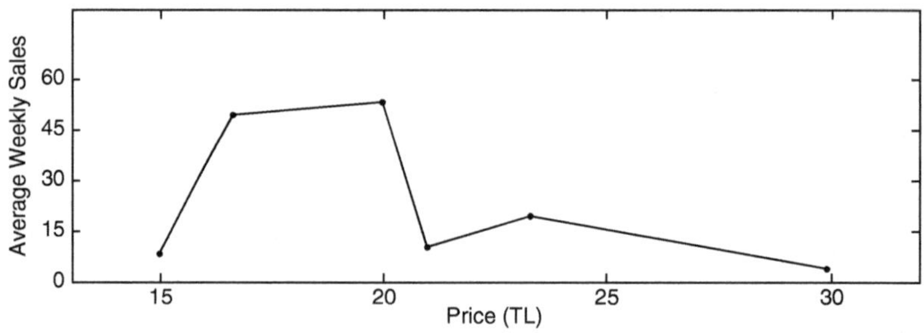

Fig. 7.3 Average weekly sales at different price points

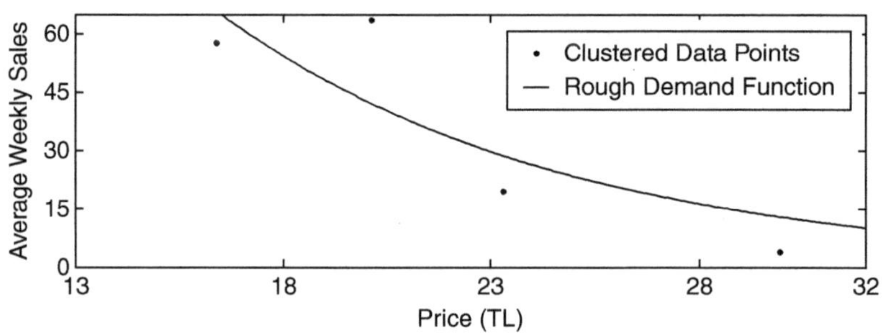

Fig. 7.4 Rough demand function estimation

Weekly averages are used because different prices remain effective for different durations. The data of weeks containing systematic events (as explained in Step 2) is ignored because of the misleadingly-high demand during these weeks. Figure 7.3 presents the results for our shirt example. Observe from the figure that demand is not necessarily a decreasing function of sales price.

Next, based on certain rules, we group the price points into a number of clusters. Then, using least squares estimation, we fit the rough demand function $D_r(p)$ as illustrated in Fig. 7.4. This function provides a rough estimate of weekly sales for a given sales price p.

Using the rough demand function, we calculate the *price factors* corresponding to price points p, which capture the effect of sales price on demand. The *normal price NP* of the product is defined as the annual average sales price of the category, which is equal to 19.81 TL (Turkish Liras) in our example. The *rough price factor* for price point p is calculated as $PF_r(p) = D_r(p)/D_r(NP)$. Note that $PF_r(p) > 1$ for prices lower than the normal price NP, whereas $PF_r(p) < 1$ for prices higher than NP.

7.2.1.4 Step 4: Rough Seasonal Pattern Calculation

To obtain the rough seasonal pattern, we normalize the price effect present in the demand data of Step 2 using the rough price factors calculated in Step 3.

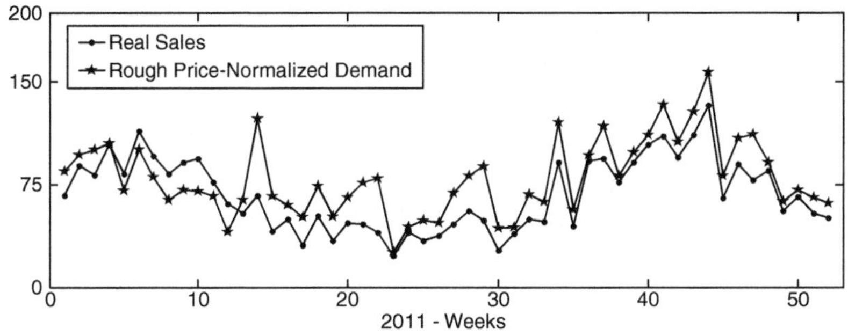

Fig. 7.5 Rough price-normalized demand values, $PND_r(w)$

To obtain the *rough price-normalized demand* PND_r in week w, we sum price-normalized sales values over all different price points p_i used in that week. That is, $PND_r(w) = \sum_i D(w,p_i)/PF_r(p_i)$ where $D(w,p_i)$ is the sales in week w at price point p_i. Figure 7.5 presents the resulting values (the starred series) to which we collectively refer to as the rough seasonal demand pattern.

Next we calculate the *rough seasonal factor* for week w as $SF_r(w) = PND_r(w)/PND_r(AA)$ where $PND_r(AA)$ denotes the rough price-normalized annual average weekly demand. A week's rough seasonal factor $SF_r(w)$ indicates how much above or below that week's demand would be due to seasonality, compared to the annual average demand if prices were normalized. For example, a seasonal factor of 1.6 indicates 60 % more sales than average in that week due to seasonality; whereas a seasonal factor of 0.7 indicates 30 % less sales then average.

Note that we have already obtained a seasonal demand pattern as shown in Fig. 7.5. This pattern, however, is based on the rough price effects of Step 3, which were calculated ignoring seasonality. Now that we have a rough estimate of seasonality, we repeat Steps 3 and 4 in Steps 5 and 6 respectively, this time taking seasonality into account in calculation of the price effect.

7.2.1.5 Step 5: True Price Effect Calculation

Next, we *deseasonalize* Step 2 demand data using the rough seasonal factors of Step 4. We calculate the *rough deseasonalized demand* in week w as $DSD_r(w) = D(w)/SF_r(w)$. Figure 7.6 presents the resulting values.

Then, we calculate the average weekly deseasonalized sales corresponding to each price point used in the store, as shown in Fig. 7.7. This is similar to Step 3, but this time we use deseasonalized sales values.

Next, we group these price points into a number of clusters and estimate the demand function shown in Fig. 7.8. This function provides the average weekly sales as a function of sales price in the absence of seasonality. Finally, we calculate the *true price factor* corresponding to price point p as $PF(p) = D(p)/D(NP)$ where NP is the normal price.

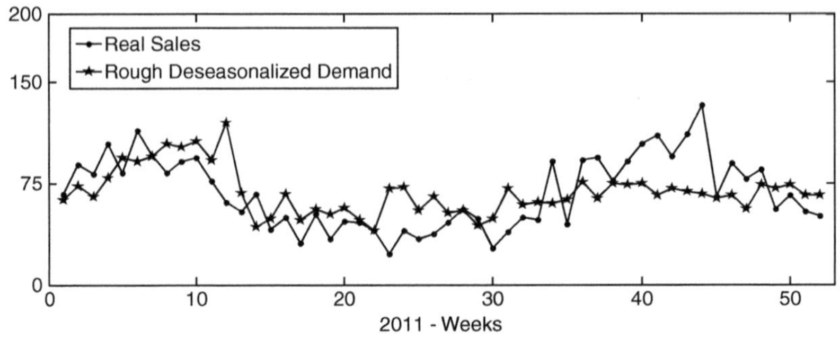

Fig. 7.6 Rough deseasonalized demand values, $DSD_r(w)$

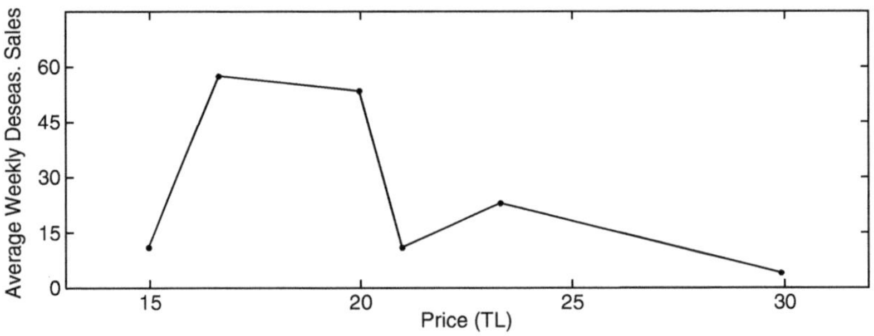

Fig. 7.7 Average weekly deseasonalized sales

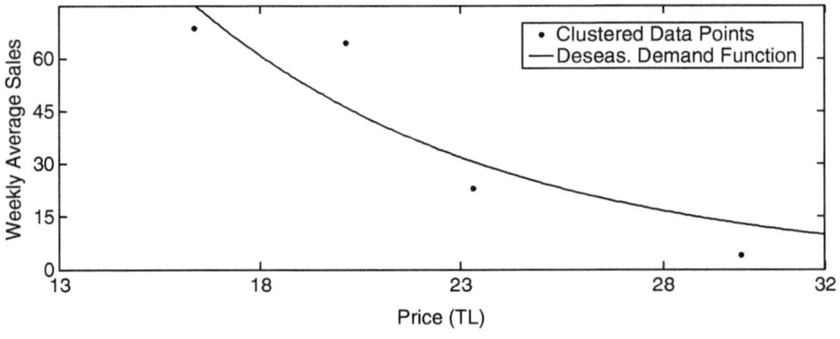

Fig. 7.8 Deseasonalized demand function estimation

Note that the demand function shown in Fig. 7.8 can also serve other purposes than demand forecasting. For instance, it can be employed as a revenue-management tool: Using the function, the level of expected sales increase in response to a certain discount rate can be calculated.

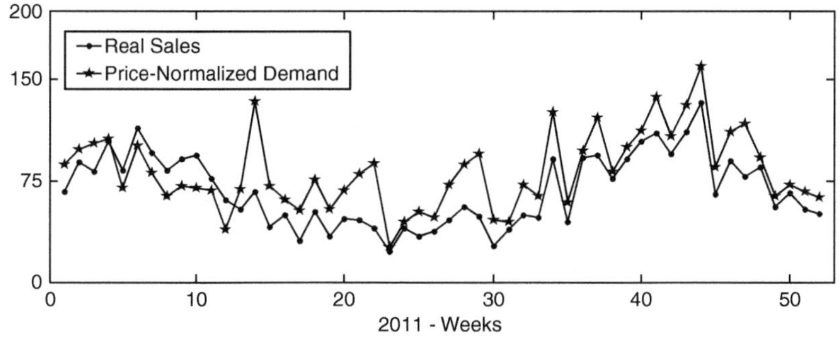

Fig. 7.9 Price-normalized demand values, PND(w) (True seasonal pattern)

7.2.1.6 Step 6: True Seasonal Pattern Calculation

In this step, we normalize the price effect that is present in the demand data of Step 2 using the price factors calculated in Step 5. To obtain the *price-normalized demand PND* in week w, we sum price-normalized sales values over all different price points p_i used in that week. That is, $PND(w) = \sum_i D(w,p_i)/PF(p_i)$ where $D(w,p_i)$ is the sales in week w at price point p_i. Figure 7.9 presents the resulting values to which we collectively refer to as the *true seasonal demand pattern*. Note that this pattern can be interpreted as the expected category demand if the sales price were fixed at the normal price of $NP = 19.81$ TL.

To summarize, the six-step procedure decouples the effects of seasonality and price on category demand. The primary output of the procedure is the seasonal demand pattern given in Fig. 7.9. This pattern predicts the distribution of demand within a sales season in the absence of stockouts, unsystematic events and price changes. Another output of the process is the demand curve given in Fig. 7.8, which estimates how demand is likely to react to possible price changes. Next, we discuss how this pattern can be used for forecasting purposes.

7.2.2 Preparing the Seasonal Pattern for Forecasting

The six-step procedure constructs a seasonal demand pattern based on the sales values of the most recent completed season, which was year 2011 in our example. The following is a list of other factors to be considered before using this pattern for forecasting the demand of an upcoming season.

Using data from multiple previous seasons: In addition to the most recent completed season, one can construct similar patterns using previously completed seasons' data (such as 2010 and 2009 weekly sales values). These patterns can then be combined using weighted averages, with higher weight given to more recent seasons. Comparison of demand patterns across consecutive seasons also gives an idea about the reliability of the underlying seasonal pattern. A pattern that repeats itself over different seasons would be dependable for forecasting purposes.

Integration of expert opinion: Beyond seasonality, price, and unsystematic events, demand is also affected by other factors that are not captured by our quantitative methodology. For example, a new fashion trend may be emerging, a competitor may be planning a large sales event, the firm may be introducing a new category that may steal sales from the studied category, or the firm may be opening a new store branch close to the store we study. Quantitatively estimating the effects of such factors on demand would be a daunting task; however, product managers are likely to have opinions. In fact, literature emphasizes that statistical methods and expert opinions have complimentary roles in achieving good forecasts. Armstrong and Collopy [1] discusses conditions under which statistical methods and judgment should be integrated. Our decision support system allows product managers to reflect their opinions by manually modifying the seasonal demand pattern. The manager can click and drag demand points on the seasonal pattern figure up or down, using an easy-to-use graphical interface. Such modifications can be made before or during the season, whenever new information on demand becomes available. One needs to be cautious about the level of modification, though: Fildes and Goodwin's [13] survey finds excessive management intervention to affect forecast performance negatively in most organizations.

Introduction of price effect: The seasonal pattern is price-normalized where normal price is defined as the average sales price in the last season. The effects of the firms' new pricing decisions for the upcoming season should be reflected on the pattern. The price factors calculated in Step 5 can be used for this purpose.

Disaggregation to SKU level: The seasonal demand pattern is constructed at category level. Yet, SKU-level forecasts are needed to support the repeat production, discounting and transshipment decisions of the managers. To obtain SKU-level forecasts, the forecast is disaggregated with respect to style, color and size. Disaggregation percentages, which are store-dependent, are determined by product managers. Our decision support system provides historical color and size distribution of the category's sales in the given store to assist managers in this decision.

7.2.3 In-Season Forecasting with the Seasonal Pattern

The weekly demand forecast values indicated in the seasonal demand pattern are not directly used in forecasting for the incoming season. Instead, we use the distribution of forecasted demand among the weeks of season. We calculate the percentage of total seasonal demand forecasted to realize in each week (referred to as the weekly weights $w_1, w_2, \ldots, w_T$). These weight values are kept constant throughout the upcoming sales season unless a product manager modifies them to reflect new information.

The product manager also makes an initial estimate of the category total demand C_0 over the upcoming season. Our decision support system aids the manager in this decision by providing past season sales values of this category and similar product categories.

During the new sales season, at the end of each week t, the total season demand estimate C is updated based on the cumulative observed demand value up to that week. The updated value is calculated as $C_t = \left(\sum_{i=1}^{t} D_i\right) / \left(\sum_{i=1}^{t} W_i\right)$.

In practical terms, this update causes the forecasts for the coming weeks to scale up (if total realized demand is higher than the total forecasts up to week t) or scale down (otherwise). To forecast the demand in a future week k, one multiplies that week's weight w_k with the latest (as of week t) total season demand estimate. That is, one calculates $F_{t,k} = w_k C_t$.

In Sect. 7.2, we explained the Seasonal Pattern Based (SPB) forecasting method, which constitutes the first contribution of this study. In our tests with sample data, we observed this method to generate quite successful demand forecasts. While the method is successful, it is well known in literature that forecast accuracy can be improved by combining forecasts from different methods. To this end, we developed a "forecast combiner". This combiner, which constitutes the second contribution of this study, is explained in the following section.

7.3 Fuzzy Forecast Combiner

We developed a forecast combiner that calculates the final forecast as a weighted average of forecasts generated by independent methods. The combiner increases the weights of the more accurate methods over time, achieving an adaptive learning process. The distinctive feature of the combiner is the use of *fuzzy logic* in forecast combination operations.

The theory of fuzzy sets is firstly introduced by Zadeh. Fuzzy sets have been used in many different areas such as control system design, decision making, clustering and optimization in the last decades. In general, a fuzzy logic system (FLS) is a nonlinear mapping of an input data (feature) vector into a scalar output (the vector output case decomposes into a collection of independent multi input single-output systems). The richness of fuzzy logic (FL) is that there are enormous numbers of possibilities that lead to lots of different mappings [23].

In literature, two different approaches are proposed for forecast combination with fuzzy systems and fuzzy sets: In the first suggestion, fuzzy systems are used as a kind of ruling model, so two or more various forecasting models are used actively at one time [15]. In the second approach, the features of fuzzy systems are brought the fore as the capability of modeling linguistic and subjective knowledge [16, 20, 27]. Different forecasting methods based on soft computing have been considered [3, 31, 35].

The proposed fuzzy forecast combiner has a flexible structure as illustrated in Fig. 7.10. Like the other FLS, the proposed fuzzy forecast combiner maps crisp

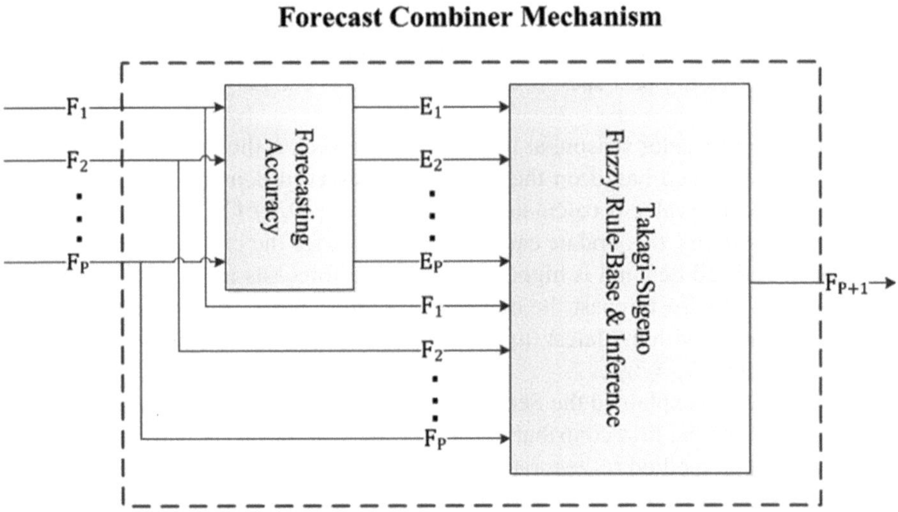

Fig. 7.10 The proposed fuzzy forecast combiner

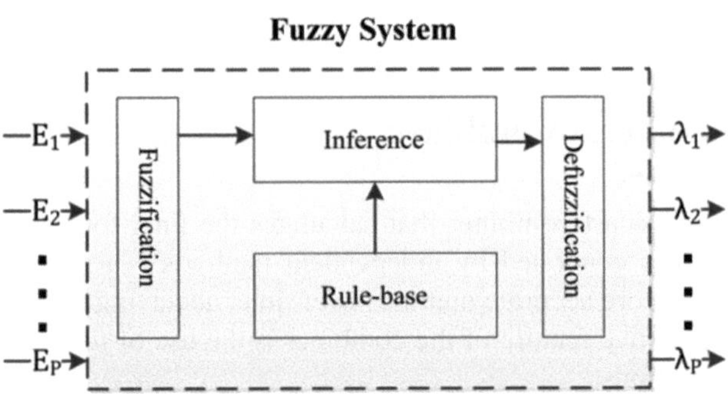

Fig. 7.11 The fuzzy system used in the proposed combiner

inputs into crisp outputs. It contains four components as seen in Fig. 7.11: fuzzifier, rules, inference engine, and defuzzifier. Once the rules have been established by the experts, fuzzy combiner can be viewed as a mapping from inputs to outputs, and this nonlinear mapping can be expressed quantitatively as $y = f(z)$.

The inputs are forecasting methods F_i and their forecast errors E_i. The total number of forecasting methods used in combiner P can be easily increased. Forecast errors E_i can be measured using one of the methods given below [20]:

- MAPE Mean Absolute Percentage Error
- MdAPE Median Absolute Percentage Error
- sMAPE Symmetric Mean Absolute Percentage Error
- sMdAPE Symmetric Median Absolute Percentage Error
- MdRAE Median Relative Absolute Error

- GMRAE Geometric Mean Relative Absolute Error
- MASE Mean Absolute Scaled Error

Rules may be provided by experts or can be extracted from numerical data using a learning algorithm. In either case, engineering rules are expressed as a collection of IF-THEN statements. Consequently, the proposed fuzzy combiner is a rule based fuzzy system where the relationships between the variables are represented by means of fuzzy IF-THEN rules as seen in Fig. 7.11. The rule-base block has the fuzzy IF-THEN rules having the following general form:

IF < antecedent proposition > **THEN** < consequent proposition >

Depending on the form of the consequent, two main types of rule based fuzzy system are distinguished: Mamdani fuzzy model and Takagi-Sugeno (T-S) fuzzy model. Mamdani-type fuzzy models have linguistic IF-THEN rules with fuzzy proposition in the antecedent as well as in the consequent. However The Takagi – Sugeno fuzzy model uses crisp functions in the consequents.

The proposed fuzzy combiner uses T-S type fuzzy rules. The antecedent propositions are forecast errors E_i $(i = 1, 2, \ldots, P)$, where P is the total number of the forecasting methods entering the combiner. Similarly, consequent propositions are weights of forecasting methods λ_i $(i = 1, 2, \ldots, P)$ which form linear combination of forecasting methods. In addition, the T-norm (and) in antecedent proposition is preferred as product operation.

The fuzzifier maps crisp numbers into fuzzy sets. There are two classes of fuzzifiers in literature as singleton and nonsingleton (triangular, Gaussian, trapezoidal, etc.). For this project, singleton type of fuzzification is preferred in order to decrease the computational complexity.

The inference engine of the FLS maps fuzzy sets into fuzzy sets. It handles the way in which rules are combined. Just as we humans use many different types of inferential procedures to help us understand things or to make decisions, there are many different fuzzy logic inferential procedures. Only a very small number of them are actually being used in engineering applications of FL.

In many applications, crisp numbers must be obtained at the output of a FLS. The output of the fuzzy combiner is the forecasted demand so this value should be also a crisp number. The defuzzifier maps output sets into crisp numbers, and so weighted average defuzzification method is used for the proposed fuzzy combiner.

The output of the fuzzy combiner F_{P+1} can be calculated as

$$F_{P+1} = \sum\nolimits_{i=1}^{P} F_i \lambda_i$$

where λ_i denotes the weight of the corresponding forecasting method F_i. Then λ_i is calculated as [26]:

$$\lambda_i = \frac{\sum\nolimits_{y=1}^{K} b^{(j,k,\ldots,l;i,p)_y} \mu_1^j \mu_2^k \cdots \mu_P^l}{\Sigma_{\mathrm{i}}^{\mathrm{K}} \mu_1^j \mu_2^k \cdots \mu_P^l}$$

Table 7.1 Parameters of the fuzzy forecast combiner

E_i	Inputs of fuzzy system $(i=1,2,\ldots,P)$
λ_i	Outputs of fuzzy system $(i=1,2,\ldots,P)$
F_i	Forecasting method $(i=1,2,\ldots,P)$
P	Total number of forecasting methods
N_i	Number of input membership functions of E_i $(i=1,2,\ldots,P)$
M_i	Number of output membership functions of λ_i $(i=1,2,\ldots,P)$
$\mathcal{U}_i$	Universe of discourse for inputs E_i $(i=1,2,\ldots,P)$ $\mathcal{U}_i = [0, 100]$
$\tilde{u}_i$	Linguistic variable input of E_i defined over $\mathcal{U}_i$ $(i=1,2,\ldots,P)$
$\mathcal{Y}_i$	Universes of discourse for outputs λ_i $(i=1,2,\ldots,P)$ $\mathcal{Y}_i = [0, 1]$
$\tilde{y}_i$	Linguistic variable output of λ_i defined over $\mathcal{Y}_i$
$\tilde{A}_i^j$	The jth linguistic value of $\tilde{u}_i$ $(i=1,2,\ldots,P$ and $j=1,2,\ldots,N_i)$
B_i^p	The pth linguistic value of $\tilde{y}_i$ $(i=1,2,\ldots,P$ and $p=1,2,\ldots,M_i)$
μ_i^j	Output of the ith antecedent proposition input of jth membership function $\mu_i^j \in [0,1]$
$b^{(j,k,\ldots,l;i,p)_y}$	Output of the ith consequent proposition function for the yth rule $b^{(j,k,\ldots,l;i,p)_y} \in [0, 1]$

where $b^{(j,k,\ldots,l;i,p)_y}$ is the output of the ith consequent proposition function for the yth rule $(1 \le j \le N_1, 1 \le k \le N_2, \ldots, 1 \le l \le N_P,\ i=1,2,\ldots,P$ and $p=1,2,\ldots,M_i)$. Here $(j,k,\ldots,l;i,p)_y$ represents y^{th} rule of decomposed multi input multi output (MIMO) rule forms into multi input single output (MISO) forms which satisfies the "completeness" (i.e., whether there are conclusions for every possible input) and "consistency" (i.e., whether conclusions that rules make conflict with the other rules) properties given below:

$$\textbf{IF } \tilde{u}_1 \ is \ \tilde{A}_1^j \text{ and } \tilde{u}_2 \text{ is } \tilde{A}_2^k \text{ and}, \ldots, \text{and } \tilde{u}_p \text{ is } \tilde{A}_p^l \textbf{ THEN } \tilde{y}_i \ is \ B_i^p$$

Here, $\tilde{u}_i$ is the linguistic variable of fuzzy system input E_i $(i=1,2,\ldots,P)$ defined over $\mathcal{U}_i$ where $\mathcal{U}_i$ is the universe of discourse for fuzzy system inputs. $\tilde{A}_i^j$ is the jth linguistic value of $\tilde{u}_i$ $(j=1,2,\ldots,N_i)$ and N_i is the number of input membership functions of E_i. Similarly, $\tilde{y}_i$ is the linguistic variable of fuzzy system output λ_i $(i=1,2,\ldots,P)$ defined over $\mathcal{Y}_q$ where $\mathcal{Y}_i$ is the universe of discourse for fuzzy system output $\mathcal{Y}_i = [0, 1]$. B_i^p is the pth linguistic value of $\tilde{y}_i$ $(p=1,2,\ldots,M_i)$ and M_i is the number of the output membership functions of λ_i. μ_i^j represents the output of the ith antecedent proposition input of jth membership function and K is the number of rules given as $K = \prod_{i=1}^{P} N_i$. Therefore F_{P+1} is the linear combination of forecasting methods F_i with their weights λ_i. The parameters of the proposed fuzzy combiner are presented in Table 7.1.

7.4 Simulation Study

In this section, we present the results from a simulation study that has two purposes. First, we illustrate how the fuzzy combiner adjusts combination weights in response to demand realizations. Second, we compare the overall accuracy of the combined forecast with the individual forecasting methods it combines, as well as with a number of other alternative forecasting methods.

The fuzzy combiner in the simulation study combines the forecasts from the following three independent forecast methods:

SPB: This is the Seasonal Pattern Based method we developed which is discussed in Sect. 7.2. The seasonal pattern is generated using the year 2011 data.

MA(2): With this two-period moving averages method, the forecast is calculated as the average of the latest 2 weeks' sales values. That is, $F_{t+1} = (D_{t-1} + D_t)/2$. Moving averages method, in general, is not designed to work with data that has long-run trend. Yet, it may work reasonably well when the trend in data series changes direction frequently, as it is the case with our data. Such simple forecasting methods are reported to often outperform more sophisticated ones such as ARIMA [14].

ZARA: This simple forecasting method is mentioned in a Zara case study [10]. The forecast F_{t+1} is calculated by multiplying the sales in the previous week D_t with a seasonality factor. The seasonality factor is simply the ratio of week $t+1$ sales to week t sales in the preceding season. That is, $F_{t+1} = D_t(DP_{t+1}/DP_t)$. Correra [10] reports this method to be successful in forecasting the demand of fashion products with short life cycles.

Note that the three methods differ in the data they use. The moving average method uses only the current season's sales data. Zara method uses sales data from previous season as well. In addition to using this season's and last season's sales data extensively, SPB method also allows input of opinions from product managers.

Forecast accuracy in the simulation study is measured with Symmetric Mean Absolute Percentage Error (SMAPE) defined as $\text{SMAPE} = (1/n)\sum_{t=1}^{n}((|D_t - F_t|)/(D_t + F_t))$. SMAPE has both a lower bound and an upper bound. It generates a percentage error between 0 % and 100 % which is easy to interpret. In addition, SMAPE is a good choice for the fuzzy rules because no input scaling factors are needed for the fuzzy rule-based system.

The antecedent proposition in the combiner has three variables, namely the SMAPE values of each forecast method. Each SMAPE is labeled by two linguistic terms (High, Low) that are defined with two trapezoidal membership functions. Therefore, for this simulation study, eight fuzzy rules are developed with the help of the experts. Below, we present the fifth and sixth rules as examples:

Rule 5: IF SMAPE_1 *High* AND SMAPE_2 *Low* AND SMAPE_3 *Low* **THEN** $f_5 = 0.1F_1 + 0.45F_2 + 0.45F_3$

Rule 6: IF SMAPE_1 *High* AND SMAPE_2 *Low* AND SMAPE_3 *High* **THEN** $f_6 = 0.1F_1 + 0.8F_2 + 0.1F_3$

The simulation uses the weekly sales data of a particular slim-cut men's shirt category in a particular large store of a Turkish apparel firm (This is the same data used in the Sect. 7.2 example). The first 40 weeks of year 2012 is considered, and data is distorted for confidentiality purposes.

At each step of the simulation, the fuzzy combiner generates a demand forecast for a particular week, by calculating a weighted average of the forecasts generated by the three input methods for that week. Initial weight of each method is set to 0.33. Next, using the realized sales data for the week, the SMAPE forecast errors of the three methods are calculated. The combination weights are then updated based on the last 2 weeks' SMAPE error values of the individual forecast methods. A method that obtains low SMAPE value compared to the other two will increase its weight at the expense of the other methods. Note that this simulation study does not involve any probabilistic input with respect to sales data. Instead, realized 2012 weekly sales values are used.

Figures 7.12 and 7.13 present the forecasts, and forecast error $F_t - D_t$ values of the three methods, and of the resulting combined forecast (denoted with FC). Figures 7.14 and 7.15 present the weekly SMAPE error values and the combination weights of the three methods. While there is no dominant winner among the three methods, we observe the SPB method to be the most accurate. The method is particularly successful in capturing the overall sales pattern, as it is designed for. The moving average method, on the other hand, is not responsive enough to catch the sharp reversals in demand trend. The ZARA method is quite accurate in the first 15 weeks, however it fails around weeks 16–20. To capture seasonality, this simple method uses only the week-to-week changes in the previous season's data. It does not attempt to decouple seasonality-related changes in demand from changes related to other factors, such as those related to price.

After illustrating the use of the fuzzy combiner using the simulation results, we next comment on its forecast accuracy. Table 7.2 compares the accuracy of the combined forecast (FC) with the three individual methods (SPB, ZARA, MA(2)), as well as some alternative methods (Moving Average with 3 and 5 weeks, as well as Exponential Smoothing with alpha 0.3 and 0.7). We observe the combined forecast to be much more accurate than all of the presented alternatives, according to MAE, MSE, RMSE and MAPE measures. Note that in addition to providing improved forecast accuracy, the forecast combiner is quite practical to use. This is because the combiner is totally automated, and because it does not require additional data input beyond what is needed by the individual forecasting methods it combines.

7.5 Conclusions

In this chapter, we present a practical approach to generate forecasts at SKU and store detail in the apparel industry. These forecasts constitute the core input of a larger decision support system that aids apparel managers in matching supply and demand across stores. Improved forecasts are likely to increase operational efficiency and profitability in this highly competitive industry.

We develop a forecasting method (Seasonal Pattern Based Forecasting, SPB) that aims to uncover the inherent seasonality in product category demand. To this end,

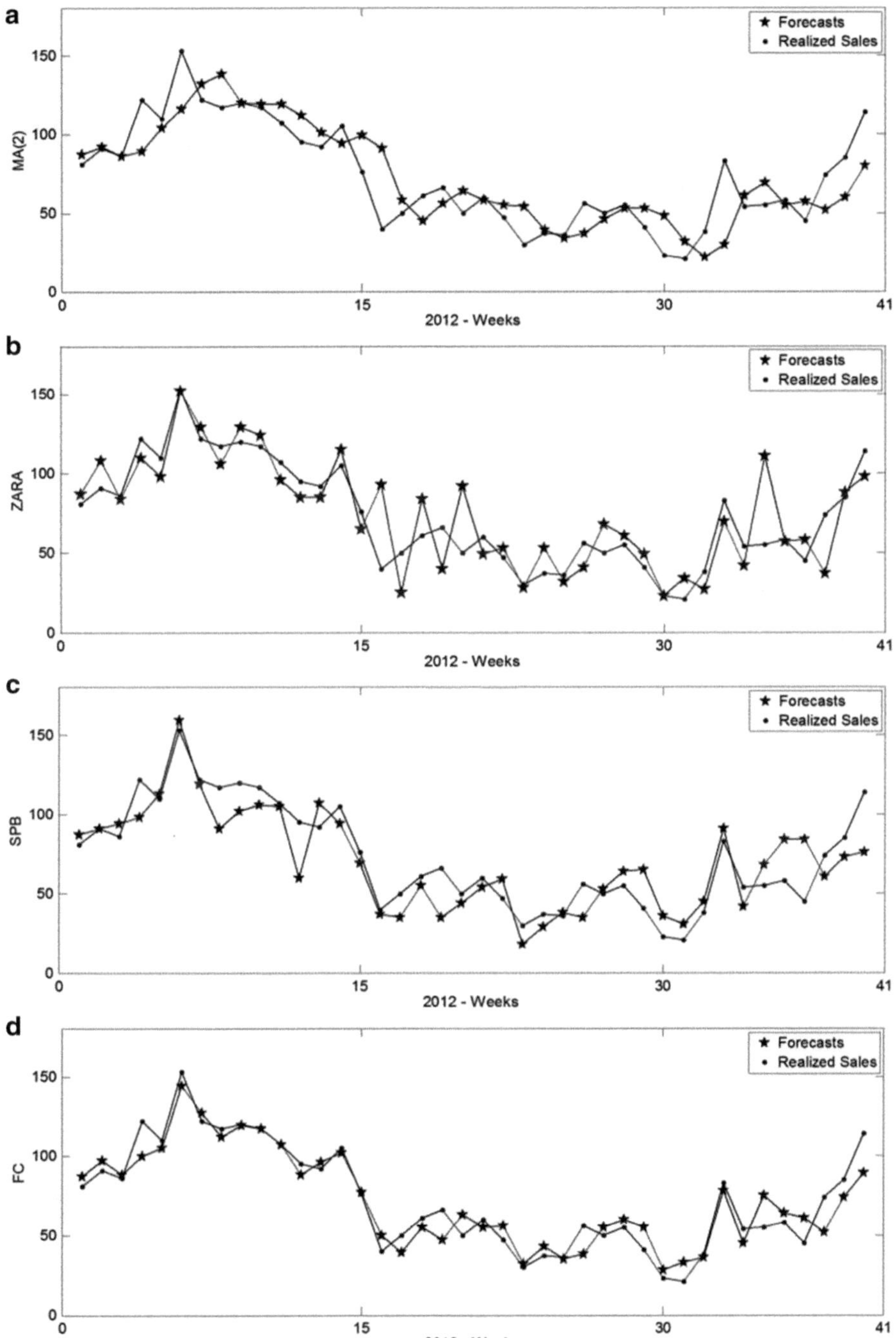

Fig. 7.12 Comparison of forecasts and realized sales

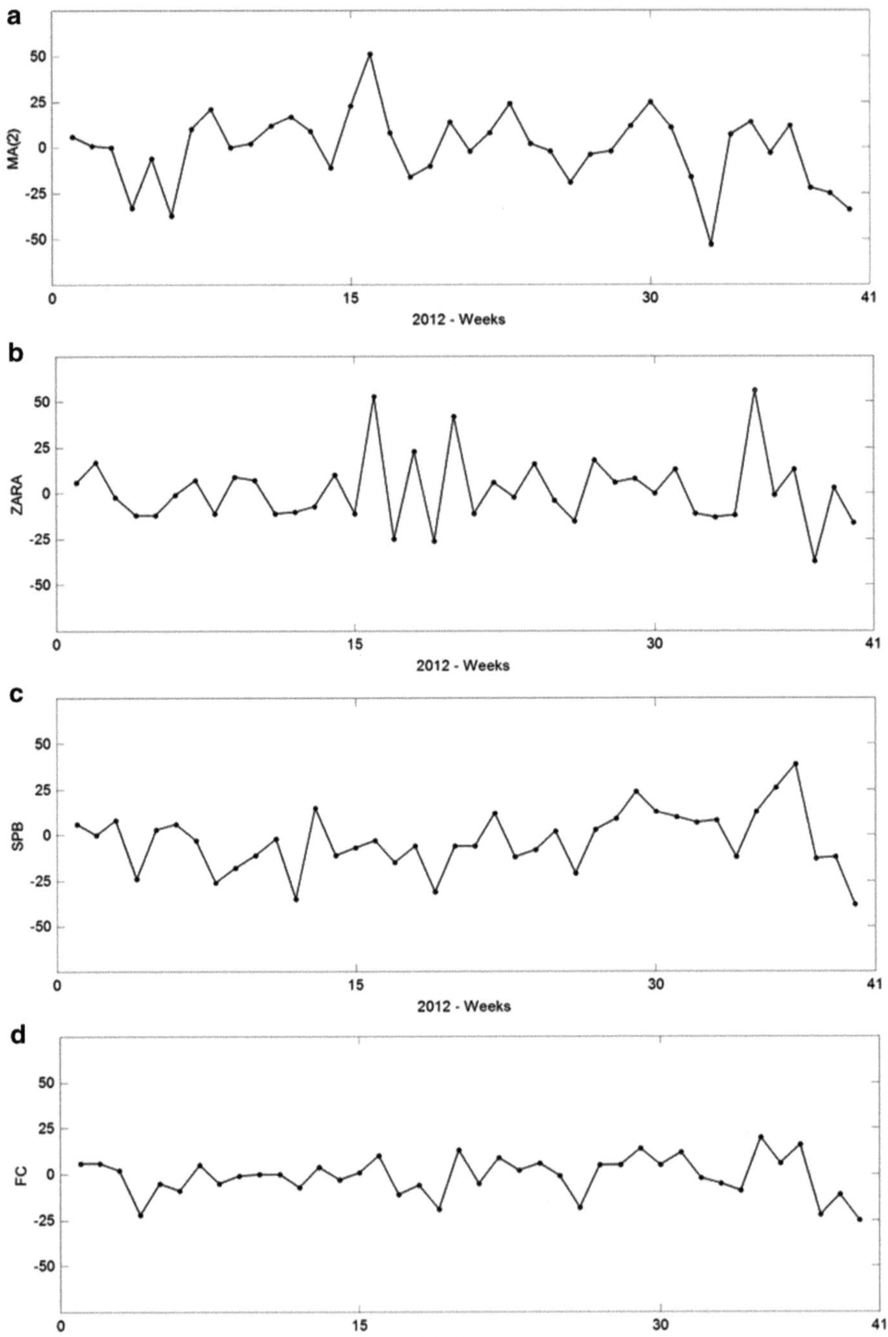

Fig. 7.13 Forecast errors (F_t-D_t)

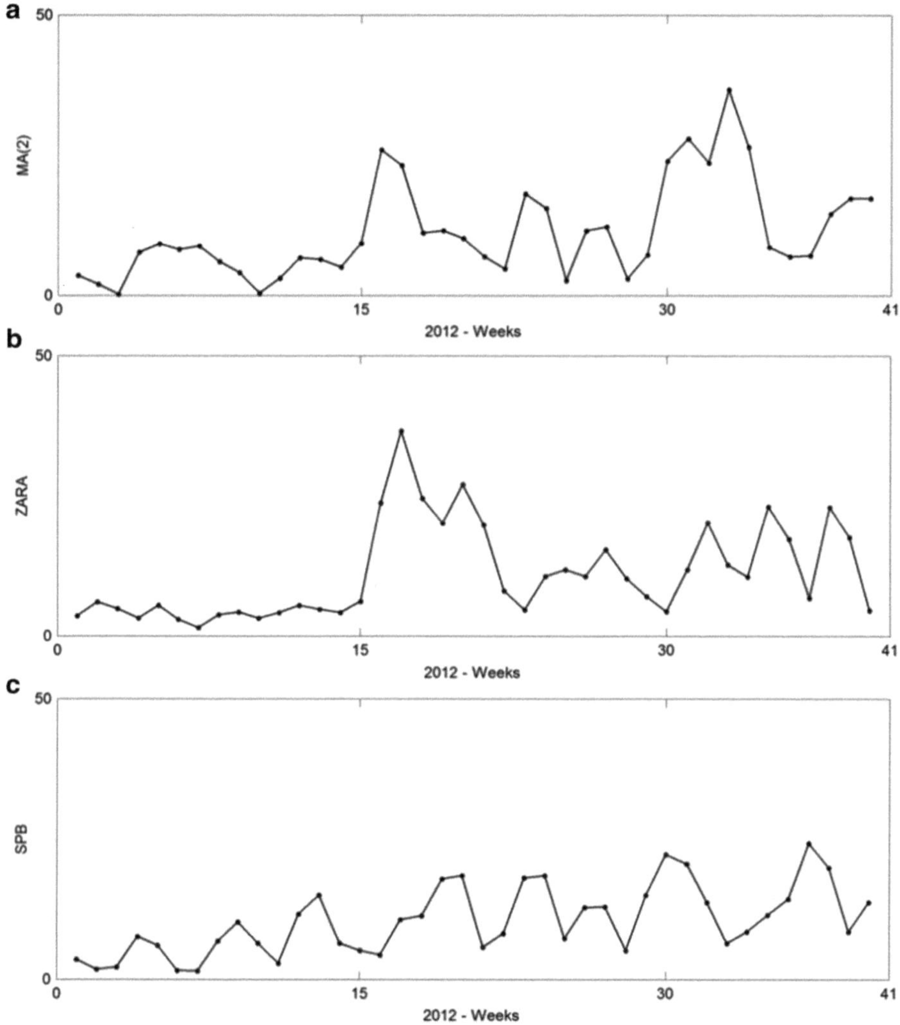

Fig. 7.14 SMAPE error values

the method estimates and removes the effects of lost sales, pricing and unsystematic events on demand. The method also allows an easy interface for product managers to reflect their related qualitative knowledge.

In addition to characterizing the underlying seasonal demand pattern, our procedure also produces estimates of lost sales, and of the effects of special events and pricing on demand. In particular, the procedure yields the category demand function that illustrates how demand changes in response to changes in sales price. This function can be used as a pricing and revenue management tool.

While the SPB forecasting method appears successful, one can achieve even better results by combining its results with other methods' results. To this end,

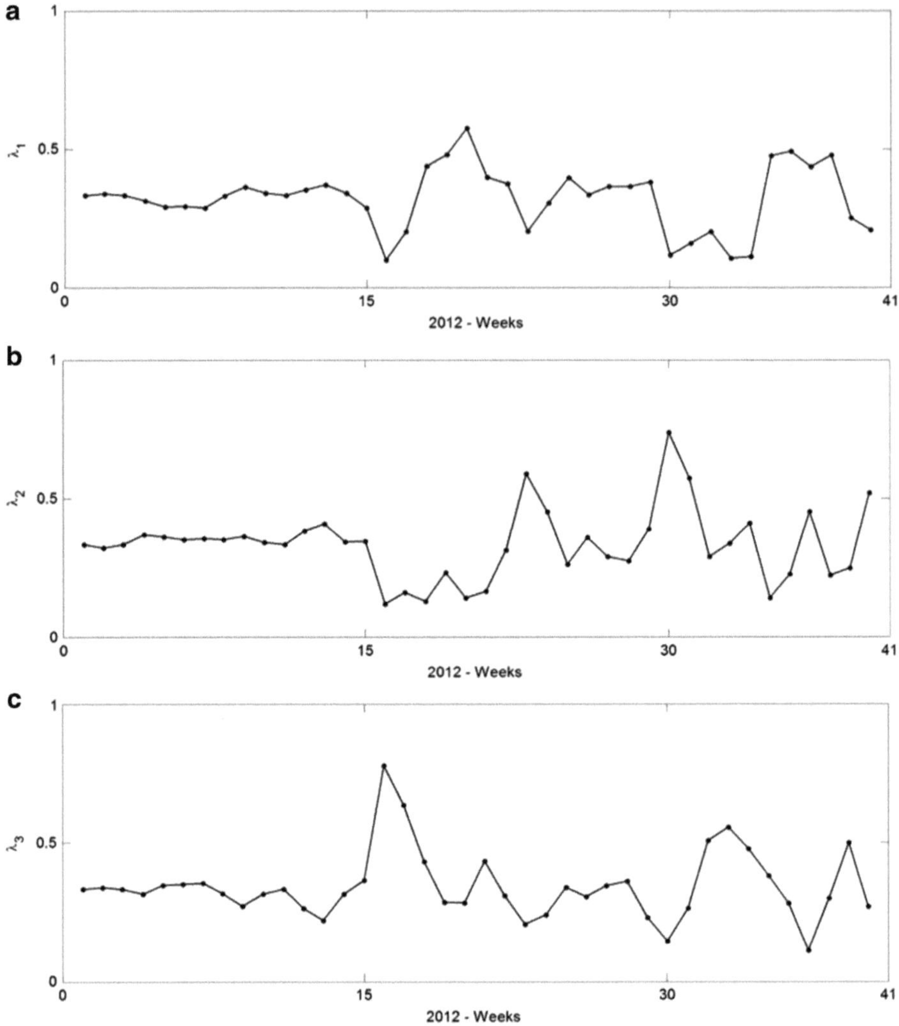

Fig. 7.15 Combination weights

Table 7.2 Comparison of forecast accuracy

Forecast accuracy	Combined forecast	SPB	ZARA	MA(2)	MA(3)	MA(5)	ES(0.3)	ES(0.7)
MAE	8.33	13.10	14.08	14.60	16.38	16.63	15.65	13.90
MSE	112.43	272.25	360.93	377.70	450.88	475.28	462.35	345.5
RMSE	10.60	16.50	19.00	19.43	21.23	21.80	21.50	18.59
MAPE	14.34 %	21.72 %	24.71 %	24.95 %	27.77 %	29.26 %	27.39 %	22.96 %

we develop a forecast combiner. Using fuzzy logic, the combiner calculates a final forecast for each week's demand as a weighted average of forecasts that are generated by different methods. The combination weights of more accurate forecasts are increased over time at the expense of less accurate methods. This adaptive approach is valuable as it is difficult to know in advance which forecasting method will be more accurate for a given store-category combination, in different phases of the selling season. As illustrated with our simulation example, the combined forecast achieves better accuracy than any of the individual forecasts.

Apparel product managers face an enormous number of store-SKU combinations that call for operational decisions. Forecasts are a key input for most of these decisions. Expecting consistently high forecast accuracy in this industry, even with the most sophisticated forecasting approach, would be unrealistic. This is especially the case for high-fashion apparel. Rather, we aim at improving forecast accuracy by making the most of available data. To obtain real benefits, the firm should complement its improved forecasting capability with efficient supply and distribution processes.

Acknowledgements This study was supported by TÜBİTAK (The Scientific and Technological Research Council of Turkey) TEYDEB Industrial Research Funding Program Grant Numbers 7100373 and 7110387, awarded to GETRON Bilişim Hizmetleri A. Ş. The authors also wish to thank Murat Ercan, Bülent Göven, Gökhan Çetin and COŞKUN HAZIR GİYİM A.Ş. (SÜVARİ) for their help in preparing this chapter.

References

1. Armstrong JS, Collopy F (1998) Integration of statistical methods and judgment for time series forecasting: principles from empirical research. In: Wright G, Goodwin P (eds) Forecasting with judgment. Wiley, New York
2. Armstrong JS (2001) Combining forecasts. In: Armstrong JS (ed) Principles of forecasting: a handbook for researchers and practitioners. Kluwer Academic, Norwell
3. Au K-F, Choi T-M, Yu Y (2008) Fashion retail forecasting by evolutionary neural networks. Int J Prod Econ 114(2):615–630
4. Bates JM, Granger CWJ (1969) The combination of forecasts. Oper Res Q 20:451–468
5. Burruss J, Kuettner D (2002) Forecasting for short-lived products: Hewlett-Packard's journey. J Bus Forecast Methods Syst 21(4):9–14
6. Chan CK, Kingsman BG, Wong H (2004) Determining when to update the weights in combined forecasts for product demand – an application of the CUSUM technique. Eur J Oper Res 153:757–768
7. Chen SM, Chen CD (2011) TAIEX forecasting based on fuzzy time series and fuzzy variation groups. IEEE Trans Fuzzy Syst 19(1):1–12
8. Clemen RT (1989) Combining forecasts: a review and annotated bibliography (with discussion). Int J Forecast 5:559–583
9. Collopy F, Armstrong JS (1992) Expert opinions about extrapolation and the mystery of the overlooked discontinuities. Int J Forecast 8:575–582
10. Correa J (2007) Optimization of a fast-response distribution network. Unpublished master's thesis, Massachusetts Institute of Technology, Cambridge
11. Deutsch M, Granger CWJ, Terasvirta T (1994) The combination of forecasts using changing weights. Int J Forecast 10:47–57

12. Elliott G, Timmermann A (2005) Optimal forecast combination weights under regime switching. Int Econ Rev 46(4):1081–1102
13. Fildes R, Goodwin P (2007) Against your better judgment? How organizations can improve their use of management judgment in forecasting. Interfaces 37(6):570–576
14. Fildes R, Makridakis S (1995) The impact of empirical accuracy studies on time series analysis and forecasting. Int Stat Rev 63:289–308
15. Fiordaliso A (1998) A nonlinear forecasts combination method based on Takagi-Sugeno fuzzy systems. Int J Forecast 14(3):367–379
16. Frantti T, Mähönen P (2001) Fuzzy logic-based forecasting model. Eng Appl Artif Intel 14(2):189–201
17. Granger CWJ (1989) Combining forecasts-twenty years later. J Forecast 8:167–173
18. Granger CWJ, Newbold P (1986) Forecasting economic time series, 2nd edn. Academic, New York
19. Hammond JH, Kelly M (1991) Quick response in the apparel industry. Harvard Business School Case Study
20. Hyndman RJ, Koehler AB (2006) Another look at measures of forecast accuracy. Int J Forecast 22(4):679–688
21. Kumbasar T, Eksin I, Guzelkaya M, Yesil E (2011) Adaptive fuzzy model based inverse controller design using BB-BC optimization algorithm. Expert Syst Appl 38(10):12356–12364
22. Makridakis S, Hibon M (2000) The M3-competitions: results, conclusions and implications. Int J Forecast 16:451–476
23. Mendel JM (1995) Fuzzy logic systems for engineering: a tutorial. Proc IEEE 83:345–377
24. Mrinalini S (2012) Fuzzy based trend mapping and forecasting for time series data. Expert Syst Appl 39(7):6351–6358
25. Newbold P, Granger CWJ (1974) Experience with forecasting univariate time series and the combination of forecasts. J Royal Stat Soc Ser A 137:131–165
26. Passino K, Yurkovich S (1998) Fuzzy control. Addison Wesley, Reading
27. Petrovic D, Xie Y, Burnham K (2006) Fuzzy decision support system for demand forecasting with a learning mechanism. Fuzzy Set Syst 157(12):1713–1725
28. Richardson J (1996) Vertical integration and rapid response in fashion apparel. Organ Sci 7(4):400–412
29. Sen A (2008) The US fashion industry: a supply chain review. Int J Prod Econ 114(2):571–593
30. Stock J, Watson M (2001) A comparison of linear and nonlinear univariate models for forecasting macroeconomic time series. In: Engle R, White H (eds) Cointegration, causality, and forecasting: a festschrift in honour of Clive Granger. Oxford University Press, Oxford, pp 1–44
31. Sun Z-L, Choi T-M, Au K-F, Yu Y (2008) Sales forecasting using extreme learning machine with applications in fashion retailing. Decis Support Syst 46(1):411–419
32. Timmermann A (2006) Forecast Combinations. In: Elliott G, Granger CWJ, Timmermann A (eds) Handbook of economic forecasting. North Holland, Amsterdam, pp 135–196
33. Winkler RL, Makridakis S (1983) The combination of forecasts. J Royal Stat Soc Ser A 146:150–157
34. Yesil E, Kaya M, Siradag S (2012) Fuzzy forecast combiner design for fast fashion demand forecasting. In: International symposium on innovations in intelligent systems and applications (INISTA2012), Trabzon
35. Yu Y, Choi T-M, Hui C-L (2011) An intelligent fast sales forecasting model for fashion products. Expert Syst Appl 38(6):7373–7379
36. Zadeh LA (1965) Fuzzy sets. Info Control 8:338–353
37. Zadeh LA (1989) Knowledge representation in fuzzy logic. IEEE Trans Knowl Data Eng 1(1):89–100
38. Zellner A, Hong C, Min C-K (1991) Forecasting turning points in international output growth rates using Bayesian exponentially weighted autoregression, time-varying parameter, and pooling techniques. J Econom 49:275–304

Chapter 8
Intelligent Fashion Colour Trend Forecasting Schemes: A Comparative Study

Yong Yu, Sau-Fun Ng, Chi-Leung Hui, Na Liu, and Tsan-Ming Choi

Abstract The colour of a fashion item is one of its key features which often play an important role on the purchase decisions of consumers. And the fashionable colours often prevail in one season, thus, it is crucial for the fashion industry to do forecasting of the fashion trends, especially on colours, prior to the beginning the production for the target season. The lead-time of forecasting becomes shorter recent years with the intensified competition of global fashion industry, and imposes pressure on the forecasting of fashion colour trends. The common practise for the forecasting of colour trends in the fashion industry are based on the ideals of field experts, and the forecasting is in nature fuzzy and hard to be substituted by analytical models. In this paper, we explore the forecasting of colour trends by artificial intelligence models, especially artificial neural network and fuzzy logic models; we observed that such models help to improve the forecasting of fashion colour trends.

8.1 Introduction

Change is the everlasting trend of fashion product in nature. And the fashion industry faces innovation all the time, mostly of which is on style instead of technical features, e.g. creativity in cut, colours and relative combinations, patterns, fabrics and their processing and finishing .... Colours, fabrics and styles are some of the key features of the design of fashion products, and the fashion product consumers often judge a fashion product based on such features and make purchase decisions based on these judgement. Colour is the especially important feature in that it influences not only the purchase decision of consumers, but also the

Y. Yu • S.-F. Ng • C.-L. Hui • N. Liu (✉) • T.-M. Choi
Business Division, Institute of Textiles and Clothing, The Hong Kong Polytechnic University, Hung Hom, Kowloon, Hong Kong, China
e-mail: 08900900r@connect.polyu.hk

T.-M. Choi et al. (eds.), *Intelligent Fashion Forecasting Systems: Models and Applications*, DOI 10.1007/978-3-642-39869-8_8,

production process of the fashion industries. The mass productive of fabrics must be prior to the sales season, often with quite a long lead time in terms of months or years because there is usually a large and sophisticated supply chain involved. Hence it is very important to conduct an accurate forecasting of the colour trend of fashion. The fashion colour trends often prevail in a whole season, and there will be no chance of remedy for a wrong forecasting discovered when the sales season begins, as the whole supply chain processes will all be influenced by the decision of colour trends. Therefore, colour trend forecasting had always been an essential part of the fashion forecasting and trend prediction.

In the common experience of fashion industry, the forecasting of colour trends often depends on the personal experience and judgement of the field experts, and such process is often found underperforming [3]. Many research works have been devoted in improving the forecasting of fashion colour trends, such as in [2, 4], soft system methodology is adopted in providing a systematically way of modelling and understanding the subjective perceptions of experts, and hence improve the forecasting results. Other researches on fashion colour trend also becomes popular recently, many of which based on the historical data analysis, or time series methodology [5]. There are many statistical models such as Bayesian forecasting, linear regression and Auto Regression Integrated Moving Average (ARIMA) which are commonly used for time series forecasting. But all such models like ARIMA come with some statistical assumptions, such as the trend and cycle components of time series are presumed in ARIMA. These models perform well when these assumptions are valid, while in practice, there may be no obvious trend and cycle in highly volatile time series, like what the fashion trend time series are, and these traditional regression based models may not always perform well.

To deal with the highly volatile feature of fashion trends, many research works seek helps from the Artificial Intelligence (AI) models. Such as in [12], a fashion sales trend forecasting based on an revised Artificial Neural Network (ANN) model is developed, and promising results are reported. In [1, 11, 15, 16], some models based on ANN or its hybrid forms with other models are explored, and the application of them on fashion sales forecasting are also found with better accuracies than traditional models. The forecasting of fashion colour trends has more volatility and fuzziness than does the sales forecasting, so when it is taken into consideration, many research works employ models which are specifically good at treating fuzziness. For example in [9], the Gray Method (GM) and some of its hybrid forms with ANN are studied, and the GM is found to produce better accuracy. In [16], similar forms of GM is devised and its performance are also found promising.

In the empirical forecasting of fashion colour trend, the practitioners in the industry often cares only on the 'key' fashion colours (http://www.fashion-era.com/), instead of foreseeing the trends for all colours. And when the above works have verified that the AI models are ideal tools for modelling the fashion sales forecasting, the fashion colour trends are substantially very fuzzy and hard to be captured, and few models are used for colour trends forecasting in the literature. In this paper, we propose to perform the forecasting of it by Fuzzy Neural Networks (FNN), which forecasting on the fashion colour time series to produce the trends by

Fuzzy terms like *popular, neutral and unpopular*..., so that the FNN models can help to identify the key fashion colour trend.

The rest of the paper are organised as follows: The colour trend data which is used in our analysis are briefed in Sect. 8.2, and the discussions on the models are given in Sect. 8.3, we present the forecasting results, comparisons and discussions in Sect. 8.4, and concluded in Sect. 8.5.

8.2 Fashion Colour Trend Data

In Table 8.1, the sales data of knitwear in seven different colours from a Cashmere knitwear company are listed. The data contain sales data from 2006 to 2009. The weight in gm of each given colour of cashmere garment is recorded. The seven colours are *Yellow, Cream, Dark Green, Purple, Light Grey, Dark Brown* and *Black*. As we have mentioned, the forecasting in the sales of colours in quantity is highly volatile and fuzzy, the data in Table 8.1 is transformed into proportional data in Table 8.2, where the proportion of the sales of each colour in the total sales in a given year is used, as is given by $X'_{t,i} = X_{t,i}/\sum_{c=1}^{7} X_{t,c}$, where t denotes the year index and $t \in [1,4]$, i is the index of a colour and $i \in [1,7]$, $X_{t,i}$ is the sales quantity of colour i of the year t, $X'_{t,i}$ is the proportion of the sales of colour i in the total sales in the year t.

Table 8.1 The sales data for cashmere of different colours (gm)

	Year			
Colour code of cashmere	2006	2007	2008	2009
Yellow	22,900	80,445	148,330	164,255
Cream	17,730	182,670	223,175	154,885
Dark green	88,990	115,050	43,320	75,760
Purple	109,375	430,615	455,150	418,230
Light grey	153,995	197,485	121,945	55,810
Dark brown	78,680	249,680	161,770	91,905
Black	156,000	78,235	14,920	31,850

Table 8.2 The popularity of colours (proportions of total yearly sales)

	Year			
Colour code of cashmere	2006	2007	2008	2009
Yellow	0.036484	0.060295	0.126929	0.165464
Cream	0.028247	0.136916	0.190975	0.156025
Dark green	0.141778	0.086233	0.03707	0.076317
Purple	0.174256	0.322756	0.38948	0.421308
Light grey	0.245344	0.14802	0.10435	0.056221
Dark brown	0.125352	0.187141	0.138429	0.092581
Black	0.248538	0.058639	0.012767	0.032084

Fig. 8.1 "Colour of the year" from Pantone

Pantone Matching System (PMS) is a proprietary colour space invented by Pantone Inc., and used in a variety of industries, such as the fashion industry with coloured fabric, and plastics (http://www.pantone.com). Annually, Pantone declares a particular colour "Colour of the Year" which indicates the colour trend for the next year. For example, the colour for 2013 was chosen in the spring of 2012. The results of the "Colour of the Year" are published in Pantone View, which fashion designers and many other consumer-oriented companies purchase to help guide their designs and planning for future products.

In Fig. 8.1, 13 consecutive years (from 2000 to 2012) of "Colour of the Year" are listed. The colours come with a descriptive name and a corresponding Pantone code, e.g. the colour of the year 2011 is 'Honeysuckle' with the code 'Pantone 18-2120'. A Pantone code in the format of 'AA-BBCC' defines a specific colour in the PMS colour space, where 'AA' is corresponding to the Lightness, 'BB' is corresponding to the Hue and 'CC' is corresponding to the Chroma. Details about the Pantone colour codes are given in the next section. Using these historical "Colour of the Year", we can analyse on the change of colour trends based on the time series analysis and provide insights on future colour trends in another profile beyond the experts' view.

8.3 Methodology

In our research, a Fuzzy Neural Network (FNN) is used in the forecasting of fashion colour trends. And some widely used forecasting models, such as ARIMA and

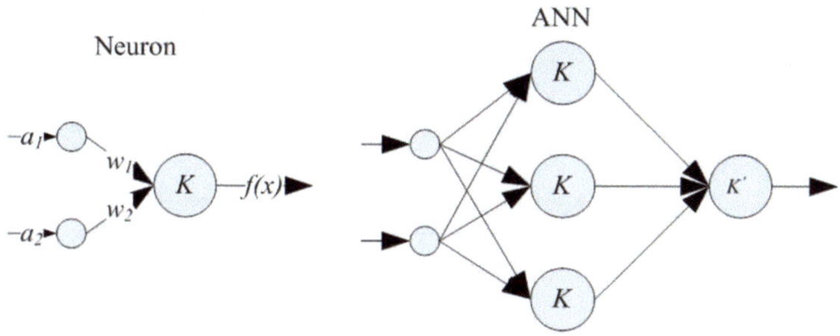

Fig. 8.2 The sample of a neuron and a feed-forward ANN

ANN, are also employed in the forecasting, and their performances are compared with the FNN. These models are discussed in the following.

8.3.1 Autoregressive Integrated Moving Average (ARIMA)

The ARIMA is a commonly used statistical model for the modelling of time series data, which can be fitted to time series data either to better understand the data or to forecast future points in the series. Given a time series of X_t, where t is an integer index and X_t are real numbers, then an ARIMA(p,d,q) model can be given in Eq. 8.1.

$$\left(1-\sum_{i=1}^{p}\varnothing_i L^i\right)(1-L)^d X_t = \left(1+\sum_{i=1}^{q}\theta_i L^i\right)\varepsilon_t \tag{8.1}$$

where L is the lag operator, the $\varnothing_i$ are the parameters of the autoregressive part of the model, the θ_i are the parameters of the moving average part and the ε_t are error terms. The error terms ε_t are generally assumed to be independent, identically distributed variables sampled from a normal distribution with zero mean, p, d, and q are non-negative integers that refer to the order of the autoregressive, integrated, and moving average parts of the model respectively. The ARIMA is widely used in the forecasting of time series, such as in [6], a hybrid model of it is used in the sales forecasting. In this work, we will employ ARIMA in the forecasting of fashion colour trend to study its performance.

8.3.2 Artificial Neural Network (ANN)

Artificial neural networks are inspired on the parallel architecture of animal nerve systems. ANN is consisted of simple processing elements called neurons, which are interconnected, and are often organised in layers, as depicted in Fig. 8.2.

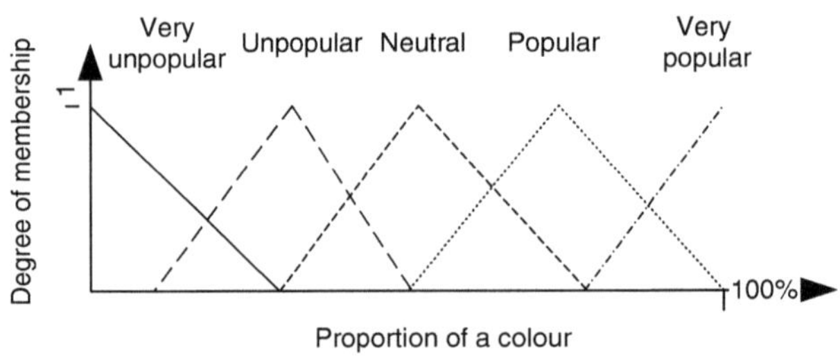

Fig. 8.3 The fuzzy membership functions

A neuron's network function $f(x)$ is defined as a composition of its inputs, which can further be defined as a composition of other functions, and the output of neuron $f(x)$ can also be an input to other neurons, and finally constitute the network structure of ANN. A widely used type of composition is the nonlinear weighted sum, where $f(x) = K\left(\sum_i w_i a_i\right)$, where K is some predefined function, such as the hyperbolic tangent, often known as activate function. The most interesting and useful property of ANN is its ability of learning. In general, an ANN can be considered as a class of functions F, learning means using a set of observations to tune the parameters in the ANN in order to find $f^* \in F$ which approximate the underlying observations in some optimal sense.

There are many variations of the ANN, among them the feed-forward back-propagation network is a popular one which is often used in data approximation and forecasting. Such as in Yu et al. [13], a hybrid form of ANN is used in forecasting of fashion sales. In this work, the feed-forward back-propagation ANN is also employed in the forecasting of fashion colour trends to study its performance as reference to other models.

8.3.3 Fuzzy Logic and Fuzzy Neural Network (FNN)

The trends of fashion colour is in nature volatile and hard to be captured by analytical models, hence the industry practitioners mostly depend on experts judgment on the forecasting of it. Even when the analytical models such as those are discussed previously can be used in such forecasting; the analytical results which are often "accurately" presented in real numbers are often not the ones that are expected to be. In fact, the forecasting of fashion colour trend is not necessarily to be as accurate as how many items of a colour would be sold in the future, instead, it is satisfactory to just identify what colours will be popular in the future. Therefore, to deal with the volatility of fashion trends and to meet the requirement for representing the forecasting result in the proper way as is expected, we proposed to used Fuzzy Logic [17] models to conduct the forecasting task. In our modelling of fashion colour time series, we define five descriptive terms, also known as Fuzzy terms with corresponding score number as: *very popular*(5), *popular*(4), *neutral*(3),

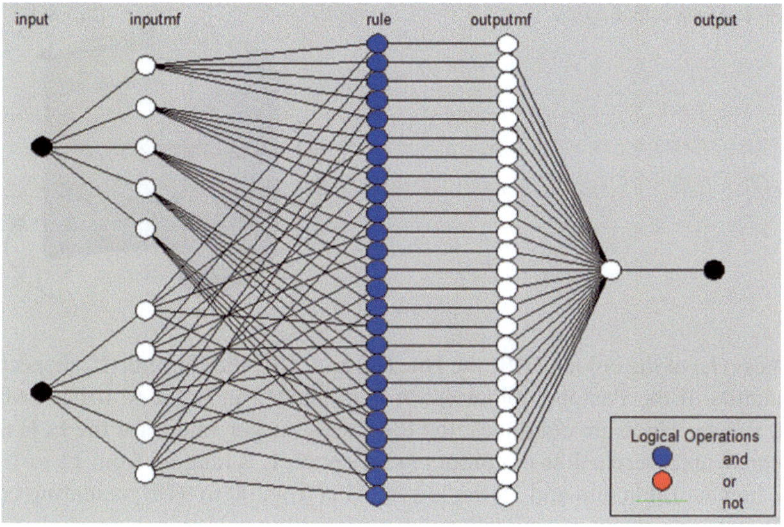

Fig. 8.4 The ANFIS structure

unpopular(2) and *very unpopular*(1). The details of these fuzzy terms are depicted in Fig. 8.3. For any sales quantity in proportions $x \in [0, 100\,\%]$, the value $\mu_{neutral}(x)$ is called the membership degree of x in the fuzzy set *neutral*. The sample membership functions are illustrated in Fig. 8.3, we observed that the shapes of the membership functions are in the shape of triangle. In fact, both the shape and the parameters defining the shape can be varied, and these are actually highly depended on the historical data, i.e. to be learnt from the observations. Therefore the ANN is used in hybridization with the Fuzzy logic to learn its membership functions. Such as Jang [8] and Yu et al. [14] have use Fuzzy Logic combine with ANN to perform inference tasks. In this paper we adopted the ANFIS [8] as an implementation of FNN, to perform the forecasting task for fashion colour trends.

A sample of the ANFIS structure is given in Fig. 8.4. In general, the ANFIS structure is also organised in layers, which is similar to that of the ANN in Fig. 8.1, while the input and output nodes of is substitute by Fuzzy sets, and connections are initiated and ended with the membership functions of terms in those nodes. By the similar back-propagation learning mechanism from ANN, the parameters of the membership functions can be set according to the historical observations, and there is no need for the forecaster to setup or identify the parameters of the descriptive terms.

8.3.4 Analysis of Colour Trends by Historical Pantone Codes

The Pantone Matching System (PMS) is widely adopted in fashion industry; it quantifies a colour by a Pantone code in the shape of 'AA-BBCC', where 'AA' is the

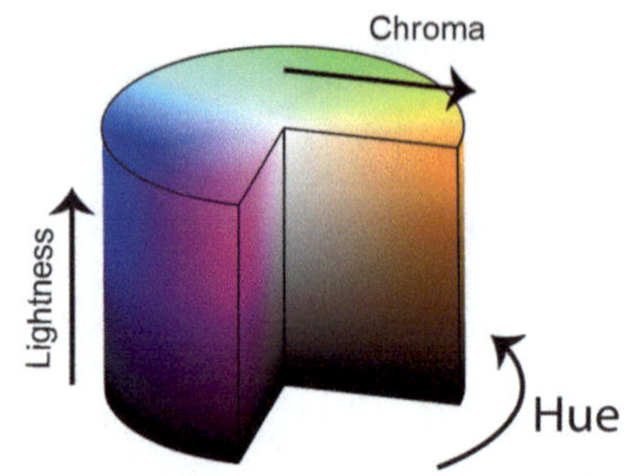

Fig. 8.5 Pantone colour space

Lightness (L) of the colour, 'BB' the Hue (H) and 'CC' the Chroma (C) respectively. The sample of the Pantone colour space is illustrated in Fig. 8.5. Instead of most colour spaces which are continues, the PMS uses integer values for the L, H and C, and represents discrete dots of colours in the space. L is ranging from 11 to 19 with 11 the highest Lightness and 19 the lowest. H is from 00 to 64 representing colours in different Hue, which is an angle value representing colour in a circularly palette, i.e. 00 is adjacent to 64. C is also in the range of 00–64, where 00 is the lowest and 64 the highest.

The colours are divided into seven colour categories by the Hue value, i.e. Green in the range of 55–64–05, Yellow 06–14, Red 15–22, Red-Violet 23–33, Blue-Violet 34–38, Blue 39–46 and Blue-Green 47–54. Although the distinction of seven colour categories helps comprehend the H value and such terms can be modelled by the FNN as discussed previously, the problem size are exponential to the size of fuzzy terms in a FNN, and with the seven terms in one value of H and plus L and C of a colour, the complexity of the forecasting problem, which often uses several historical colours (four in our case) as inputs, are often intractable and short of memory on general computers. Therefore, instead of FNN, we employ the ANN model in the forecasting of colour trends. To further break down the problem size, we conduct separate forecasting on the L, H and C values. The colours of the past 4 years are used as the inputs to forecasting for the colour of the next year. The past 4 years of L are used to forecast the L of the next year, and so does for the H and C, and the forecasted L, H and C are combined to generate the final forecasted colour. The structure of the ANN was depicted in Fig. 8.6.

8.4 Results and Discussion

8.4.1 Forecasting on the Sales of Colours

In our analysis, the three models as discussed in the previous section: ARIMA, ANN and ANFIS are applied on the forecasting of the data in Table 8.2. The observations from the years 2006–2008 are used in the approximation or training

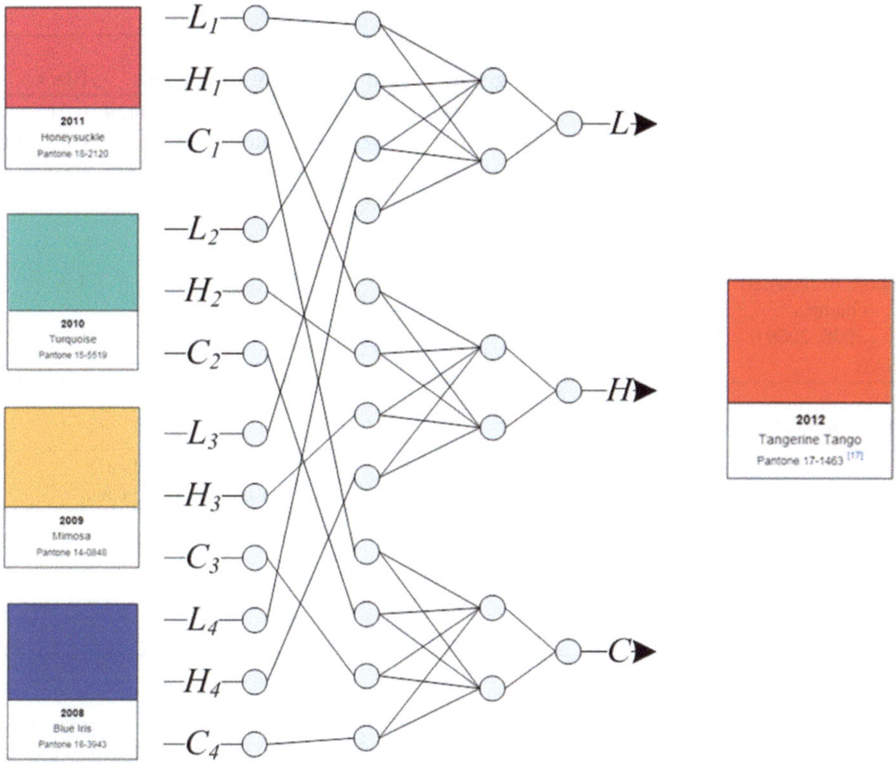

Fig. 8.6 The ANN structure for the forecasting of the colour of 2012 by the historical colour from 2008 to 2011

Table 8.3 The terms of description of change of colour trends

Term	Change in percentage	Score
Very popular	+32 % and beyond	5
Popular	+15–32 %	4
Neutral	+/−14 % of current	3
Unpopular	−15–32 %	2
Very unpopular	−32 % and beyond	1

of the models and the observations from the year 2009 is used for the verification of the forecasting performances. Instead of forecasting of the actual sales for specific colour, we forecast the changes of the fashion colour trends. We set five terms for describing the changes of trends, and a k-means clustering with $k = 5$ is executed on the change of data, and the differentiation of terms are thus obtained and as is described in Table 8.3.

In the analysis by ARIMA and ANN, the mapping between forecasted real values to the terms follows what is described in Table 8.3. As for the analysis of ANFIS

Table 8.4 The ARIMA forecasting result

	Yellow	Cream	Dark green	Purple	Light grey	Dark brown	Black
2008	0.126929	0.190975	0.03707	0.38948	0.10435	0.138429	0.012767
2009	0.165464	0.156025	0.076317	0.421308	0.056221	0.092581	0.032084
2009 forecasted	0.10246	0.15386	0.0321	0.35981	0.09568	0.12734	0.00713
Score (actual changes 2008–2009)	4	2	5	3	1	2	5
Score (forecasted changes 2008–2009)	2	2	3	3	3	3	1
SAE	11						

Table 8.5 The ANN forecasting result

	Yellow	Cream	Dark green	Purple	Light grey	Dark brown	Black
Score (actual changes 2008–2009)	4	2	5	3	1	2	5
Score (forecasted changes 2008–2009)	3	2	3	3	3	3	1
SAE	10						

Table 8.6 The ANFIS forecasting result

	Navy	Light grey	Burgundy	Black	Ivory	Dark grey	Dark green
2008	0.126929	0.190975	0.03707	0.38948	0.10435	0.138429	0.012767
2009	0.165464	0.156025	0.076317	0.421308	0.056221	0.092581	0.032084
2009 forecasted	0.0860	0.1986	0.0825	0.2011	0.0359	0	0.0486
Score (actual changes 2008–2009)	4	2	5	3	1	2	5
Score (forecasted changes 2008–2009)	3	4	5	2	3	3	3
SAE	9						

where fuzzy neural network is involved, the initial mapping of terms follows the sample in Fig. 8.2, and the actual mapping will be identified by the learning from data.

The forecasting results of the ARIMA, ANN and ANFIS are shown in Tables 8.4, 8.5, and 8.6 respectively. The forecasting results are presented in forms of scores, corresponding to terms as is listed in Table 8.3, and the measurement for errors is given in the Sum of Absolute Errors (SAE) of the forecasted and actual scores, given as $\mathrm{SAE} = \sum_{c=1}^{7} |X_c - X_c'|$, where X_c is the actual proportional sales of colour with index c, and $X_c{}'$ the corresponding forecasted one. The SAEs represent how far

Table 8.7 The historical colours in Pantone L, H, C codes

Year	2000	2001	2002	2003	2004	2005	2006	2007	2008	2009	2010	2011	2012
L	15	17	19	14	17	15	13	19	18	14	15	18	17
H	40	20	16	48	14	52	11	15	39	8	55	21	14
C	20	31	64	11	56	17	6	57	43	48	19	20	63

Table 8.8 The forecasted colours in L, H, C

Year	2009	2010	2011	2012	MAE	MAPE
L	17	19	14	15	3.25	36 %
H	13	66	14	14	5.75	8 %
C	52	48	03	23	22.5	35 %
MAPE	15 %	34 %	27 %	28 %		26 %

the forecasted colour trend in terms of popularity described as in Table 8.3, when translated into SAE of scores, the errors of the models can be directly compared, with the lower SAE means better forecasting and vice versa. Observing from these results, we can find out that the forecasting of ARIMA with SAE = 11, and by using ANN, the forecasting is improved by the SAE = 10, and the ANFIS further improves the SAE to be nine. By employing ANFIS, the forecasting errors are reduced, and the forecaster need not bother to set or identify the mapping between the descriptive terms and the actual real values, and he can also retrieve managerial indicator of the popularities of colours directly. In this way, the forecasting of fashion colour trends is improved and simplified.

8.4.2 *Forecasting on the Colour Trends*

The historical colours as is depicted in Fig. 8.1 are converted into PMS codes in Table 8.7. Our forecasting uses past 4 years of colours to predict the colour of the year following, as what is illustrated in Fig. 8.5. Therefore there are totally nine data points (forecasting for 2004–2012) can be modelled and we use the first five points for the training of the ANN, and the following four points for the testing of the accuracy of our model.

The forecasting results for the years 2009–2012 are listed in Table 8.8. The colours are also represented in L, H, C values, and the errors are given Mean Absolute Error (MAE) and Mean Absolute Percentage Error (MAPE). The MAE of L is given as MAE $= \sum_{\mathrm{i}} |L_i - L_i'|$, where L_i are the actual L values of the years and L_i' the forecasted ones. Unlike traditionally the MAPE is calculated using the actual value as the dominator, in our analysis, it is calculated by using the extension of the values as the dominator, so that the MAPE will give the concept how far does a forecasted value deviated from the real one comparing to the whole possible length of the value, i.e. the MAPE is given as MAPE $= \sum_{\mathrm{i}} \frac{|L_i - L_i'|}{L_e}$. As is discussed in Sect. 8.3.4, $L_e = 11$, $H_e = 64$, and $C_e = 64$.

Table 8.9 The comparison between actual and forecasted colours

	2009	2010	2011	2012
Actual Colour	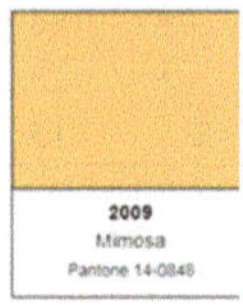	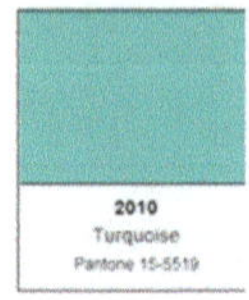	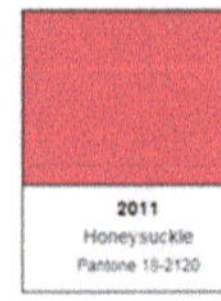	
Forecasted Colour				

Observing from Table 8.8, the forecasting for the Hues are with very good accuracy with MAPE = 8 %, and the errors for Lightness and Choma are rather high with MAPE = 36 % and 35 % respectively. While considering how the forecasted colour is difference with respect to the actual one, the forecasting for the year has the best match with a MAPE = 15 %, the errors are higher with the years 2011 and 2012, and the max error are found for the year 2010 with MAPE = 34 %.

With the forecasted L, H and C values, we can construct the Pantone code and search the real colour in the Pantone database. The forecasted colours are shown the Table 8.9 with comparison to their actual counterparts. Note that the Pantone colours are discrete ones and the actual colour with a given L, H, C value pair may not exist, and we show the abject colour instead in such cases. In Table 8.9, we can found the matching is quite good for the year 2009, following by the years 2011 and 2012, and the matching is poor for the year 2010. Such results conforms to the MAPEs as are listed in Table 8.8, with lower MAPE means better matching and vice versa.

8.5 Conclusions

The forecasting of fashion colour trends has long depended on the experts' opinions, and is proved to be not very accurate and efficient. When the traditions of the fashion industry, especially of the fashion design, are highly subjective process, the forecasting of colour trends which have great impact on the design and every parts of the fashion supply chain, may not necessarily be subjective. In this paper, we tried to employ statistical and artificial intelligence models in the forecasting of colour trends, where the historical observations of fashion colour sales are used for the learning of patterns of the changing of trends, and therefore, to learn and forecast of the colour trend objectively from the time series data. This may not be a method that can totally substitute the traditional and subjective forecasting of fashion colour trends, but can be used as a very good complementary to it as an objectively managerial decision support.

Comparisons among the analytical models are studied, and we identified that when the statistical models like ARIMA can produce sound forecasting results, the artificial models like ANN and ANFIS performs slightly better. Additionally, with FNN models like ANFIS, the forecaster do not need to pay attention on the settings of terms which corresponding to the changing of colour trends, while get the forecasting result in the forms of descriptive terms directly from the model. This improved the forecasting accuracy as well as the usability of the models.

Although the AI models are objective, and are discovered useful and accurate in this work, the forecasting of the fashion colour trends can always help from the in-depth exploration of the colour features with respect to fashion items. By analysing the colour tones represented by the Hue values, Lightness and Chroma, knowledge can be obtained from data analysis on fashion colour trends time series by ANN models, and forecasting can be conducted from learning from historical colours. The forecasting is found with good accuracy and offer an interesting options besides the forecasting of popular fashion colour by experts opinions. Our experiments show that forecasting for the Hue value is with quite high accuracy, whereas it is not the case for the Lightness and Chroma values, and these values do influence on the perception of colours, and future research one these issue are required to further improve the forecasting for colours.

References

1. Au K-F, Choi T-M, Yu Y (2008) Fashion retail forecasting by evolutionary neural networks. Int J Prod Econ 114(2):615–630
2. Cassidy TD, Cassidy T (2012) Using soft systems methodology to improve the colour forecasting process. J Int Colour Assoc 7:27–50
3. Cassidy G, Kamlet MS, Nagin DS (1989) An empirical examination of bias in revenue forecasts by state governments. Int J Forecast 5(3):321–331
4. Cassidy TD (2007) Personal colour analysis, consumer colour preferences and colour forecasting for the fashion and textile industries. Colour Des Creativity 1(1):1–14
5. Chang L-X, Gao W-D, Zhang X (2009) Discussion on fashion color forecasting for textile and fashion industries. J Fiber Bioeng Inform 2(1):15–21
6. Choi T-M, Yu Y, Au K-F (2011) A hybrid SARIMA wavelet transform method for sales forecasting. Decis Support Syst 51(1):130–140
7. Fashion-era (2012) http://www.fashion-era.com/
8. Jang JSR (1993) ANFIS: adaptive-network-based fuzzy inference system. IEEE Trans Syst Man Cybern 23(3):665–685
9. Lin JJ, Sun PT, Chen JJ-R, Wang LJ, Kuo HC, Kuo WG (2010) Applying gray model to predicting trend of textile fashion colors. J Text Inst 101(4):360–368
10. PANTONE (2012) http://www.pantone.com
11. Sun Z-L, Choi T-M, Au K-F, Yu Y (2008) Sales forecasting using extreme learning machine with applications in fashion retailing. Decis Support Syst 46(1):411–419
12. Wong WK, Guo ZX (2010) A hybrid intelligent model for medium-term sales forecasting in fashion retail supply chains using extreme learning machine and harmony search algorithm. Int J Prod Econ 128(2):614–624

13. Yu Y, Choi T-M, Au K-F, Sun ZL (2010) Applications of evolutionary neural networks for sales forecasting of fashionable products. In: Olivas ES, Guerrero JDM, Martinez-Sober M et al (eds) Handbook of research on machine learning applications and trends: algorithms, methods, and techniques. IGI Global, pp 387–403
14. Yu Y, Hui C-L, Choi T-M (2010) Intelligent fabric hand prediction system with fuzzy neural network. IEEE Trans Syst Man Cybern C Appl Rev 40(6):619–629
15. Yu Y, Choi T-M, Hui C-L (2011) An intelligent fast sales forecasting model for fashion products. Expert Syst Appl 38(6):7373–7379
16. Yu Y, Hui C-L, Choi T-M (2012) An empirical study of intelligent expert systems on forecasting of fashion color trend. Expert Syst Appl 39(4):4383–4389
17. Zadeh LA (1965) Fuzzy sets. Inform Control 8(3):338–353

Chapter 9
Neural Networks Based Forecasting for Romanian Clothing Sector

Logica Banica, Daniela Pirvu, and Alina Hagiu

Abstract Clothing industry enjoys a high level of attention on all world markets, despite the prolonged economic crisis. Companies have turned to knowledge and research, processing and analyzing information obtained from the market analysis, surveys, their own and their competitor's sales evolution, and are making use of short- and medium-term forecasts as powerful tools for the top management. The paper presents a twofold approach regarding forecasting of the financial indicators and trends related to the Romanian clothing industry, firstly at macroeconomic level, taking into account the interest of potential investors in this field, and secondly at microeconomic level, representing the analysis of the results for an operational company.

Keywords Clothing industry • Forecasting software • Financial indicators

9.1 Introduction

The prolonged economic crisis felt by the entire business world has sharpened even more the competition inside the fashion and clothing industries. In this context, companies have turned to knowledge and research, processing and analyzing information obtained from the market analysis, surveys, the own and the competitors sales evolution and making short and medium term forecasts as powerful tools of top management.

A complex instrument that supports efforts in this field consists in the software products, like: designing applications, web-based marketing campaigns and also

L. Banica (✉) • D. Pirvu • A. Hagiu
Faculty of Economics, University of Pitesti, Pitesti, Romania
e-mail: olga.banica@upit.ro; ddanapirvu@yahoo.com; alinahagiu@yahoo.com

T.-M. Choi et al. (eds.), *Intelligent Fashion Forecasting Systems: Models and Applications*, DOI 10.1007/978-3-642-39869-8_9,

business intelligence software, useful for companies in their effort to obtain current situation viewed from different angles, and projections that support decision-making strategy.

Fashion, as the "princess" of the clothing industry, is not only a target for rich people, but now appeals to the mass market — people with incomes below average who become more resistant to buying when the economy shrinks.

Fashion becomes a reason of pride and also weakness, something imposed by media, good quality clothes from famous fashion companies also add up to the sales. Even after 5 years from the beginning of the global crisis, fashion is an important clothing industry branch, and the companies which are able to achieve a balance between the need and luxury are the ones who become successful on market.

In this article we focused on two approaches of forecasts in clothing industry in Romania: firstly at macroeconomic level, taking into account the interest of potential investors in this field and secondly, at microeconomic level, representing the analysis of the results of an operational company and the identification of trends that could improve its performances.

From the point of view of investors, the priority consists in obtaining reliable information concerning the evolution of the Romanian fashion and clothing industry during 2004–2011, in the context of the European Union integration. The analysis of the key performance indicators, and the usage of GMDH Shell software in order to forecast the financial indicators for 2012–2013, offer a consistent overview for a future investor in this domain [1].

The other approach refers to the intelligent tools that a manager may use to have complete and correct information about the sales of the company, and to forecast the production for the next period, based on analysis and research.

Romanian companies can assert on domestic and foreign markets, although they are constantly competing with the subsidiaries of large companies and with foreign firms, which try to dominate the market by quality, by low pricing, by rapid distribution of models presented at fashion events (fast fashion) and by "cool hunting".

To plan the future actions, the company management includes three financial elements: profit and loss, cash flow and the balance sheet. These three documents collectively and separately demonstrate the impacts of profitability, liquidity and growth on business matter over the planning horizon chosen. In order to know the pulse of business it is important to understand these financial management tools and the way they interact. Using financial forecasting is important for measuring the performance for the previous period and making a new business plan, which may be presented to investors [2].

We used artificial neural network (ANN) because of their capability to learn (modeling) from their environment, without requiring specific expert knowledge on the problem in order to complete the task, as the statistical models are usually do [3]. This feature is useful in complex applications where other type of solutions are impractical, due to the capacity to detect patterns from complex or fuzzy data, extract patterns and detect trends.

There are many types of ANN, and choosing the right artificial neural network type depends on application and data representation.

Feed-forward ANNs allow information to move from input nodes to output nodes, through the hidden layers, without loops in the network. They are extensively used in pattern recognition.

Recurrent (feedback) ANNs have information moving in both directions, by introducing loops in the network. Feedback networks are very powerful and dynamic, aiming to reach the equilibrium point [4].

The main weakness of the previous ANN models is the relatively more time consumed to perform forecasting. In the fashion industry, forecasting is challenging because there are so many product varieties and prompt result is required.

Another known model is Extreme Learning Machine (ELM) for single-hidden layer feed-forward networks, faster than the traditional feed-forward network learning algorithms. However, ELM's forecasting outputs are unstable in comparison with the traditional ANN and statistical models [5].

The SVM (Support Vector Machines) concept represents a binary linear classifier that uses supervised learning to infer from a set of examples to which of the two defined output classes the input data belongs to. This kind of pattern recognition is not suitable for the goal of the paper, as the output data should be much more detailed and cannot be enclosed in just two categories.

The concept of *forecasting software* for business refers to the software applications used for gathering and analyzing data about a company, discovering pattern and proposing the appropriate prediction model, in order to supply the best business decisions.

The most interesting forecasts are in fashion trends and the big companies can afford marketing research, sales analysis on types and colors, in order to establish which are the customers preferences and thus to prefigure the future production.

Two of the well known forecasting tools are GMDH Shell and DTREG software. First of them is a professional neural network software, that solves time series forecasting and data mining tasks by building feed forward network based on a quadratic polynomial function [1].

DTREG predictive modeling software is capable to build classification and regression decision trees, neural networks, support vector machines (SVM), GMDH polynomial networks and offer full support for time series analysis [6].

Based on the Romanian National Institute of Statistics (RNIS) data of the clothing industry during the period 2004–2011, and using GMDH Shell forecasting software, we analyzed key performance indicators and we applied various forecasting models in order to obtain a prediction of financial indicators for Romanian clothing industry in 2012–2013.

We also made the analysis of annual sales of a company, on clothing categories and color preferences and we obtained a forecast for short-term, then we made an assessment of the accuracy of predictions, comparing partial data realized by the company with GMDH Shell forecast and we analyzed the mismatch causes.

9.2 What About the Romanian Clothing Industry?

Having available a set of data from the RNIS, and also statistics on textiles and clothing from EUROSTAT and the World Trade Organization, we will present the particularities of the Romanian garments industry, the internal market demand and the volume of exports on foreign markets.

Regarding the number of companies producing clothing in 2004–2010 periods, the overall situation and on category of companies is as follows (Table 9.1).

It is noted that in the 2004–2007 period, the number of firms has remained almost constant, in 2008 there was a slight decline, in 2009–2010 a severe drop, so that in 2010 there were about 24 % fewer companies than in 2008.

Regarding the average number of employees, taking into account the data from the RNIS, we obtain the following structure on categories of manufacturing clothing firms (Table 9.2 and Fig. 9.1).

According to EUROSTAT, the report "Exports of goods and services by Member States of the EU/third countries in current prices" (Table 9.3) shows that Romania has an upward trend that will preserve also in 2013, according to the estimates (Fig. 9.2).

Table 9.1 The evolution of clothing companies by number and employees

Year	Total number	0–9 employees	10–19 employees	20–49 employees	50–250 employees	over 250 employees
2004	5,628	3,068	523	782	981	274
2005	5,849	3,361	552	772	921	243
2006	5,743	3,331	592	762	845	213
2007	5,698	3,356	605	793	764	180
2008	5,336	3,228	575	722	660	151
2009	4,841	3,127	492	560	531	131
2010	4,078	2,469	426	566	500	117

Source: RNIS

Table 9.2 The evolution of labor force in clothing companies

Year	0–9 employees	10–19 employees	20–49 employees	50–249 employees	over 250 employees	Total number
2004	8,821	7,419	24,823	109,025	167,608	317,696
2005	9,213	7,749	24,765	99,020	145,467	286,214
2006	8,983	8,278	24,493	91,930	122,205	255,889
2007	9,040	8,349	25,425	81,255	100,125	224,194
2008	8,653	8,050	22,842	69,620	79,276	188,441
2009	7,810	6,883	17,537	56,902	64,167	153,299
2010	6,187	5,882	17,655	54,564	57,157	141,445

Source: RNIS

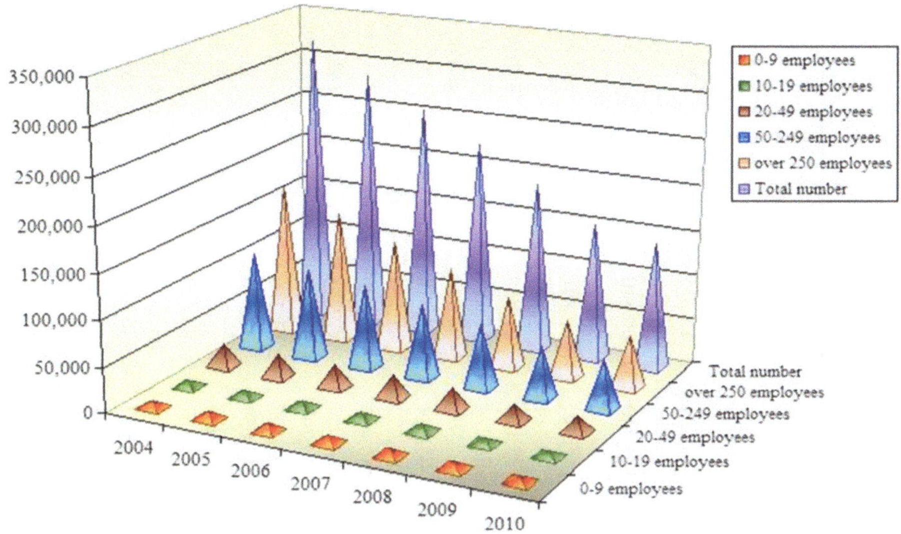

Fig. 9.1 Graphical evolution of labor force in clothing companies (Source: RNIS)

Regarding the clothing industry, the RNIS data, summarized in Table 9.4 and plotted in Fig. 9.3, we see a similar trend, which records a peak in 2008, a strong decrease in the worst year of the crisis (2009) and a revival in 2010.

Also, in the same figure is depicted a strong decrease of the turnover in 2009 and the fact that the downwards trend continued in 2010, but less severe, while exports reached the turnover, which means that almost all production is for export.

It was noticed that the products of the clothing industry are mainly for export, so approximately 85 % of the clothing products of our country are exported especially to the European community's countries [7].

The clothing industry in our country indicates a similar evolution as those in the whole European Union during this last period. Unfortunately, the products of the Romanian clothing companies launched on the internal market are different to the products sold on international markets – in terms on quality and prices. The poor competitive nature of the internal market clothing companies is due both to the ineffective sales and marketing activities, as well as to the decreased purchasing power of the population [7]. It is to add to these weaknesses also the low investment level, which means insufficient funds for supporting research and for design and manufacturing of advanced equipment (Table 9.5).

Despite the modest purchasing power of the population, the annual statistics on 2012 indicate a high share of consumption expenditure (72.1 %) in total household expenditure structure (Table 9.6 and Fig. 9.4).

Table 9.3 Exports of goods and services by member states of the EU/third countries – current prices (million euros)

GEO/Time	2005	2006	2007	2008	2009	2010	2011	2012	2013
European Union (27 countries)	4,118,920	4,632,732	4,976,644	5,154,309	4,338,454	5,010,675	5,524,424	5,768,225	5,931,512
Belgium	238,737	257,498	277,203	294,186	248,035	284,533	311,931	319,034	323,637
Bulgaria	9,427	16,206	18,299	20,627	16,596	20,698	25,605	26,430	27,822
Czech Republic	67,417	79,225	89,983	99,423	83,829	99,832	113,335	118,837	120,567
Denmark	101,587	113,901	118,815	128,700	106,517	119,105	128,423	133,328	136,662
Germany (until 1990 former territory of the FRG)	919,070	1,053,140	1,145,410	1,191,190	1,006,540	1,173,340	1,300,810	1,362,590	1,391,898
Ireland	132,526	140,707	152,389	150,181	146,369	157,810	166,791	177,134	183,869
Greece	44,807	48,298	53,088	56,271	44,514	49,414	52,248	52,309	53,578
Spain	233,387	259,130	283,331	288,217	250,667	285,110	321,819	338,014	352,980
France	452,871	485,914	506,724	520,974	440,683	495,274	538,191	568,417	583,103
Italy	371,639	412,377	448,408	448,227	360,880	412,509	454,783	474,177	488,665
Luxembourg	47,171	57,617	65,956	67,934	58,918	68,784	75,228	75,918	79,328
Hungary	58,538	69,653	80,842	86,188	70,920	83,972	91,169	92,612	98,057
Netherlands	357,453	393,475	424,229	453,442	393,050	460,493	499,620	524,719	546,525
Austria	132,037	145,996	161,397	167,575	138,253	154,950	172,283	177,672	182,938
Poland	90,643	109,802	126,756	144,895	122,534	149,791	167,145	175,952	185,899
Portugal	42,669	49,713	54,498	55,802	47,236	54,109	61,168	64,073	64,981
Romania	26,401	31,553	36,547	42,532	36,170	44,039	52,576	52,693	55,493
Finland	65,744	75,413	82,383	86,958	64,352	72,005	77,251	77,261	79,372
Sweden	144,496	162,608	175,292	178,388	140,261	173,157	193,672	199,126	204,536
United Kingdom	497,842	569,444	555,449	539,471	453,634	522,108	567,423	602,351	613,130
Norway	107,839	122,958	126,937	145,566	109,291	128,677	146,396	159,079	165,647
Switzerland	147,230	164,148	178,978	194,130	184,914	215,144	243,751	251,675	261,460
United States	1,049,031	1,171,551	1,212,477	1,255,643	1,138,084	1,391,265	1,504,454	1,699,876	1,746,414

Source: Eurostat 06.05.2013

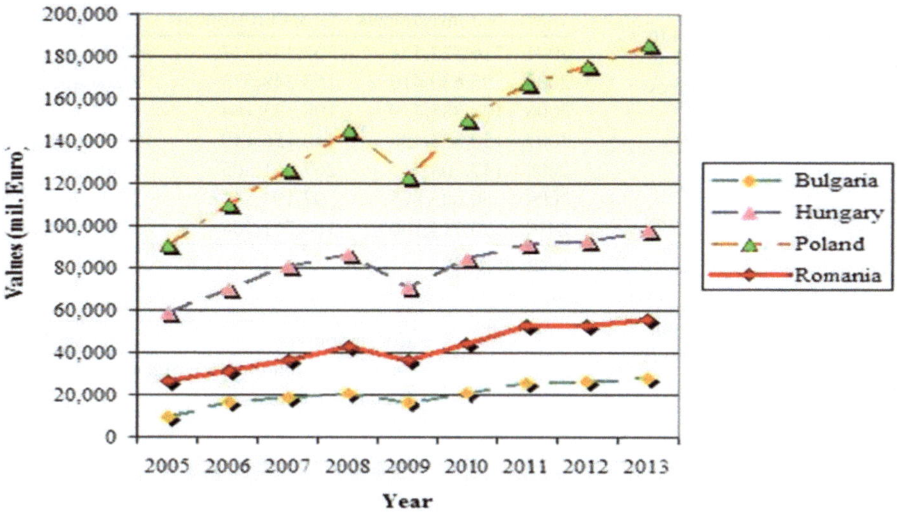

Fig. 9.2 Comparison between the volume of exports of goods and services of Romania and several Member States of the EU (Source: Eurostat 06.05.2013)

Table 9.4 The cumulative turnover and exports of Romanian firms of manufacturing garments (million dollars)

Year	Total turnover	Total exports
2004	22,842	13,829
2005	22,645	14,326
2006	23,643	15,206
2007	25,731	15,701
2008	25,096	16,642
2009	17,212	13,383
2010	14,678	14,089

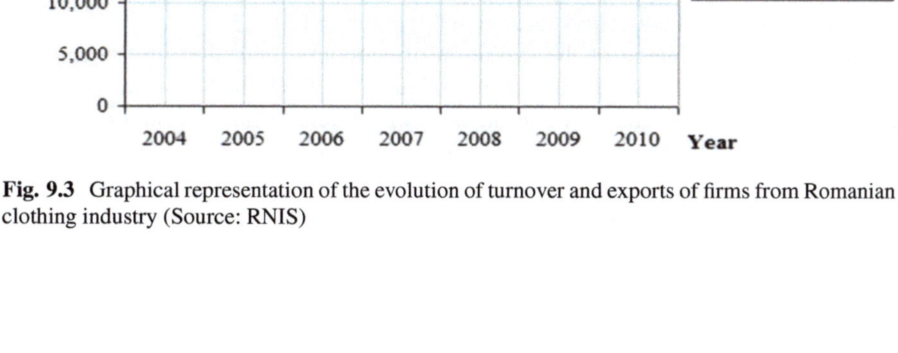

Fig. 9.3 Graphical representation of the evolution of turnover and exports of firms from Romanian clothing industry (Source: RNIS)

Table 9.5 Evolution of turnover and investments in clothing sector during 2004–2010 (constant prices in dollars)

Year	Net investments	Gross investments	Total turnover
2004	216,522,451	307,248,537	2,284,209,202
2005	95,630,410	153,748,573	2,264,455,605
2006	128,385,479	198,533,164	2,364,337,916
2007	150,323,126	440,756,149	2,573,073,107
2008	147,208,713	267,061,505	2,509,557,965
2009	50,605,875	97,197,842	1,721,204,418
2010	90,714,190	106,511,768	1,467,840,443

Source: RNIS

Table 9.6 The structure of household expenditure on III quarter of 2012

Consumption expenses	72.1 %
Taxes, contributions, fees, charges	16.5 %
Production expenses	6.0 %
Other expenses	3.5 %
Investment expenses	1.0 %

Source: RNIS

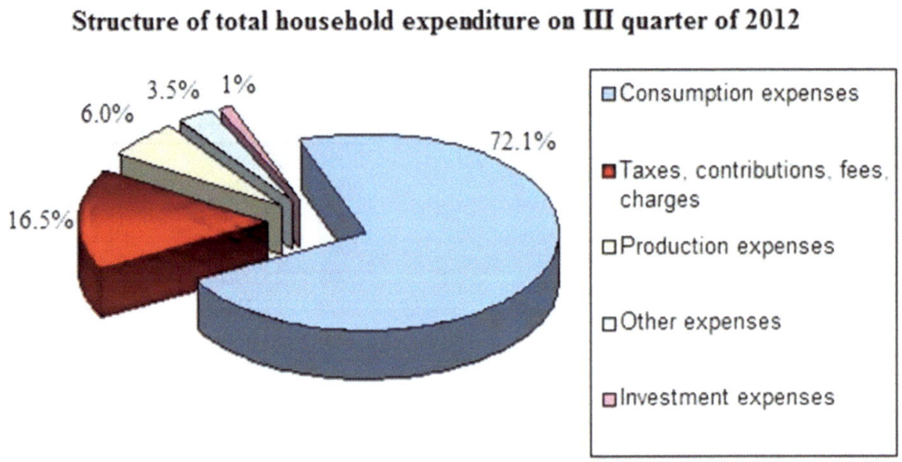

Fig. 9.4 Household expenditure (Source: RNIS)

We also note that the Romanians allocate 5.3 % of total consumption expenses on clothing and footwear, a percentage greater than that allocated to health, communications and education, as shown the graph in Fig. 9.5.

To have a clear image of the evolution of economic indicators in the clothing industry, we turned the statistical data provided by the RNIS from constant prices in current prices, because the last one includes the general effects of inflation during the analysis period. The conversion formula we used it is the following:

$$\text{Current Prices} = \text{Constant Prices} * \text{Consumer Price Index}$$

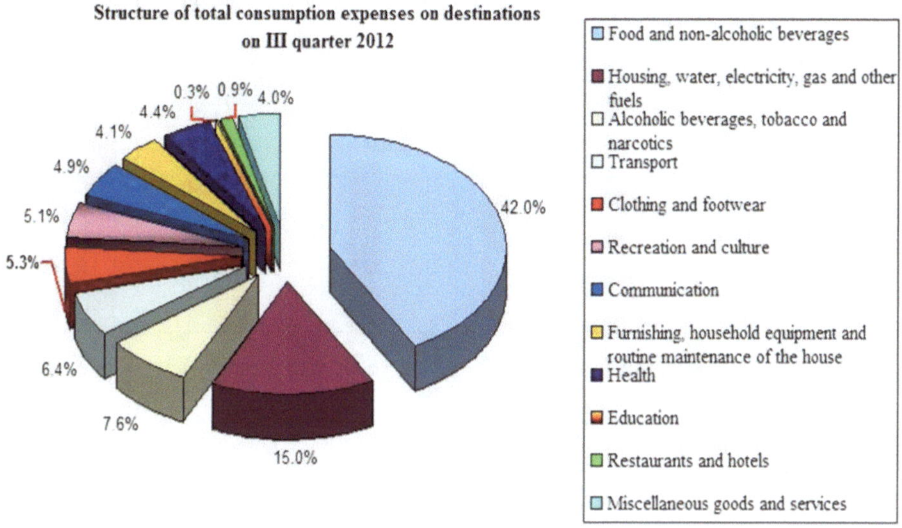

Fig. 9.5 Total consumption expenses (Source: RNIS)

Table 9.7 The evolution of Romanian export and imports

Values in million of euro	2007	2008	2009	2010	2011	2012
Exports (FOB)[a]	29,549	33,725	29,084	37,368	45,041	45,043
Imports (CIF)[b]	51,322	57,240	38,953	46,902	54,824	54,607
Commercial balance	−21,773	−23,516	−9,869	−9,534	−9,783	−9,564

Romanian international trade yearbook, 2011
[a]Free on board
[b]Cost insurance and freight

9.2.1 The External Market of Romanian Clothing Industry

From the assessment of Romania's international trade developments in the 2007–2010 period it is clear that, after a decrease of nearly 14 % of the exports in 2009 compared to 2008, in 2010 they rose by over 28 % compared to 2009, even above the level reached in 2008, in the context of the global economic recovery, including that of the EU markets. At the same time, imports, after a decrease of 32 % in 2009, rose by almost 20 % in 2010 (see Table 9.7), remaining though below the levels achieved in 2008 and even in 2007 [8] (Fig. 9.6).

In 2011 the exports totaled 45,041 million Euros, increasing with 20.5 %, and the imports increased by 16.9 % and reached 54,824 million Euros, resulting in a deficit of 9,783 million Euros, similar to the one in 2010 [9, 10].

In 2012, FOB exports amounted 45,043 million Euros while CIF imports were 54,607 million, so that Romania's trade balance recorded an increasing deficit in 2012.

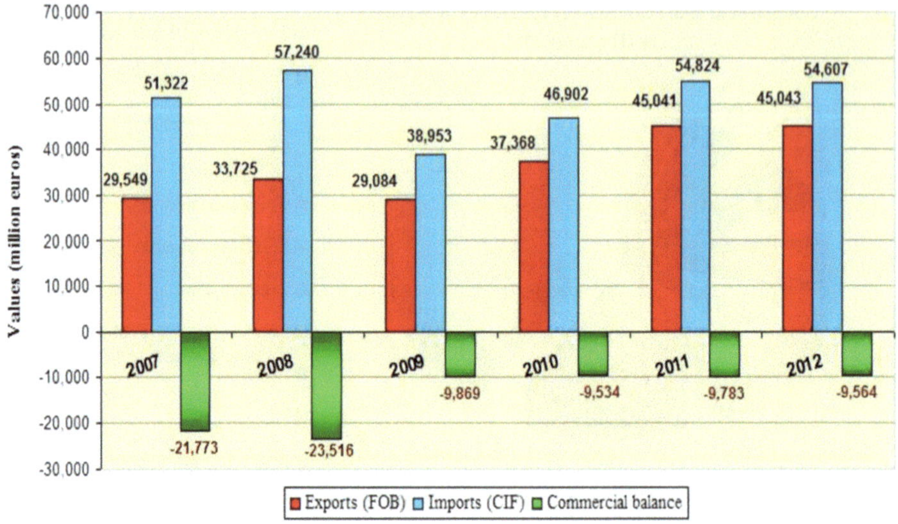

Fig. 9.6 Graphical evolution of Romanian export and imports (Source: Romanian international trade yearbook, 2011)

"Compared to 2011, exports increased by 4.6% at values expressed in lei (decreased by 0.5% at values expressed in euro) and imports increased by 4.5% at values expressed in lei (decreased by 0.6% at values expressed in euro)", according to an RNIS statement.

Significant shares in the values of exports and imports are held by product groups of machinery and transport equipment (40.4 % at export and 33.7 % at import) and other manufactured products (34.1 % at export and 29.3 % at import).

According to the Romanian International Trade Yearbook, 2011 [9], the structure of exports and imports according to the classification of products by activity, in the 2008–2010 period is as follows (Table 9.8):

Extracting data regarding the clothing sector (Fig. 9.7), it is noted that exports predominate compared to imports, with a medium difference of 5.86 %.

In 2012, Romania's exports were supported mainly by the sale of machinery and transport equipment, which held 40.5 % of total exports, while imports in the same area were 33.6 % [11].

On the next position stood "manufactured goods", which includes clothing, footwear and accessories, and which holds a percentage of 34.3 % of total exports. The same product category represents 29.6 % of total imports, according to the RNIS for the same period. Romania's clothing exports are addressed mainly to EU countries (over 90 % during 2004–2009).

The exports for UE follow two main directions [7]:

– Developed countries, that abandoned the industry of consumer goods for the production of luxury goods in short series, dominating the international fashion;

Table 9.8 The structure of Romanian exports and imports during 2008–2010

	Exports %			Imports %		
Class of products	2008	2009	2010	2008	2009	2010
Total	92.6	93.0	92.9	91.6	92.5	92.7
Products of agriculture and hunting	4.1	4.5	4.9	2.2	2.7	2.6
Crude petroleum and natural gas				9.3	7.0	6.7
Refined petroleum products	9.0	5.5	4.8	2.5	2.1	3.1
Food products	1.3	1.8	2.3	4.8	6.4	5.4
Textile products	1.8	2.2	2.0	4.2	4.9	4.7
Wearing apparel	8.4	7.7	6.3	1.5	1.8	1.5
Leather and leather products	3.2	3.5	3.2	1.7	2.2	2.2
Metallurgical products	9.2	5.5	6.9	7.8	5.7	6.5
Wood and products of wood (except furniture)	2.8	3.2	3.2	1.0	0.9	0.8
Furniture	3.3	3.4	2.8	0.9	0.8	0.6
Computer, electronic and optical products	5.2	8.2	9.5	8.0	9.6	10.7
Machinery and equipment	7.6	7.2	7.1	10.6	10.0	9.5
Motor vehicles, trailers and semi-trailers	12.8	16.2	16.3	11.6	7.1	7.4
Other transport equipment	4.0	5.1	3.5	1.0	0.9	0.9
Electrical equipment	7.2	7.2	7.4	6.3	7.6	8.3
Rubber and plastic products	3.4	3.9	4.2	4.2	4.8	4.8
Chemicals and chemical products	5.5	3.6	4.0	6.3	8.1	7.8
Other product classes	3.8	4.3	4.5	7.7	9.9	9.2

Source: Romanian international trade yearbook, 2011

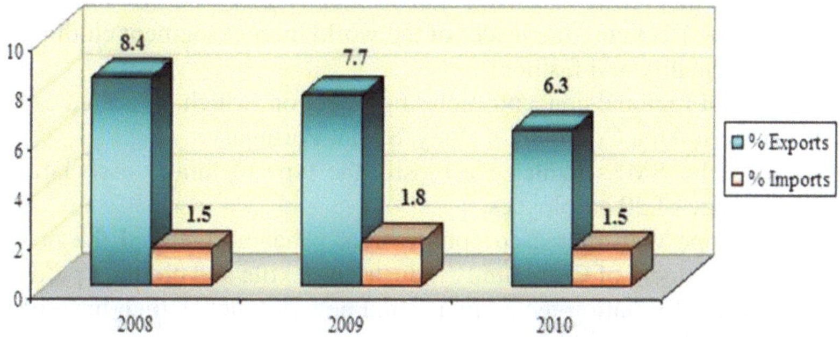

Fig. 9.7 Exports and imports for clothing sector (Source: Romanian International Trade Yearbook, 2011)

- Developing countries, the major owners of raw materials, with skilled, low cost labor and favorable industrial policies that promote exports and look for new markets.

As the clothing industry exists in all countries of the European Union and especially developed in Italy, Germany, France and England, is difficult for Romanian products to penetrate the markets of these countries. Another disadvantage is represented by the household budgets declining and the quickly changes in fashion domain.

The phenomenon of "fast fashion" was present at famous companies' level and began to generalize to other companies, so that the outfits presented at fashion events become available in stores in a few weeks [12].

Through aggressive market policies and market research, companies are turning to certain segments of the population, especially young people in order to facilitate the access to clothes with a high content of fashion.

Another example of intelligent strategy is the Swedish company H&M that hired young designers whose job was to produce as quickly and as cheap as possible "high fashion" clothes, the products of H&M at that time being called also "disposable fashion", "trendy" clothes that you can throw in the trash after the passing of the fashion [7].

The company Inditex, that produce Zara clothes, applied the same policy as H&M, by employing a core of 200 young designers, creating 40,000 models of clothes per year, some of them arriving in stores, about one-fourth, the rest being useless.

Having an advanced communication system, Zara branches quickly registers the success or the failure of a model and the company decides to withdraw or to extend the production.

The reports from the European Commission highlight several features of the clothing sector in the European Union, the most significant being in the list below [13]:

1. A long tradition, innovation and product diversity;
2. Concentrating on products with high added value, quality, design, innovation and technology, the EU being the leader of the world market segment clothing with a high level of quality and fashion;
3. High degree of regional concentration of production, which is located especially in the Southern Area Community (Italy, Spain, Portugal);
4. Is dominated by SMEs, which are mostly the type of family associations and have an average of 20 employees;
5. In order to cope with increased competition, it has accelerated the process of structural adjustment of Community industry of textile and clothing products, by applying new information technologies and new products which have benefited from the overall Structural Funds of the EU, but also by improving the activity of subcontracting.
6. EU textile and clothing industry widely uses the labor force from East Europe, Asia and North African countries.

Among developing countries possessing raw materials and cheap skilled labor detaches China, the world leader in production and export of textiles and clothing. In 2011 China was the leading exporter of textiles and clothing with more than 250 billion dollars having the European Union and the United States as major markets for clothing [14].

Regarding the export situation in Romania, the data presented in Table 9.4 show a decline of 20 % in total exports recorded in the clothing industry of our country in 2009 compared with 2008 and an increase with 5.2 % in 2010 compared with 2009 [13].

9.2.2 *What About Internal Market?*

Romania was and still is an attractive market for investments in the garments retail sector due to following factors:

- The important percentage of population that lives in town and cities;
- The young people is interested to spend money on clothing and fashion;
- The development of shopping centers all over the country during 2004–2008.

In 2009, the most severe year of the economic crisis, the retail clothing sector in Romania recorded a significant decline. In 2010, the clothing retail sector continued the decline, but it was a soft decrease and by aggressive marketing promotions with price decreases or by offers that included discounts they diminished the losses and stimulated the consumption.

The fashion sector in Romania addressed to the high-income consumers was not as seriously affected by the crisis as the one of medium-income or low-income persons, though the sales pace slowed down significantly and the traffic in the fashion stores became more unpredictable and fluctuating.

Famous fashion companies have entered on the Romanian market, such as:

- C&A was launched in Romania in April 2009 by five stores;
- The first Sasch store in Bucharest was opened in November 2009, and in December they launched the second one;
- At the beginning of 2010 the company GHP Management opened the first store Gerard Darel in Bucharest.

Despite the decline of the retail clothing consumption in 2010, the foreign companies implemented their long-term development strategy. Also, other famous companies, such as H&M, opened new stores in our country [13].

Some of the most important foreign clothing brands in Romania are (Fig. 9.8):

- ZARA, introduced by the Spanish retailer Inditex in 2007; in 2012, Inditex developed its network up to 90 stores;
- Kenvelo, having a decline in 2009 and a revitalization of sales in 2010;
- New Yorker, introduced by the German retailer in 2007 and having in 2010 a network that includes 14 stores;
- BSB Fashion Romania, a local subsidiary of the BSB Greek retailer opened in 2004 and having a network of 10 stores;

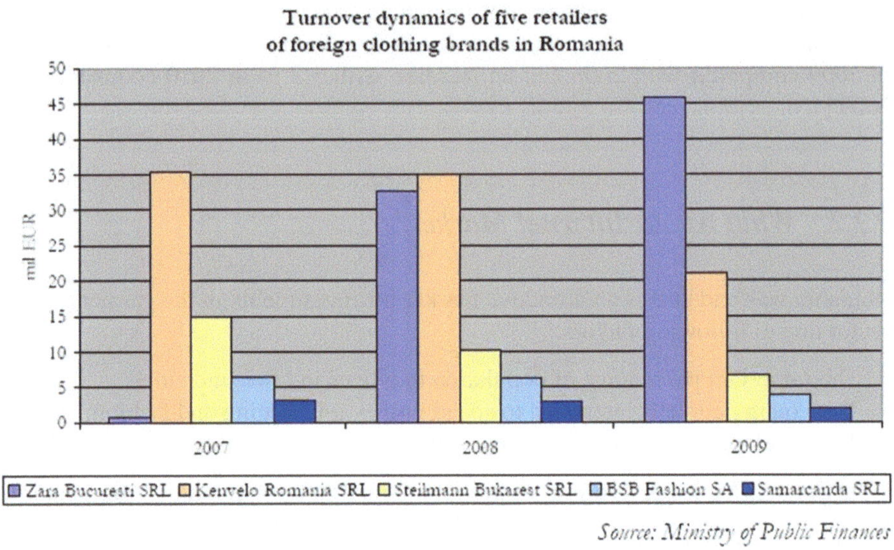

Fig. 9.8 The evolution of turnover for the main retailers of clothing brands in Romania

- Steilmann brand, entered Romanian market in 1992 and has a retail network of 46 stores in 2009;
- Flo&Jo brand, represented by the company Samaranda and including 14 stores in 2010.

Main Romanian clothing and fashion brands are (Fig. 9.9):

- House of Art, produced by Staff Collection and supported by a network of 62 stores.
- Braiconf, a clothing producer from 1950 and privatized in 1996; the company has 17 stores and is listed on the Bucharest Stock Exchange;
- TinaR brand is controlled by the company TinaR, including 14 stores in Romania;
- Seroussi brand produced by J&R Enterprises and sold by the stores named "No.36";
- Yokko brand controlled by Yokko Fashion company, having a network of 10 stores in 2010.

We must underline the unfair competition that runs on the internal market, among Romanian clothing producers and foreign producers.

The Romanian companies tried to conserve quality standard and tradition without a significant increase of prices, but the foreign producers have two advantages:

- The low-prices of the products, preferred considering the modest purchasing power of the population;
- The aggressive penetration of the foreign products, many of them being equal or superior to the range of Romanian products.

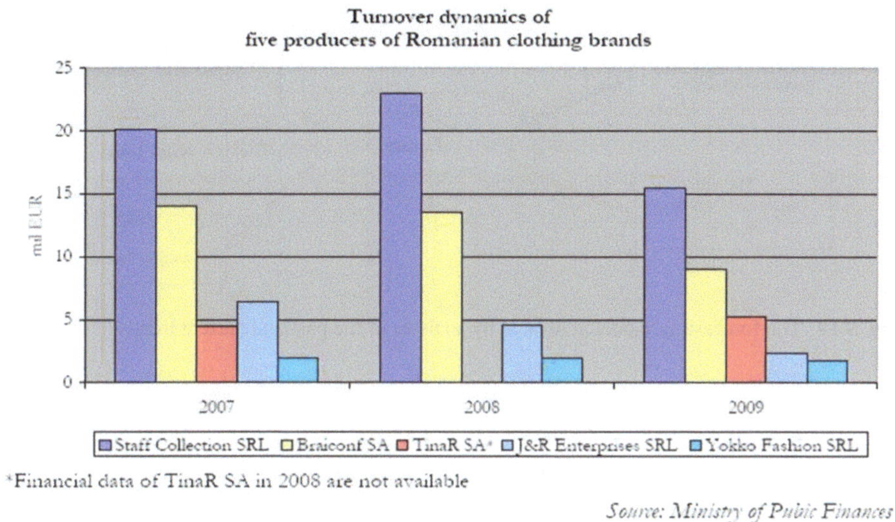

Fig. 9.9 The evolution of turnover for the main producers of Romanian clothing brands

9.3 Two Ways to Approach Fashion Forecasting

9.3.1 Choosing GMDH Shell as Forecasting Software

In a strongly competitive environment as the fashion one, company's managers must use the whole range of instruments of knowledge and research to analyze in depth the statistics of the prior period and the reports of current situation in order to improve the future operational efficiency – Fig. 9.10.

The main objective is to make realistic forecasts in order to optimize resource allocation and consumption, and also to avoid possible problems that could have a negative impact on their business [15].

Economists use forecasting also to extrapolate how trends will change in the next year or as a benchmark for a long-term perspective of business. The further out the forecast, the higher the chances that the estimate will be less accurate [16].

Inspired by the human brain structure and functions, artificial neural networks (ANNs) have a large application area in forecasting the economic phenomena [17].

In this paper we propose the forecasting based on neural model, using the GMDH Shell software. Professor A.G. Ivahnenko from the Cybernetic Institute from Kiev discovered in 1968 the method indicated for solving the forecasting issues and for obtaining the large dimension models, generally for regression phenomenon. The method is based on problem model decomposition in simple models and reassembling them, after a preliminary selection. His method is based on obtaining a forecast model of a function according to previous values of the function, at points in time equal sequenced.

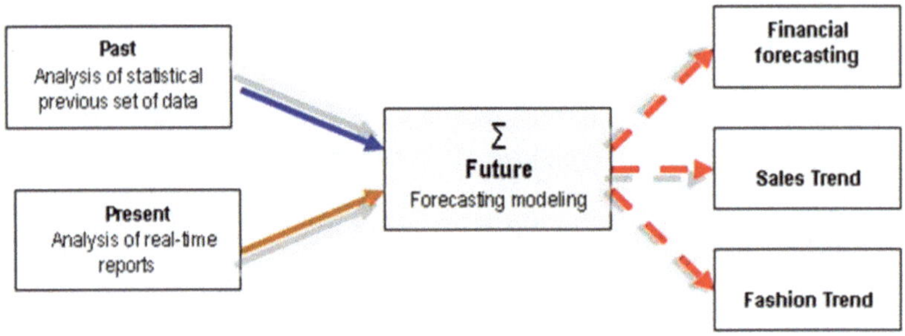

Fig. 9.10 The forecasting model generated by analysis of the past and current trends

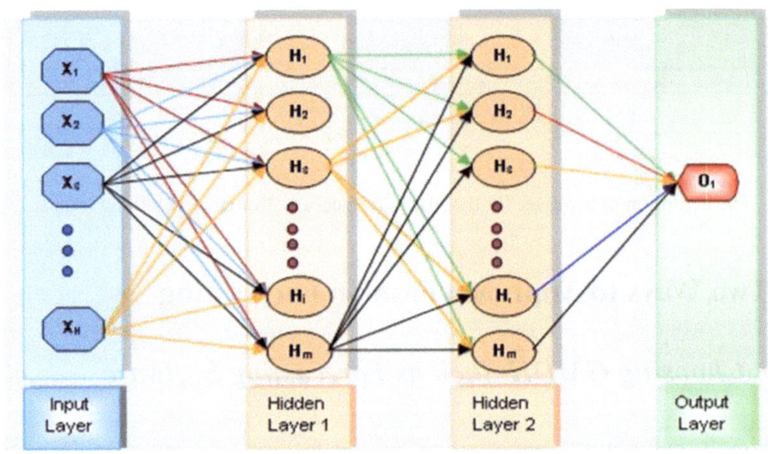

Fig. 9.11 Neural network architecture

According to [18] "Artificial neural networks (ANNs) are one of the most accurate and widely used forecasting models that have enjoyed fruitful applications in forecasting social, economic, engineering, foreign exchange, stock problems".

Neural network architectures can be trained to predict the future values of the dependent variables. The characteristics that recommend the ANNs for scientific forecasting are:

- The capacity to approximate any continuous function, with a target of accuracy;
- The usage of nonlinear methods, similarly with most of the real systems;
- Data-driven self-adaptive methods, opposed to the traditional model-based methods;
- The capacity to generalize the forecasting process, after learning the data set;
- The parallel-distributed processing of data.

The most popular model is the "one hidden layer feed forward network" [19]. In Fig. 9.11 is presented the model structure, containing three types of layers for processing units connected by acyclic links. The role of the input layer neurons is to transfer the input data to the hidden layers as this layer doesn't have an activation function. Neurons may be linked to further neurons (synapses), designing multiple layers configuration. Weights and numbers of layers are typically optimized over an estimation interval (training set) and are then used for prediction on the test dataset and on the selected architecture.

Starting from certain assumptions, forecasting projects the trends into the future using different models, such as neural networks, Delphi method, exponential smoothing, moving averages and regression analysis [17].

Our experiment is based on *neural network – time series* model, used for forecasting the future behavior of variables. Neural networks are nonlinear sophisticated modeling techniques, able to modeling complex functions. They can be applied to problems of prediction, classification or control in a wide spectrum of fields such as finance, medicine, engineering, and physics.

Neural networks have been widely used to process time series in forecasting: most often these are feed-forward networks which employ a sliding window over the input sequence [15, 16].

The algorithm used in the case study presented is *neural networks*, usually chosen when the exact nature of the relationship between inputs and output is known. A key feature of neural networks is that they learn the relationship between inputs and outputs through training, so we split the input variables on two groups, having the training/test ratio: 60 %/40 %. The accuracy of expectations which can be formulated for the selected cases of forecasts in Romanian clothing industry leads to a correct decision for the potential investors or allows clothing sector managers to allocate resources and concentrate their sales in order to maximize profits.

The precision of information depends on sources and volumes of collected data and the selection of descriptive variables for chosen predictive model. Even if some factors are not relevant, the model assesses the most important and assigns them much more weights [2].

In this manner, the relevance of the results depends on the development of the following three stages of forecasting system:

1. Accessing large amounts of historical data and giving an appropriate weight to each factor within the input data;
2. Using a forecasting software to prepare data processing – meaning the import of data into the application, separate the training data from test data, establish the number of neuron layers and the output variable(s). In case of non-continuity or outliers of dataset, it must be additionally specified a method for data estimation. If the software detects missing values, they must be replaced, by an interpolate value, by an average value or by zero etc. If erroneous data is discovered, it must be removed or the process stops.
3. Choosing the appropriate model for forecasting and evaluation the accuracy of prediction – is a matter of trust and of goal seeking. Current forecasting software gives enough information (graphs, reports, performance, indicators etc.) to an experimented manager in order to make an evaluation of the accuracy of the results. It depends on his option to share input data between the learning and the validation set and also, on his choice regarding the configuration of neural network: number of layers and neurons.

With a powerful graphical interface is easy and it is recommended to test several models on the same input data in order to compare the forecasting results.

Neural network architectures can be trained to predict the future values of the dependent variables. A *feed-forward neural network* consists of an input layer, one or several hidden layers and an output layer. The main idea is to create layers of neurons with two or more inputs, saving a set of neurons that will contribute to the next layer. Every new layer is based-on two or more neurons from previous layers [1].

Another approach is known as the partially *recurrent neural network* that can learn sequences as time evolves and responds to the same input pattern differently at different times, depending on the previous input patterns [20].

So, the ANNs components are:

- The network architecture: neurons, layers, inputs and outputs;
- Describing inputs and outputs;
- The training set and the validation dataset;
- The training process;
- The measure of the error.

As we can see in the Fig. 9.11, a neural network is a system that connects an input dataset to a set of outputs in a non-linear mode. In a general time-series context, the output is the value to be forecasted and the inputs are the previous-known values of the series and of other explanatory variables. The connections between inputs and outputs are made via one or more hidden layers of neurons, also called *nodes*. Choosing the architecture of a neural network implies to establish the number of layers, the number of neurons in each layer, and how the inputs, hidden layers and output(s) are connected [21].

The structure is the *feed-forward* type without feedback loops. A suitable architecture for a given problem has to be determined from the context, using some of the external considerations and the properties of the data. The model structure depends on its performance and the measure of error at each level is an indicator to choose an appropriate number of hidden layers.

The architecture presented is for a typical neural network for time-series forecasting with *N inputs*, *two or three hidden* layers of *m neurons*, and *one output* (the forecast). Each input is connected to all neurons, and the neurons are connected to the output. The *strength* of each connection is measured by a parameter called a *weight*. There may be a large number of such parameters to estimate. A numerical value is calculated for each neuron at each time period, *t*, as follows.

The output variable, $\boldsymbol{y}$ at $\boldsymbol{t+1}$ moment depends on inputs until the chosen moment $\boldsymbol{t+1-i_x}$ and also on its values at previous moments ($\boldsymbol{o_x}$). The model can be estimated as:

$$\mathrm{y\,(T) = f(x\,(T-i1)\,, x\,(T-i2)\,, \ldots x\,(T-im)\,, y\,(T-o1)\,, \ldots y\,(T-om))} \tag{9.1}$$

where $\mathrm{y_j}$ are the outputs, $\mathrm{T = t + 1}$ the time of estimation and $\mathrm{x_i}$ are the inputs.

The next step consists of choosing a nonlinear function, the *activation function*, for transforming the values of *y* into values for the neurons. The most important advantage of a neural network is represented by the ability to represent nonlinear relationships and to *learn* from the previous behavior of the data being modeled [22, 23].

The goal of the neural network is to create several models and select the function that correctly maps the input to the output using the training data.

From the generated models, is selected the model that approximate better the *real* function on tested values. This is a process that refers to the comparison of the *test set* or *validation set* with the last two actual observations.

The final step is the *forecasting stage* that aims to compute the network response for the new inputs, leading to a specific target output.

In some cases, the researchers use a univariate model, where a single variable is taken into account by the ANN such as the target indicator time series. So, we have a time series of daily, monthly or annual intervals, and an ANN with an input or more input layers of N neurons and output layer with only one neuron.

The input layers then hold the time series data points of T consecutive periods, and after the ANN is computed the output layer would hold the prediction for the (T + m)th periods. Usually a multivariate model is preferred, in which several input variables are taken into account and we must emphasize that some of them are more important than others for the forecasting, these being preferred in the ANN model [2].

In the first stage, we will decide the input data, and how it should be split between training and test data. As for the second stage, choosing the number and size of the hidden layers in the ANNs, we will demonstrate that the optimal structure for a given problem is based on trial-and-error calculated values [17, 24, 25].

The results of two different implementations are compared based on the value of Mean Squared Error (MSE) [26, 27]:

$$\mathrm{MSE} = \frac{1}{N}\sum_{i=1}^{N}\left(\hat{Y}_i - Y_i\right)^2 \tag{9.2}$$

where $\hat{Y}_i$ is the vector of predictions and Y_i is the vector of true values.

Also, the accuracy may be evaluated taking into account the Root Mean Square Error (RMSE) [27, 28]:

$$\mathrm{RMSE} = \sqrt{\mathrm{MSE}\left(\hat{\theta}\right)} \tag{9.3}$$

where $\hat{\theta}$ is an estimator.

Modeling results will be depicted tabular and graphical so that we may compare the accuracy of the representations.

Concerning the forecasting software offered by the IT market, we believe that GMDH Shell environment is appropriate to build the forecasts due to more features: data acquisition, integration, neural network modeling, analysis and forecasting.

According to the documentation of the Group Method of Data Handling (GMDH): "GMDH Shell is an advanced but easy to use tool for predictive analytics and data mining, able to automatically detect usable data inside a file, transform data according to a problem type, drop irrelevant inputs and, finally, construct a set of predictive models at the base of optimal complexity detection and self-organization principals" [1].

Analyzing the features of this forecasting software we made a summary of its strengths [2]:

1. Graphical User Interface for Windows is very friendly and consists of multiple panels: Data Manager (input dataset, target variables), Solver options, and Simulation results.
2. GMDH Shell accept the input dataset from XLS and CSV files, organized on columns and rows, some of them being the input variables and others the forecasting targets.
3. GMDH Shell is able to solve different types of forecasting problems, especially Time-series forecasting which is a complex type of continuous value forecasting
4. Applications of time-series forecasting include: financial management, evaluation of alternative economic strategies, production and capacity planning. To obtain a reliable model, time-series forecasting GMDH Shell treats and considers the validation dataset as important as that for training. *Time series preprocessor* panel allows the choice of core algorithms to learn from a training input data: neural networks or combinatorial type. We interested in neural networks algorithm, able to iteratively create layers of neurons with two or more inputs and to use a limited set of optimally neurons.
5. Viewing and saving the results as graphical and tabular presentation of model performance and the importance of each indicator (as input variable) to the accuracy assessment for the modeled dataset. The current model for the target variable and also, other models of the same target are shown in visualization panels, using the Model browser panel [1].

Figure 9.12 indicate the steps to be followed to perform a forecast using the neural network algorithm of GMDH Shell.

From the software's online documentation, several operating principles of the forecast algorithms based on neural network are inferred [1]:

- Algorithm focuses on the two-level validation approach, the second validation level, called *hold-out sample*, is not implicated in estimation of model structure, but it is used to validate the modeling attempt, the performance of processed predictions. This second validation may alert about over-fitting or about low quality model.
- The model complexity can be increased by using built-in validation strategies in order to improve forecast accuracy. The main idea is to create layers of neurons

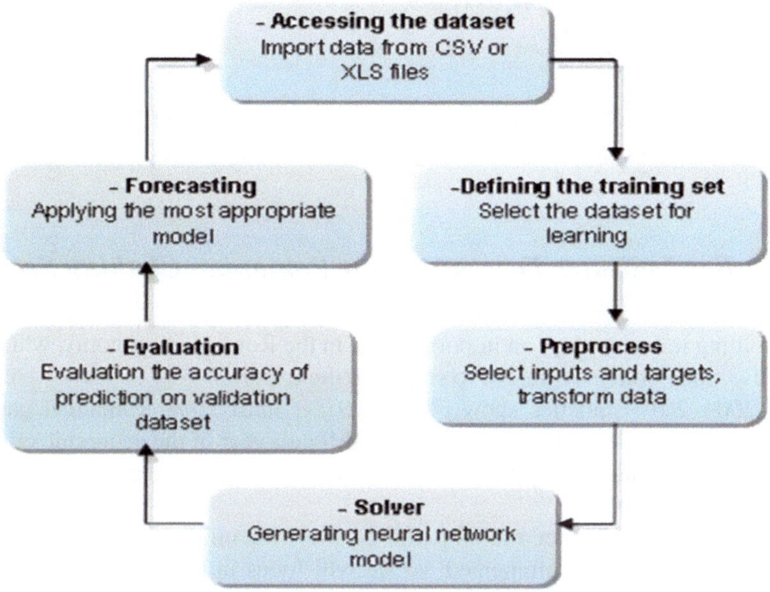

Fig. 9.12 Sequence of operations for performing a forecast using GMDH Shell [17]

with two or more inputs, keeping a set of neurons that will contribute to the next layer. So, every new layer is based-on two or more neurons from previous layers.

- The process of creating layers ends in one of the following cases:
  - The most recent layer did not provide a better accuracy than previous layer;
  - The testing error was reduced by less than 1 %;
  - The number of layers has reached the configuration limit.

In this paper, we will highlight the advantages of using this kind of tools to improve investment-decisions based on *Key indicators forecasting* Romanian clothing sector, and to increase profits whilst reducing costs and risks based on *Company sales forecasting*. We emphasize the advantages of using GMDH Shell for managers: applying various types of models on same input financial data in order to define the future values of performance financial indicators.

The authors aim to test and perform comparative analysis of the obtained results by using a different software application, DTREG, which implements an important set of forecasting models.

DTREG is forecasting software that offers powerful modeling methods [6]:

- Multilayer Perceptron Neural Networks
- Probabilistic Neural Networks
- General Regression Neural Networks
- GMDH Polynomial Neural Networks
- Cascade Correlation Neural Networks

- Support Vector Machine (SVM)
- Decision Trees
- Linear Regression

Next paragraphs briefly describe these steps recommended for building a forecasting system and which have been applied to the case studies.

9.3.2 *Key Indicator Forecasting for Romanian Clothing Sector*

The clothing industry plays an important role in the Romanian economy, which uses the active trade policies oriented to stimulate the exports.

As 2004–2010 statistics show (Table 9.9), if until 2008 Romanian garments recorded an upward trend, in 2009 the most difficult year of the economic crisis, the number of companies in the field, the total number of employees and the turnover dropped considerably.

In the previous chapter the situation of the Romanian clothing industry was presented in detail and commented, so we will focus in the following part on the forecast of some financial indicators.

The improvement of some indicators in the last years, justifies the increase of the Romanian and abroad investors interest for this sector.

Key performance indicators highlighted in our study case demonstrate:

Operating profit margin $= \frac{\text{gross\_result}}{\text{turnover}} * 100$ – express what proportion of a company's revenue is left over after paying for variable costs of production such as wages, raw materials, etc. The clothing's total operating margin increased between 2004 and 2008 and decreased during 2008–2009 (Fig. 9.13).

Return on equity (ROE) $= \frac{\text{gross\_result}}{\text{share\_capital}} * 100$ – The *ROE* has a similar trend as operating profit margin (Fig. 9.14).

Operational profit margin (EBIT) $= \frac{\text{gross\_operating\_surplus}}{\text{turnover}} * 100$ The EBIT registered a powerful decrease in 2008 and an increase during 2009–2010 (Fig. 9.15) (Table 9.10).

This section will explain how to prepare data, choose the model, and make the configuration in GMDH Shell to obtain a forecasting for three key performance indicators on 2011–2012: Return on equity, Operating profit margin, Operational profit margin.

Return on equity – reflects the efficiency of shareholder's invested capital. In the presented case study, it is observed that the rate of financial return was maintained at affordable levels (Fig. 9.14), with the exception of 2009.

Following the sequence of operations shown in Fig. 9.12, first step is the import of data from an Excel file (Fig. 9.16).

Second action refers to establish the input variables that may affect the target ("Return on equity" indicator): Gross result, Turnover, Share capital.

Table 9.9 The evolution of main financial indicators on Romanian clothing sector (constant prices in dollars)

Year	2004	2005	2006	2007	2008	2009	2010
Number of companies	5,628	5,849	5,743	5,698	5,336	4,841	4,078
Average number of employees	317,696	286,214	255,889	224,194	188,441	153,299	141,445
Average number of employed persons	320,402	287,684	257,243	225,367	189,635	154,453	142,326
Personnel expenses	745,413,067	776,982,151	803,738,834	904,161,286	809,513,509	551,961,892	381,263,970
Salary expenses	563,315,102	589,042,071	624,085,056	708,479,254	641,502,797	436,854,538	1,570,963,062
Total turnover	2,284,209,202	2,264,455,605	2,364,337,916	2,573,073,107	2,509,557,965	1,721,204,418	1,467,840,443
Yearly output	2,182,606,772	2,119,024,956	2,161,238,286	2,360,912,239	2,235,621,476	1,543,285,372	671,249,337
Gross added value at factor cost	1,016,908,629	996,864,603	1,007,317,442	1,062,417,092	1,140,670,751	746,465,999	190,715,746
Gross operating surplus	271,495,562	219,882,452	203,578,609	158,255,806	331,157,242	194,504,107	198,758,918
Direct exports	1,382,901,903	1,432,631,543	1,520,627,778	1,570,149,147	1,664,186,290	1,338,257,445	1,408,869,179
Gross return of the year	155,127,392	112,233,878	126,698,217	892,539,602	46,248,635	36,839,848	50,101,986
Net investments	216,522,451	95,630,410	128,385,479	150,323,126	147,208,713	50,605,875	90,714,190
Gross investments	307,248,537	153,748,573	198,533,164	440,756,149	267,061,505	97,197,842	106,511,768
Equity at December 31	112,302,367	116,471,345	139,932,629	219,368,421	160,472,505	143,502,984	106,511,768

(Source: author's calculations based on data from RNIS)

Fig. 9.13 Evolution of operating profit margin during 2004–2010

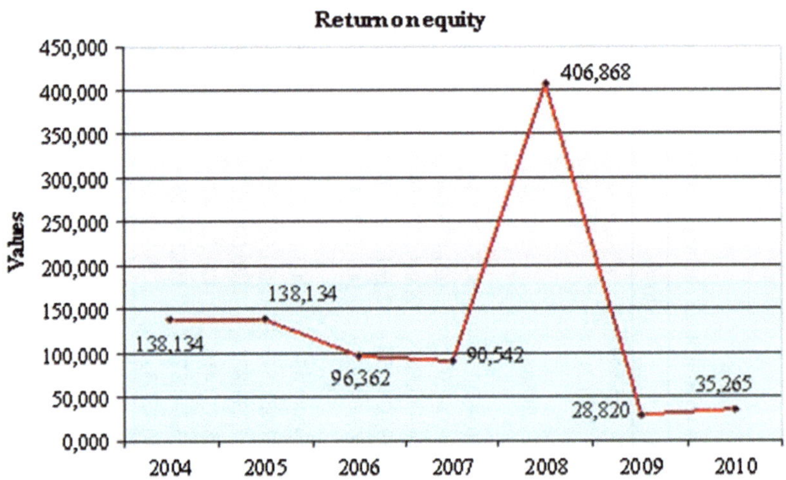

Fig. 9.14 Evolution of ROE during 2004–2010

An important step is to indicate on Configuration – Workflow the Time-series options: window size, forecast horizon.

As we mentioned above, the predictions are based on learning algorithm, defined as a procedure that controls model optimization process. The related learning algorithms chosen, available in GMDH Shell is Neural-type networks. Also known as polynomial neural networks, this method employ combinatorial algorithm for optimization of neuron connection.

The algorithm iteratively creates layers of neurons with two or more inputs. The Configuration of Solver settings includes model generation algorithms

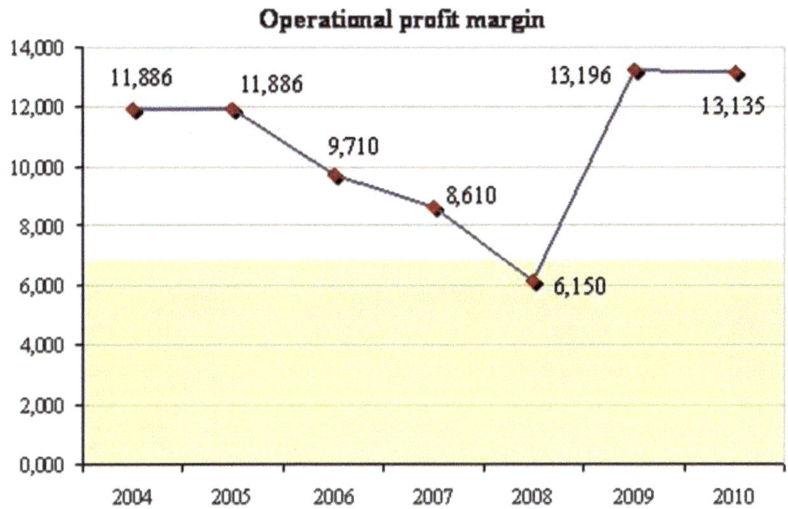

Fig. 9.15 Evolution of operational profit margin during 2004–2010

Table 9.10 The evolution of financial indicators during 2004–2010

Year/financial indicator	2004	2005	2006	2007	2008	2009	2010
Operating profit margin	6,791	6,791	4,956	5,359	34,688	1,843	3,279
Return on equity	138,134	138,134	96,362	90,542	406,868	28,820	35,265
Operational profit margin	11,886	11,886	9,710	8,610	6,150	13,196	13,135

(Core algorithm-Neural type), validation strategy (Training/Testing), validation criterion (RMSE), and Neuron inputs (2), Maximum number of layers (5), as it is indicated in Table 9.11.

Whole data testing is a validation strategy that splits dataset, trains model using the training part, but uses both parts for testing. We used also *Training/testing* option that splits dataset into two parts, uses the training part to find model coefficients and uses the testing part to compare all generated models.

In order to see the accuracy estimations, this software provides the Performance panel with at least a small number of actual values of the target variable that we are trying to model.

The performance panel shows Maximal positive, Maximal negative, Mean absolute and Root mean squared values of error. Error values are either absolute or normalized by range of the output variable or normalized by values of the target variable. The range of target variables are always calculated only for data-points that fall under training and testing parts.

The panel **Simulation results** have many components**:** Plot, Table, Importance and Model browser (Fig. 9.17). **Plot** tab helps visually estimate quality of regression or time series models: blue curve with red addition (predicted for next time horizon chosen) that marks model forecast, gray curve for actual data.

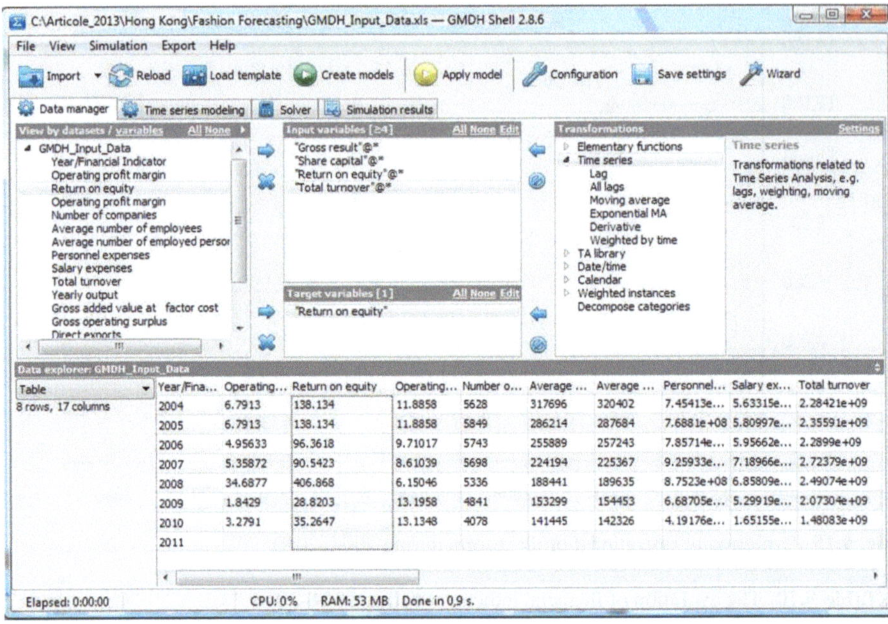

Fig. 9.16 Import of dataset from an excel file

Table 9.11 Configurations of Solver settings for ROE forecasting

Criteria	First simulation		Second simulation	
Validation strategy	Training/testing	60/40	Training/testing	60/40
Validation criterion	RMSE		RMSE	
Core algorithm	Neural-type		Neural-type	
Neuron Inputs	2		3	
Neuron function – quadratic polynomial	$a_0 + a_1 \cdot x_i + a_2 \cdot x_j + a_3 \cdot x_i \cdot x_j + a_4 \cdot {x_i}^2 + a_5 \cdot {x_j}^2$		$a_0 + a_1 \cdot x_i + a_2 \cdot x_j + a_3 \cdot x_i \cdot x_j + a_4 \cdot {x_i}^2 + a_5 \cdot {x_j}^2$	
Maximum number of layers	5		5	

In the same figure, it may be observed that the forecast value for 2011 is 156,645 following the trend of the years 2009–2010 and using the Solver settings configuration on left frame.

In Fig. 9.18 we can see that, by choosing the value of 3 for Neuron inputs, the forecasting is different having the value 187,303.

As presented in Table 9.12, the assessed accuracy of the model is determined via RMSE (root-mean squared error) and MAE (mean absolute error) and we can see that the second simulation is better than the first simulation.

We made similar steps to obtain other key performance indicators, such as: *Operational profit margin*.

Choosing the method of forecasting Neural-type, with two neuron inputs and two layers, it is observed that there is a difference between the actual value and the one projected in 2010 (Fig. 9.19), which means that the model can be improved.

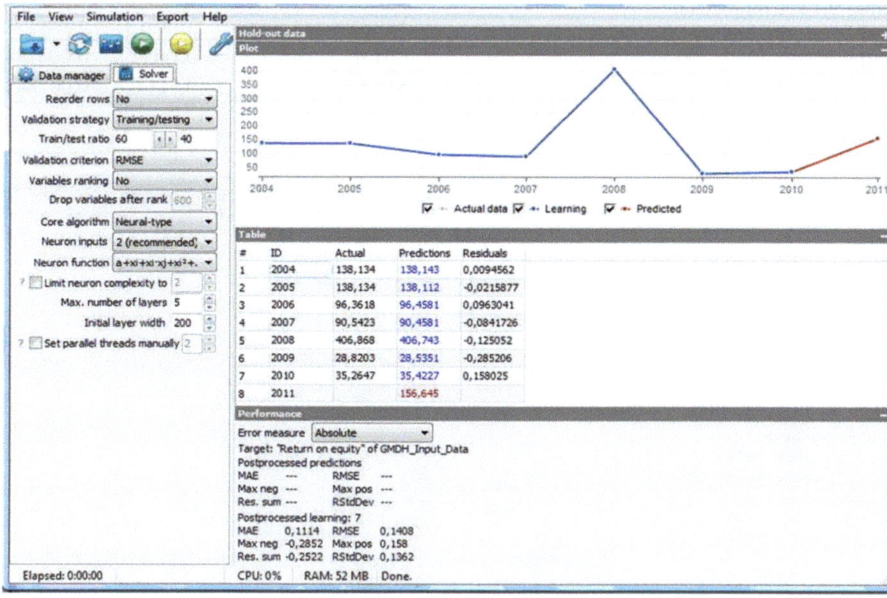

Fig. 9.17 ROE forecasting by a configuration of Solver settings with two input neurons

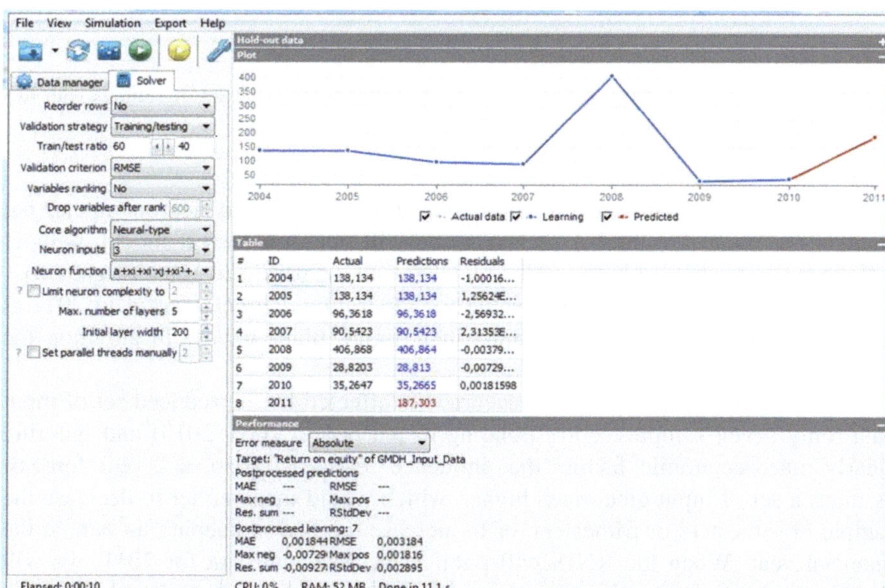

Fig. 9.18 ROE forecasting by a configuration of Solver settings with three input neurons

Table 9.12 Comparison between the accuracy of the models

Validation criterion	Model 1	Model 2
RMSE	0.1408	0.003184
MAE	0.1114	0.001844

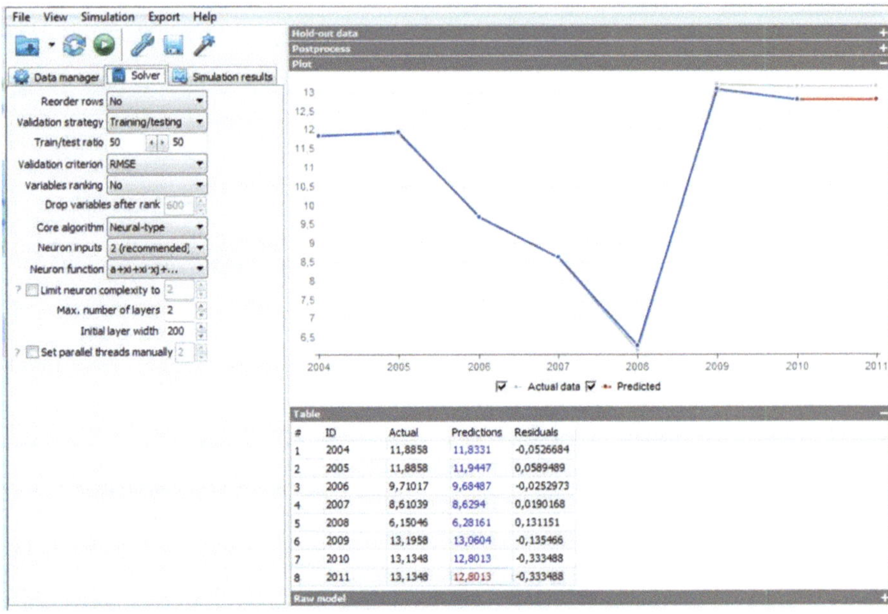

Fig. 9.19 *Operational profit margin* forecasting by a configuration of Solver settings with two input neurons and two layers

So, keeping the same neural type algorithm and the two neuron inputs, but changing at three the number of layers, we will obtain a correct model, without differences in testing set between the real data and the predicted value (Fig. 9.20).

In conclusion, the forecasting value for *Operational profit margin* in 2011 is reliable and the managers may adjust their future plans having in attention the mentioned forecast.

In our experiment, the forecast accuracy is affected by the reduced set of input data (only seven samples, corresponding to the period 2004–2010) and ignoring clearly macroeconomic factors that influence forecasts. Also, a 2-year forecast assumes a set of input data much higher, which would mean either to decrease the sample in semesters or trimesters, or to increase the period keeping as sample the financial year. When the RNIS will publish the financial data for 2011, we will be able to check the quality of forecasts for 2011 and we will do the forecast for 2012.

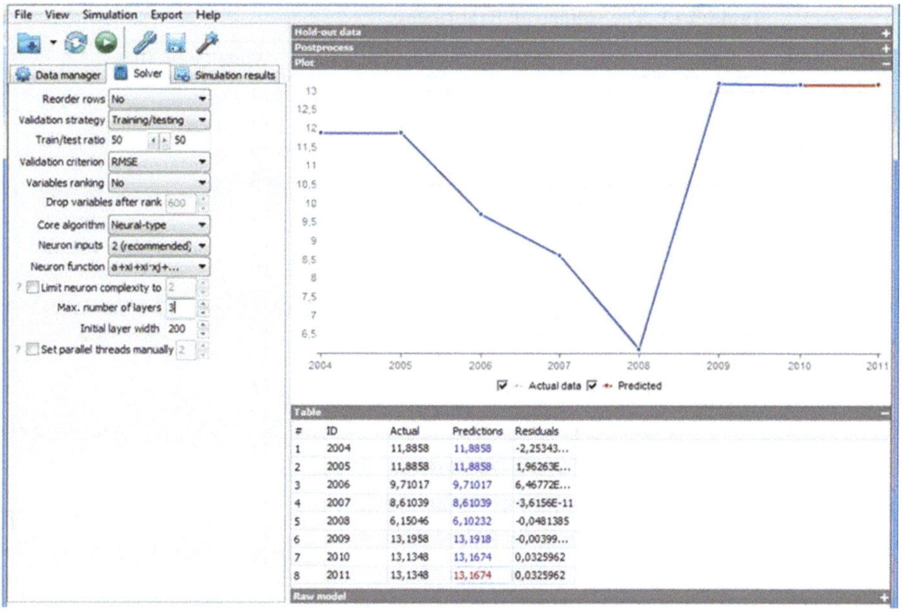

Fig. 9.20 *Operational profit margin* forecasting by a configuration of Solver settings with two input neurons and three layers

9.3.3 Company Sales Forecasting

For the manager of a company that produces and sells clothing is very important to know at any time what types of products or what colors are the top choices of consumers. In this way he can plan manufacturing focusing on those products. This is also the most appropriate method to apply "fast fashion" on scientific bases.

The forecast of future fashion trends is a very important activity for a company in the field which wants to maintain or to increase its level of efficiency compared with the one of its competitors. Nowadays this activity is also known as "cool hunting", is managed by special departments and embodied in trend books (printed papers in which are identified colors, materials, lines and emerging forms, that can be used as a source of inspiration and adaptation to what is new), and involves two main activities: the first is based on observing the fashion system by periodically discussions with the mangers of the production factory and by analyzing the competitors activity, and the second on observing the changes in the consumers style [29].

"However, if the fashion forecasting is an endogenous activity for the fashion system, aiming to identify color, line and fabric trends, the cool hunting tries to understand the social trends linked to lifestyles." [29]

Table 9.13 The volume of T-shirt sales

Color/month	Black (×1000)	Green (×1000)	White (×1000)
Prev 1	14	15	14
Prev 2	13	14	15
Prev 3	16	16	16
Prev 4	15	18	15
Prev 5	16	17	15
Prev 6	17	15	16
Prev 7	16	18	18
Prev 8	20	18	13
Prev 9	22	17	15
Prev 10	20	13	16
Prev 11	16	15	15
Prev 12	16	12	12
1	15	14	11
2	14	12	12
3	17	16	12
4	13	21	11
5	14	20	18
6	17	18	16
7	16	18	18
8	23	17	13
9	22	15	14
10	26	16	19
11	21	17	18
12	25	20	20
Next 1			

Fashion companies have two main possibilities in their activity: to create a style or to follow market trends. These two activities shouldn't be considered independently but must complement each other in order to obtain a balance between defining a brand style and compliance with current trends.

We will demonstrate in this section how to proceed in order to predict the sales evolution for a product by the color chosen by consumers. The chosen product is the T-Shirt and, from the previous sales, three favorite colors (black, green and white) were picked. We have the monthly volume of sales in the past 2 years (Table 9.13 and Fig. 9.21) and we want to do the forecasting for the next period.

Using GMDH Shell software the sales forecasting can be made on short term (1–2 months) for each product category. Updating entry dates is made in the Excel table, at the end of each month, and in the forecasting software is sufficient to activate the *Reload* command.

After importing the data, we establish the target variables, corresponding to the three colors of selected product. Using the Solver settings configuration on the left frame (Fig. 9.22), we will obtain the forecasts for all three variable.

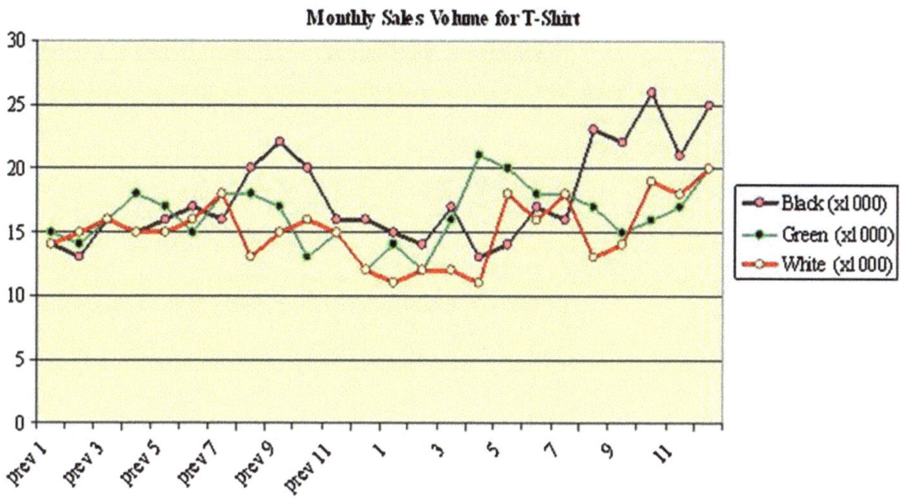

Fig. 9.21 The evolution of T-shirt sales

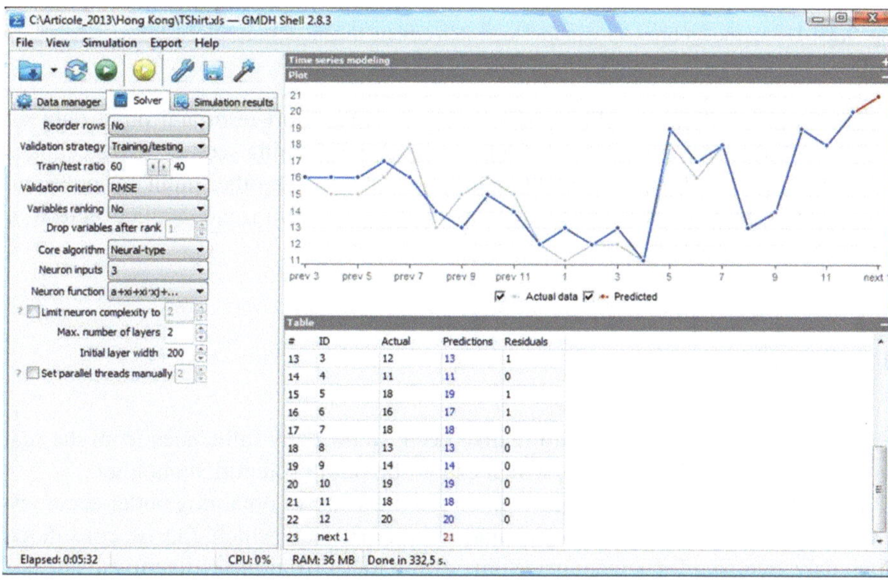

Fig. 9.22 The forecasting for green T-shirt

In *Model browser* frame are available the three forecasts for the chose colors of T-Shirt products: Green, White and Black.

The *Times series report* window contains the values predicted compared with the last actual values, and the *Plot* window presents the graphical result for each model selected from *Model browser* (Fig. 9.23).

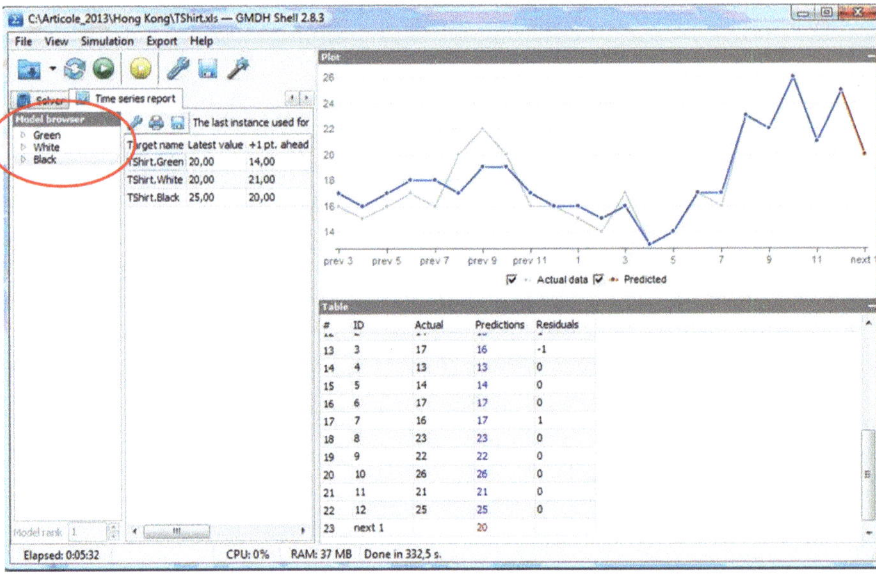

Fig. 9.23 Using model browser window to switch among the models of forecasting

The forecast of sales volume of a company is on short-term and input data set must be reduced at the last months in the case of the clothing sector, where changes are very frequent. The model could be improved by adding other input variables, on which the target variable depend, such as season, the color trend, cyclical return of certain fashion trends.

9.4 Conclusions

Forecasting fashion is difficult to realize because of many influences from the real world, objective and subjective, which cannot be put in scientific containers.

But equally true is that its improvement, in the sense of obtaining better accuracy, even on short term, it is necessary and it is a criterion which can be considered obviously, decisive for a manager. Some of the ideas from these diagnostic checks, and from the related activity of forecast monitoring, are helpful in the case studies presented, namely comparing the relative accuracy of several different forecasting methods on the same data.

Reaching this point, the authors of this paper find natural to ask themselves:

Is the financial forecasting in the fashion sector a method to improve the foreign direct investments in Romania?

Are the company sales forecasting a method to increase the profit and improve the company management?

The answer in both cases is certainly *Yes,* but we must verify the prediction before applying it.

First, it is mandatory to do a comparative forecasting, using the initial dataset: from $\boldsymbol{n}$ samples, we can choose a number $\boldsymbol{m} < \boldsymbol{n}$ as historical data, while the second part of data, $\boldsymbol{m}$-$\boldsymbol{n}$, will be forecast and compared with real ones. After the analysis of comparison the forecast to actual, it is indicated to recommend the method that made the most accurate forecasts.

Secondly, it is necessary to make an assessment of the accuracy of predictions, comparing with real data obtained from the next sample and, if there are notable differences, analyzing the mismatch causes. Obviously, forecasts must look at future trends; the real test of a forecasting method is whether it produces appropriate predictions for real data. In other words, we are interested to know if a method works for real-time conditions.

We assume as future work the extensions of this experiment in two main directions: the update of the data volume used for prediction and the comparison with a second simulation software (like DTREG) that uses different ANN models.

As increasing pressure is put on managers to make better decisions and more accurate estimates, it becomes more important to provide a decision support system that will allow them to review in detail past and current performance, as well as to predict future conditions and activities. As a result, the demand for the integration of advanced modeling and forecasting techniques into top management applications will rise to meet those needs.

Romania is one of the European countries which recorded an economic growth of 0.2 % in 2012 in comparison with 2011, the number of employees in the economy rose by 70,000 in April 2012 – February 2013, unemployment decreased by about 7 % in February 2013, the unemployment rate being twice lower than the one in the euro area countries.

Adding to these accomplishments the fact that Romania isn't following anymore the on debt model, the short-term external debt at January 31, 2013 being down by 3.6 % compared to 2012, we have reason to aim for a local economic recovery in 2013, in foreign capital inflows for the country.

The clothing sector and its fashion component will be in the attention of many foreign investors, based on Romania's tradition in this area, and on cheap skilled labor force.

References

1. http://www.gmdhshell.com/docs/. Latest accessed 8 Dec 2012
2. Banica L, Pirvu D (2012) Intelligent financial forecasting, the key for a successful management. Int J Acad Res Accounting Finance Manage Sci 2(3):192–206. ISSN: 2225–8329
3. Yu Y, Choi T-M, Hui C-L (2011) An intelligent fast sales forecasting model for fashion products. Expert Syst Appl 38(6):7373–7379
4. Christos S, Dimitrios S (1996) Neural networks.http://www.doc.ic.ac.uk/~nd/surprise_96/journal/vol4/cs11/report.html

5. Huang GB, Zhu QY, Siew CK (2006) Extreme learning machine: theory and applications. Neurocomputing 70:489–501
6. http://www.dtreg.com/DownloadManual.htm
7. Avrigeanu AF, Anghel FG (2012) Romanian clothing industry: external market vs. internal market. Rom Econ Bus Rev 6(1):67–76
8. Georgescu G (2012) The global crisis impact on Romanian trade structure. Available online at http://mpra.ub.uni-muenchen.de/36339/
9. Romanian International Trade Yearbook (2011) Institute National of Statistics Romania. pp 36–37
10. Romania's Trade balance for 2012: increasing deficit. http://www.wall-street.ro/articol/Economie/144079/balanta-comerciala-a-romaniei-pe-2012-deficitul-in-crestere.html
11. Secrieru A (2013) The most popular Romanian export goods. http://mpra.ub.uni-muenchen.de/36339/1/ MPRA_paper_36339.pdf
12. Masson R, Iosif L, MacKerron G, Fernie J (2007) Managing complexity in agile global fashion industry supply chains. Int J Logist Manage 18(2):238–254
13. Fashion and clothing retail sector in Romania – a FRD center market entry services Romania report, 2010. Available online at http://www.frdcenter.ro/assets/Fashion-and-Clothing-Retail-Sector-Romania-2010-DEMO-REPORT.pdf
14. http://www.wto.org/english/res_e/statis_e/its2012_e/its12_highlights2_e.pdf
15. Kotorov R (2009) Enhancing decision-making, cost-efficiency, and profitability with predictive analytics. Information Builders
16. Walczak S (2001) An empirical analysis of data requirements for financial forecasting with neural networks. J Manage Inform Syst 17(4):203–222
17. Banica L, Pirvu D, Hagiu A (2012) Financial forecasting using neural networks. Int J Adv Manage Econ 1(6):70–79, Vol. Xxx, ISSN: 2278–3369
18. Khashei M, Bijari M (2010) An artificial neural network (p, d, q) model for timeseries forecasting. Expert Syst Appl 37(1):479–485
19. Zhang G, Patuwo BE, Hu YM (1998) Forecasting with artificial neural networks. Int J Forecast 14:35–62
20. Aamodt R (2010) Using artificial neural networks to forecast financial time series. http://130.203.133.150/viewdoc/summary?doi=10.1.1.174.7142. Latest accessed 4 Dec 2012
21. Chirita M (2012) Usefulness of artificial neural networks for predicting financial and economic crisis. Annals of "Dunarea de Jos", University of Galati, Fascicle I. Econ Appl Inform XVIII(2):61–66
22. Khashei M, Bijari M (2011) Which methodology is better for combining linear and nonlinear models for time series forecasting? J Ind Syst Eng 4(4):265–285
23. Filik UB, Kurban M (2007) A new approach for the short-term load forecasting with autoregressive and artificial neural network models. Int J Comput Intell Res 3(1):66–71
24. Elder J (2012) The best and the worst of predictive analytics: predictive modeling methods and common data mining mistakes, Elder Research, Inc. Workshop. http://docs.media.bitpipe.com/io_10x/io_105908/item_564128/worst_practice_wp.pdf
25. Xia M, Chu W (2010) Adaptive neural network model for time-series forecasting. Eur J Oper Res 207(2):807–816
26. http://en.wikipedia.org/wiki/Mean_squared_error. Latest accessed 2 Dec 2012
27. Marchetti S, Tzavidis N, Pratesi M (2010) Non-parametric bootstrap mean squared error estimation for M-quantile estimators of small area averages, quantiles and poverty indicators. Comput Stat Data Anal 56(10):2889–2902
28. http://en.wikipedia.org/wiki/Root_mean_square_deviation. Latest accessed 2 Dec 2012
29. Pedroni M (2010) From fashion forecasting to coolhunting. Previsional models in fashion and in cultural production. Available online at http://www.academia.edu/1672430/From_Fashion_Forecasting_to_Coolhunting_Previsional_Models_in_Fashion_and_in_Cultural_Production

MIX
Papier aus verantwortungsvollen Quellen
Paper from responsible sources
FSC® C105338

FSC
www.fsc.org

If you have any concerns about our products,
you can contact us on
ProductSafety@springernature.com

In case Publisher is established outside the EU,
the EU authorized representative is:
Springer Nature Customer Service Center GmbH
Europaplatz 3, 69115 Heidelberg, Germany

Printed by Libri Plureos GmbH
in Hamburg, Germany